THE WESTMINSTER LIBRARY

A SERIES OF MANUALS FOR CATHOLIC PRIESTS AND STUDENTS

EDITED BY

THE RIGHT REV. BERNARD WARD
BISHOP OF BRENTWOOD

AND

THE REV. HERBERT THURSTON, S.J.

Nihil Obstat

F. Thomas Bergh, O.S.B.
Censor Deputatus

Imprimatur

Edmundus, Canonicus Surmont
Vicarius Generalis

Westmonasterii
die 1 Septembris, 1919

PREACHING

BY THE
REV. W. B. O'DOWD

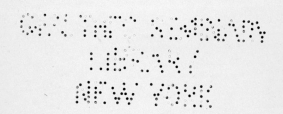

LONGMANS, GREEN AND CO.
39 PATERNOSTER ROW, LONDON
FOURTH AVENUE & 30TH STREET, NEW YORK
BOMBAY, CALCUTTA, AND MADRAS
1919

PREFACE

NONE but the very unreflective can be unaware of the grave problems which Christian doctrine and morality are now being brought to face—not to mention others, still thinly veiled from us, but certainly about to emerge from the wreck of many institutions, ideals, and delusions, which, but a few years ago, seemed to defy destruction.

Some of these problems can be safely handled only by the expert ; and the wise man who is not an expert may well shrink from rushing in light-heartedly to cope with them. The priest charged with the care of souls cannot usually equip himself with the wide and detailed knowledge of the specialist ; his work lies elsewhere.

Already we hear the rumours of fresh activity in which he is able to bear a part ; guilds and leagues and societies are gathering their forces with the object of giving a Catholic direction to the new aspirations—social, educational and industrial—of the strange, though, apparently, no better world that is coming to birth. That the parochial clergy should have a share in these enterprises is a good thing, nay, there is positive danger if they hold themselves aloof.

But danger no less grave may be apprehended if they let themselves be led away from the recognition of the power for good which Providence has placed in the exercise of that essential ministry in the Church of Christ—the ministry of preaching.

Doctrine, in the Catholic economy, is the soul of religion ; and doctrine is set forth and applied to the changing needs of the faithful through the normal channels of instruction, which is preaching. It would be foolish and disastrous for us to put our whole trust in extraordinary means of propaganda, to the neglect of what is still the most general and pervasive influence at our command. The decision taken at the lengthy committee-meeting, the inspiring manifesto, the enthusiastic resolution carried at the great popular demonstration are insignificant in their appeal, compared with the steady power of the instructions given Sunday by Sunday at the parochial Mass.

It is with the purpose of rendering the Catholic pulpit even a little more effective, and of helping the average preacher, that this book has been written. It is not a guide to sacred eloquence ; if by that phrase is meant the accomplished forms of preaching, suited to very special occasions or very special audiences. In writing it, I have tried to bear in mind the actual equipment of a newly-ordained seminarist, and the conditions of pastoral work under which he will exercise his ministry, as well as the ideal, so far as I can discover it, which the Church has traced for the preacher's guidance.

The Council of Trent expressed this when it charged pastors " to feed the flock committed to them with whole-some words, suited to their own capacity and that of their hearers ; teaching whatever is necessary to all for salvation, announcing with brevity and simplicity of discourse the sins they must avoid and the virtues they must strive after, that they may escape everlasting punishment and attain to the glory of heaven.[1]

The Council says nothing about rhetoric ; what it commends is wholesome, popular, clear instruction upon the main doctrines of the Faith and the chief duties of the Christian life.

The recently issued code of Canon Law speaks in the same sense when it commands preachers to exercise " an evangelic ministry," to suit their sermons to their people's capacity, and to avoid pretentious and artificial styles of oratory.[2]

This may seem too unexciting a programme for those

---

[1] Sess. V., *De Ref.*, c. 2.

[2]   *De catechetica institutione.*

Can. 1332.—Diebus dominicis aliisque festis de præcepto, ea hora quæ suo iudicio magis apta sit ad populi frequentiam, debet insuper whose watchword is " professional ambition,"—that fetich of mediocre souls—but the task will not be thought easy by men who understand what it exacts. Clear, interesting, vivid exposition does not come at call ; it is far less facile, for instance, than what Swift has called " low sublimity."

The patient duty of instructing his people by a process of steadily growing enlightenment is the work of the parish priest ; he cannot lay it upon other shoulders or supply its place by the vicarious efforts of missioners or special preachers. If the parochial clergy will not do this, their proper work, it will be left undone ; if they are perfunctory and slipshod in doing it, the spirituality of their people will slowly but surely decline and become more and more mechanical, languid and unintelligent.

If, then, the average man must leave to others the solution of the sharp problems lying about the path of the expert,

---

parochus catechismum fidelibus adultis, sermone ad eorum captum accommodato, explicare.

De sacris concionibus.

Can. 1344.—Diebus Dominicis ceterisque per annum festis de præcepto proprium cuiusque parochi officium est, consueta homilia, præsertim intra Missam in qua maior soleat esse populi frequentia, verbum Dei populo nuntiare.

Parochus huic obligationi nequit per alium habitualiter satifacere nisi ob justam causam ab Ordinario probatam.

Can. 1345.—Optandum ut in Missis, quæ fidelibus adstantibus, diebus festis de præcepto in omnibus ecclesiis vel oratoriis publicis celebrantur, brevis Evangelii aut alicuius partis doctrinæ christianæ explanatio fiat ; quod si loci Ordinarius id præceperit, opportunis datis instructionibus, hac lege tenentur non solum sacerdotes e clero sæculari, sed etiam religiosi, exempti quoque, in suis ipsorum ecclesiis.

Can. 1346.—Curent locorum Ordinarii ut tempore Quadragesimæ, itemque, si expedire visum fuerit, tempore Adventus, in ecclesiis cathedralibus et paroecialibus sacræ conciones frequentius ad fideles habeantur.

Can. 1347.—In sacris concionibus exponenda in primis sunt quæ fideles credere et facere ad salutem oportet.

Divini verbi præcones abstineant profanis aut abstrusis argumentis communem audientium captum excedentibus ; et evangelicum ministerium non in persuasibilibus humanæ sapientiæ verbis, non in profano inanis et ambitiosæ eloquentiæ apparatu et lenocinio, sed in ostensione spiritus et virtutis exerceant, non semetipsos, sed Christum crucifixum prædicantes.

Here follow some canons having reference to jurisdiction and faculties required by preachers.

his is yet no mean task : for on his unrecorded and unpretentious zeal depends the preservation and the progress of the Faith among the multitudes for whom Christ spent Himself, and whom His compassion and sympathy most readily sought.

I will add one word concerning the Appendices at the end of the volume. The first three are translations of three important documents issued from Rome during the last quarter of a century. Appendices are often left unread, but I would ask that one of them at least—the letter of the present Pope—should be excepted from that fate. After these comes a plan of Sunday instructions for a three years' course, with references to some reading matter for each sermon. These references are made exclusively to stated works, likely to be found in a priest's private library. This restriction has its drawbacks, but it has also some compensating advantages. The priest who has these books—and all of them are standard works—can, by following the indications given, supply himself with sufficient material, out of which his own personal labour can fashion a substantial discourse. It is hoped that the references will save him time and trouble, and suggest possible ways of treating the chosen topics ; they are not designed to dispense him from the salutary labour of composing a sermon which will be, in a true sense, the work of his own intelligence.

I am grateful to many friends for much suggestive counsel ; and I must not omit to offer special thanks to the general Editors of this Series, who have interpreted their editorial duties generously, and given me a measure of help and encouragement to which I had no claim.

W. B. O'DOWD

St Charles' House, Oxford
   June 1919

CONTENTS

APPENDICES

ERRATA

p. 89, *line 6 from bottom, for* numbers *read* members.

p. 95, *line 23, for* Maker *read* matter.

p. 135, *line* 14, *for* prophesy *read* prophecy.

CHAPTER I

CHRISTIAN preaching, unlike Christian literature, proceeds directly from the Person of the Incarnate Son of God. Jesus Christ, the Founder of the Christian Church, and the Object of its worship, wrote nothing. He delivered his doctrine orally to the first groups of believers, chosen witnesses of His life and hearers of His words, to be carried by them as a spoken message to the ends of the earth.

John the Baptist, the forerunner and herald of the new Dispensation, gave to Our Lord the point of departure for His preaching when he announced the nearness of the Kingdom of God. The Gospel, the "Good News of the Kingdom," is the subject of Christ's preaching in the synagogues and by the lake side of Galilee; it is the theme of the Sermon on the Mount. If some elements of this preaching are as old as the Law and the Prophets, others are original and personal. It is no mere repetition or scholastic commentary of any former teaching, it is a doctrine of His own, seeking a home in the heart and conscience. With increasing distinctness its Preacher proclaims Himself the Revealer of God, the Saviour of men, the Good Shepherd, the Lord of a spiritual Kingdom.

During His public ministry Our Lord is seen gathering round Himself a number of disciples, who live in familiar intercourse with Him and listen to His instructions. He shows His intention concerning certain of these followers, at the very time when He invites them to His discipleship. "Jesus, walking by the sea of Galilee saw two brethren, Simon who is called Peter and Andrew his brother, casting a net into the sea, for they were fishers. And He saith to them : Come ye after Me and I will make you fishers of men" (Matt. iv. 18,

19). Twelve out of the number of followers are definitely chosen to the special vocation of the Apostolate. " And it came to pass in those days, that He went out into a mountain to pray, and He passed the whole night in the prayer of God. And when day was come He called unto Him His disciples ; and He chose twelve of them, whom He also named Apostles, Simon, whom He surnamed Peter, and Andrew his brother, James and John, Philip and Bartholomew, Matthew and Thomas, James the son of Alpheus, and Simon who is called Zelotes, and Jude the brother of James and John, and Judas Iscariot, who was the traitor " (Luke vi. 12-16).

These chosen men are prepared for a special mission distinct from the personal obligations that flowed from their discipleship. They are initiated into the Mysteries of the Kingdom of God, and receive clear and open explanations of doctrines which are communicated to the rest of the disciples in the obscurity of figure and parable. Special functions are assigned to them in the Kingdom which is being founded, and authority is conferred upon them to proclaim the Gospel to the world at large. They are fortified by the prayer of their Master, and the promise of His unfailing help and presence. The Holy Spirit is to be their teacher and consoler, He is to be their prompter when they are called to answer for their mission before the powers of this world. Even during the lifetime of their Master they are sent as His heralds and witnesses, and He explains to them in detail how they are to act during these first essays of their apostolate (Luke ix. 1-6). Thus the years of Our Lord's public ministry are for them years of training for the work which is to be theirs as soon as He shall have returned to the Father.

We gather from all this that the Apostolate was established as an essential feature of the Kingdom of God ; it was to remain as a permanent function in the Church of Christ. It is unnecessary to explain at length the expansion which took place in the Apostolate itself. Before the Apostolic age closed, the authority of " the twelve " came to be shared by others who were not of the number immediately chosen by Our

Lord. St Paul, St Matthias, St Barnabas, with others, were gathered in different ways into the group of the Apostles. They shared with those originally chosen the vocation and mission, as well as the name of "the twelve." Yet, even to the last of the New Testament Scriptures, the apostolic office was referred to its origin—the special choice of Jesus of these twelve ; the writer of the Apocalypse shows the Church, the New Jerusalem, reared upon twelve foundations upon which are written the twelve names of the twelve apostles of the Lamb (Apoc. xxi. 14). If other missionaries and teachers made good their claim to the title of Apostle it was in virtue of the mission which they had come to share with the original twelve, the accredited envoys of Christ.[1]

The Apostolate, in its original form, gradually passed away by the death of its constituent members, and with it disappeared certain incidental gifts which were of their nature temporary and provisional — the personal infallibility in the official teaching of each Apostle, and the jurisdiction which each of them possessed unlimited by any territorial boundary.

The Charismata, extraordinary gifts such as prophecy and the gift of tongues, which held a place during the early days side by side with the authoritative rule of the Apostles, fell into some disrepute and at length ceased. In the generation which succeeded that of the constitution of the Apostolic college, there grew up, in one place and then in another, the stable institution of local bishoprics. The transformation of the missionary system into that of the territorial episcopate, though it began in the Apostolic period, was not effected all at once, nor did it come into being simultaneously in every place ; the middle of the third century, however, found it general and on the way to becoming universal, and the fourth saw it as the normal organization of all the churches. The episcopate, as it was becoming solidly established, had

---

[1] For an account of the significance of the Apostolate in the first Christian generation, see Batiffol, " The Christian Apostolate," *Irish Theological Quarterly*, Oct. 1906, and at greater length, Moran, *The Government of the Church in the First Century* (Dublin, 1913).

and expressed the consciousness of its ancestry; and during its emergence from the primitive institution, the voice of early Christian writers, St Clement of Rome, St Ignatius of Antioch, St Irenæus of Lyons, and Tertullian of Carthage accordantly attribute the authority of the Bishop to his inheritance of the Apostolic mission.[1] Then, and ever since, the duty of preaching the Christian faith to Christian people has been regarded by the Catholic Church as the special duty of Bishops. They represent the Apostles to their own generation, and derive their right of teaching from them. Priests exercise the care of souls in the capacity of coadjutors of the Bishop, of whom they are the delegates. Thus the priest's care of souls derives from the Apostolic succession, through the delegation of the Bishop, and every priest with the care of souls becomes to his people an accredited teacher and apostle. On every preacher who has legitimate mission falls the responsibility of prolonging the voice of Christ and His first witnesses, of commending Christ's teaching to his people, of witnessing to His law, and of heralding His second coming.

I

On the day of Pentecost, a short time after the Resurrection of Jesus Christ, twelve fishermen, who had taken refuge in an upper chamber in Jerusalem, formed almost the whole Christian Church.

Long before the last of their number had passed away their doctrine had established itself, not only in the city where they were assembled, but in Rome, in Antioch, in Athens, in Alexandria, and in many other cities of the Eastern and Western world.

The Church had broken through the envelope of Jewish thought, and Christ was preached to " Greeks and barbarians." " A rapid flash proceeding from Syria, lighting up almost instantaneously the three great peninsulas of

[1] *First Epistle of Clement*, xlii.; St Ignatius, *Magnesians*, chap. vi.; *Smyrnæans*, chap. viii.; Tertullian, *De Præscrip.*, chapters xxxii. and xxxvi.

Asia Minor, Greece, and Italy, soon followed by a second flash, which embraced almost all the Mediterranean coasts : such was the first manifestation of Christianity. The course of the apostolic ships was always practically the same. Christian preaching seemed to follow a former track, which was none other than that of Jewish emigration. Like a contagion which, starting in the depths of the Mediterranean, suddenly makes its appearance at certain points of the littoral, by some secret correlation, Christianity had its ports of arrival in some measure marked out in advance. One might compare the state of things to a train of gunpowder, or, better still, to a sort of electric cable, along which the new idea flew in almost instantaneous fashion." [1] Such was the first expansion of the teaching of " the twelve."

In the New Testament is to be sought the substance of that victorious teaching ; there we may read the beliefs, the promises, the hopes, the menaces which worked the marvellous change, and turned the current of history into new channels. These lie openly upon the face of the sacred pages, yet of the manner in which the message was delivered by the Apostles to their hearers, we have only occasional and fragmentary evidence.

The Acts of the Apostles give the most direct account of the way in which the first missionaries went about their work. The author of the Acts does not indeed record any single discourse from beginning to end, but he does in several places put us in possession of what we may call the tactics of the first Christian preachers.

The first sermon reported in the Acts is that of St Peter to the crowds gathered in Jerusalem for the feast of Pentecost. Many among his audience had known Our Lord by sight, and most of them by report, since His trial and execution had taken place in that very city less than two months before.

The subject of the discourse was the inauguration of a new dispensation of Grace, of which Jesus was the Revealer, and His twelve companions the witnesses. The life, the miracles, the death and resurrection of Jesus were set before this crowd of Jews as the fulfilment of the indestructible

[1] Renan, *The Apostles*, Eng. Trans. (Watts), p. 109.

Messianic hope which had lived on in the heart of Israel for centuries. St Peter opens the book of the nation's oracles : Isaias, Joel, David—and interprets the recent events by their aid. To this ancient witness St Peter adds his own and that of his fellow Apostles, and reminds his hearers that they also have had direct experience of the facts which he is interpreting to them. " Ye men of Israel, hear these words : Jesus of Nazareth, a man approved by God among you by miracles and wonders and signs which God did by him, in the midst of you as you also know ; this same being delivered up, by the determinate counsel and foreknowledge of God, you by the hands of wicked men have crucified and slain." [1] Then under the features of David the Apostle introduces the risen Messias—David had spoken of a Holy One who was not to be permitted to see corruption, yet David did not prophesy this of himself, but of One who was yet to come. The Apostle raises his hand and points to a sepulchre close at hand in which the bones of David had crumbled to dust. Jesus their Master was the One of whom David had spoken ; He had been raised from death and set as a heavenly Messias on the right hand of God

This foundation laid, Peter calls all to penance and to fellowship with him in Christ. "Do penance and be baptized, every one of you in the name of Jesus Christ, for the remission of your sins, and you shall receive the gift of the Holy Ghost ; for the promise is to you and to your children, and to all that are afar off whomsoever the Lord our God shall call." [2]

St Peter's sermon is, in the main, that of an apologist ; its aim was to lead the Jews to recognize in Jesus the Messias foretold by the prophets. The same may be said of two other discourses given in Chapters iii. and iv. of the Acts ; there is reference to Old Testament prophecy, insistence on the holiness of Jesus, and on His dignity as God's Son, blame of the Jews and Gentiles responsible for His death, exhortation to faith in the name of Christ and to conversion of heart.

With these discourses may be grouped another, the one delivered on the occasion of the converson of the soldier Cornelius. This supplies us with a typical instruction given

---

[1] Acts ii. 22, 23. [2] Acts ii. 38, 39.

to those who were to be received into the membership of
the Church. " You know," says St Peter to Cornelius and
his kinsfolk, " you know the word which has been published
through all Judæa, for it began from Galilee after the baptism
which John preached, Jesus of Nazareth ; how God anointed
Him with the Holy Ghost, and with power, who went about
doing good, and healing all that were oppressed by the devil,
for God was with him. And we are witnesses of all things
that He did in the land of the Jews and in Jerusalem, whom
they killed, hanging Him upon a tree. Him God raised
up the third day and gave Him to be made manifest, not
to all the people, but to witnesses preordained by God, even
to us who ate and drank with Him after He arose from the
dead. And he commanded us to preach to the people, and
to testify that it is He who was appointed by God to be judge
of the living and the dead. To Him all the prophets give
testimony, that by His name all receive remission of sins who
believe in Him." [1]

The first ten chapters of the Acts, then, show that the
current oral tradition concentrated upon the miracles and
signs worked by God through Jesus of Nazareth—Christ
and Saviour and the Judge of all. In each of these early
discourses, the purpose of which was to lead those who listened
towards the Christian faith, the great miracle of the resurrection is seen to be the main object of the Apostolic
testimony, and the capital argument in favour of the new
teaching.

Turning from the ministry of St Peter to that of St
Paul we find the same scheme. The preaching of St Paul
to the Jews at Antioch and elsewhere does not appear to
have differed in its substance from that of St Peter. There
are a few personal touches which mark them off from St Peter's
sermons, but the essence and the method are the same as his.

The sermon at Antioch reported in the thirteenth
chapter of the Acts of the Apostles is in all probability typical
of St Paul's missionary preaching before a Jewish audience.
Its three themes, each introduced by the apostrophe, " Men,
brethren " (verses 15, 26, 28), are the providence of God

[1] Acts x. 37 and following.

towards Israel, then the central dogma of the Messiahship of Christ, and finally an exhortation to belief and hope in Him.

The discourse to the Athenians (Acts xv. 16-33) transports us to a totally different theatre. The Apostle is now addressing a pagan audience in the public place of a city steeped in heathenism. The circumstances are exceptional, and the sermon is unlike any other recorded in the New Testament. It is possible that it owes something to ancient classical oratory, and if that is so, it is the only recorded sermon of apostolic times in which traces of such influence appear.

Before such an audience there could be no question of invoking the authority of the Law and the prophets, philosophical speculation must take the place of scriptural interpretation. The address, though it interested its hearers at first, failed in its purpose—it was interrupted by the mockery of some and the polite irony of others among the bystanders ; yet its opportunism, as well as its eloquence, lend to it a very special interest. The Apostle sought to insinuate into the minds of his superstitious or sceptical hearers the first principles of religious faith. In an agnostic formula carved on the base of a statue, the Apostle discerned some evidence of the wistful hopes that burned dimly in the hearts of heathens. Mankind had been appointed the task of searching out God, whom a pagan poet had spoken of as the father of the race of men. This divinity of which their sages had written could not be worshipped fitly as an idol of " gold or silver or stone, the graving of art and device of men." The days when God might have tolerated such blind religion had passed, and the Lord of heaven and earth had appointed His own day for judging the world. The predestined witness had appeared, and had been raised from the dead. The first mention of the resurrection turned the curiosity of the Athenians into incredulous suspicion. The Apostle was not allowed to finish his appeal, his hearers turned away from him before he had even pronounced the name of Jesus, and " Paul went out from among them."

We can gather from these types of discourses the fashion of preaching employed by the first missionaries. They give a sketch only and not a finished picture ; still it is possible to infer from them how these early preachers accommodated their words to the dispositions, capacities, and religious outlook of the men whom they addressed. If we seek a common characteristic of these primitive sermons it will not be found in a uniformity of literary or oratorical style : for it is precisely there that their most obvious differences lie. What does appear as common quality is their appropriateness. Each sought an entrance into the conscience by the gates that seemed most accessible. One kind of hearer was confronted by the Gospel under the guise of a completion of the prophecies in which he already believed, another was invited to see in it the solution of the problems that lay half awake in the depths of man's moral nature.

We are not to imagine that the written records of such discourses as we have noted adequately represent the fulness of the Apostolic preaching. The whole of the New Testament proceeds from the earliest Christian tradition, and this body of tradition was preached even more fully than it was written, not indiscriminately, but with a wise discretion which fitted it to the spiritual and intellectual needs of the different Churches. The written sermons show only the first approaches of the missionary towards his task of instruction and conversion ; it is the New Testament in its entirety which stands as a witness to the teeming variety of religious ideas upon which the first Christian preachers drew at will.

And again, behind these written records are the men. It is not difficult to conjecture how such men must have preached. Much that they wrote is, in fact, quite in the style of spoken discourse, for in substance, and frequently even in form, it gives the impression of an address delivered in Christian assemblies. When we read, for instance, the First Epistle of St Peter, we feel that what is there set down might serve almost as well for a sermon as for a letter. It is direct, personal, natural, such as one might imagine a pastoral address to have been. There is earnest exhortation and sympathetic warning and practical counsel. It is the testimony of an eye-witness whose mind turns spontaneously to the memory of past experiences, the facts of the life of Our Lord rather than to doctrinal refinements or profound

religious speculation. The humility, endurance, charity
of Our Lord, the final judgment which He is to exercise
when He shall appear again, are the motives upon which
St Peter grounds his exhortation to patience under trials,
to the perfect performance of all Christian duties, and to
an unfailing hope of a future reward. Such thoughts have
been the *loci communes* of Christian moralists in every age ;
and we may be certain that they were common sources of
the earliest Christian preaching.[1]

St Paul's Epistles indirectly exhibit another type of
preacher. We are safe in assuming that the Epistles as they
stand do not represent his normal style of preaching, which
must usually have been much more simple. A study of the
Epistles, in fact, reveals a graduated method of spiritual
instruction. The letters themselves presuppose, as already
known to his hearers, the main facts of the life of Christ, and
the great Christian truths. He himself plainly refers to a
simpler *catechesis* which he had delivered to his Corinthians
soon after their conversion.[2] " It would be a grievous mistake
to suppose that we have in the Epistles a complete summary
of Paul's preaching ; for him as for the twelve, the first and
essential duty was to rehearse the discourses and great deeds
of the Master, as contained in that spoken Gospel, which the
missionary was never tired of repeating and explaining to his
catechumens." [3]   Yet, we may be certain that St Paul's writings, so alive with spontaneous and fervid eloquence, give the
clue to the manner and style of his spoken utterance. The
wisdom which he spoke " among the perfect " must have
been of the same quality as the messages which he wrote,
or rather dictated, for the edification of the Churches. It
needs no great power of imagination in an attentive reader
of the Epistles to evoke a picture of St Paul the preacher.
Logic and mysticism united in the depths of his spirit,
his exceptionally vivid imagination forged abstract doctrines

---

[1] In Chapter xx. of Sienkiewicz's novel, *Quo Vadis*, there is a re-
construction—and a very truth-like one—of St Peter's preaching
in the Catacombs.

[2] I Cor. xv. 1-8.

[3] Fouard, *St Paul and his Missions*, chap. x. p. 249.

into palpable and visible realities ; his power of dramatic imagery, the refinement and warmth of his temperament, his mastery of language, and that gift of sympathy which Newman in a well-known sermon so delicately illustrates—all these qualities must have rendered his preaching at once masculine and tender, instinct with a faith which saturated every faculty of his being, so that he had but to reveal himself in order to manifest Christ living within Him.

This rapid summary suffices to indicate the general character of the earliest Christian preaching. It was plainly traditional inasmuch as there lay at its base the salient facts of Our Lord's life and the doctrine of the Kingdom which He preached. Upon this background each Apostle worked, from this common fund each drew the essential ideas of his message. Nevertheless, the preaching was individual and personal. It was no mere echo. No one of the Apostles, for instance, seems to have used the method so frequently employed by Our Lord, of conveying instruction by allegories and parables. We know, indeed, that the Apostles repeated the words of their Master, still they refrained from adopting a style of instruction so familiar to Him. The first missionaries did more than repeat what they had heard, they sought to unravel the wide implications of the original deposit given over to their keeping. In this steadfast grip upon tradition and this living and personal contemplation of its contents, they are the models of all Christian preachers. The faith was the same in all, the expression of it was peculiar to each. There was room in the first band of preachers for St Peter with his fatherly wisdom and St Paul with his abrupt and impetuous movement, and St John who declared with such steady serenity the doctrine which he drew from his contemplation of God and His eternal Word.

An examination of scriptural preaching will save us from narrow views on what is called " the style of the pulpit." There are examples in the New Testament of every kind of style, familiar and ornate, didactic and exhortative. Sometimes the intellectual element is more prominent, at other times the imaginative and dramatic. Simple exposition of

doctrine, plainly worded moral exhortation hold their place
there as well as sublimity of diction and acute dialectic.
Literary forms were subordinated to the practical purpose
of instructing, warning, illuminating the faithful.

Each preacher may rightly use whatever authentic gifts he
possesses for the high purpose of bettering his hearers, for it
is only empty, pretentious, unreal, unspiritual preaching that
can justly be denied an apostolic ancestry. That muddy
stream flows from baser springs—from vanity, or listlessness,
or convention, or worldliness.

Moreover, a sermon is not to be condemned merely because
it is modern in its outlook—the Apostles were modern to
their own contemporaries. They understood their message,
they realized the attitude of their hearers, their sincerity
was absolute, and when the champions of any cause are of
this quality, they level the path that leads to its triumph.
What was true of them should be true also of every one
in whom the Apostolic office is renewed.

II

So much of this work will have to be taken up with what
may be called the intellectual aspect of preaching, that the
necessity of saying something about its spiritual aspect is
peremptory. Most of us have many imperfections to
be corrected in our preaching, but those which attach
to our ideal of what preaching ought to be, are the
most dangerous and the most destructive of the influence
of our ministry. Let me explain this a little more
exactly. Every priest who has even the average, current
views about the obligations of his state, appreciates the
sacredness of the functions which regard the essence of his
priesthood. He knows what a great and solemn privilege
is his to stand at the altar, offering the Holy Sacrifice for
living and dead, to bind and loose in the tribunal of Penance,
to comfort the sick, and prepare the dying for their journey
from this world to the next. It is possible for use and
custom to dim the vivid sense of the sacredness even of
these offices ; but as long as a vestige of the priestly spirit

survives in a man, he never completely loses the feeling that these works are the most momentous of his life. His conscience occupies itself with them, and gives him trouble when he performs them carelessly. At special periods, such as times of retreat, he takes stock of his attitude towards them, and endeavours to realize them afresh so as to regain the first fervour of the early days of his priesthood. He habitually recognizes, with more or less distinctness, that the discharge of these functions is the real work of his life. He was attracted to the altar by their sacredness, he accepted the trials of his state in the hope that these would be his aid and his stay, and he foresees that when the account of his stewardship is rendered, his fidelity to these duties will be his final consolation and his crown. Can it be said that priests are thoroughly convinced that preaching is as serious a duty as the sacramental offices of their ministry ?

In the first place, a priest has probably thought but little about this particular duty during his years of preparation. His vocation to be a priest did not include in any very explicit way any vocation to be a preacher. In a vague and general fashion he foresaw that in the ordinary course he would have to preach sermons ; but his attitude towards this part of his mission was rather that of one who knows that he will have to perform a task than of one who looks forward to enjoying a privilege. When he is ordained, he brings with him this inadequate estimate which he has imperceptibly formed. If it is not corrected it will keep him back from doing untold good to his own soul and to his people.

This matter has been temperately and justly stated in a passage which I quote from a privately circulated booklet written by one whose life has been spent in training students for the priesthood :

" At the beginning the priest's preaching has been a struggle to get through without breaking down. When he has been sufficiently long at it for this danger to have passed away he has still the practical feeling—his aim is to fill up the requisite amount of time with respectably good matter so as to discharge his duty. It has really hardly at all come before him in the light of a privilege to speak the Word of God, a source of grace to himself as well as to others, an expression of his own spiritual life and nourishment, put forth for the benefit and instruction of those intrusted to his pastoral charge. And it seems to me that this very inadequate view—to use a mild word—which we take of the work of preaching is responsible to a very large extent for the want of fervour in our sermons, and also their want of soul and interest. Let me not be misunderstood. I do not mean that *no* priests think of the work of preaching in its true light, or even that in any priest such thought is entirely absent. Many of our clergy on the English mission are models of zeal and hard work, and lead thoroughly supernatural lives. And they fulfil the words of St Paul to the letter by preaching not themselves, but Christ and Him crucified. But I am speaking of the average priest, and it does appear to me that, though the true view of preaching may not be entirely absent, it is often far too much in the background. His predominant idea is that his sermon is a task, and, as such, he discharges it, with the results already alluded to." [1]

Another circumstance tending to obscure the true conception of the office of preaching, is that in our times, for one reason or another, there is a tendency and a temptation to depreciate the efficacy of preaching. We are all more or less in danger of being inoculated with this error, especially as it seems on a superficial view to correspond with the findings of our own experience. We hear on all sides that the pulpit is a spent force, and almost an anachronism; or again that there is something radically defective in the subject-matter of preaching, so that the only hope for a revival of interest in it is the transformation of preaching into something else which is nothing like itself. Ecclesiastics, one hears, have lost touch with the thought and aspiration of the times: they live in a closed-up, antiquated world of their own. The age of preaching has gone by as truly as the Stone and Bronze age, and the great Journalistic Period has

[1] Mgr. Ward, *Preaching as a Part of Pastoral Work*, pp. 2 and 3.

taken its place. We listen to this, and may be we seem to see in our own experience a confirmation of this widespread, but not always impartial and disinterested, view. A priest preaches to the best of his ability Sunday after Sunday, and when after a time he tries to cast up the result of his efforts, he acknowledges that he sees very little improvement in anybody. He is disappointed and disheartened, and wonders whether preaching is, all things considered, worth the while.

We will look this difficulty in the face. It is undoubtedly true that the influence of newspapers and periodicals is enormous, and that secular interests now fill in the mental life of the average man a large space which was formerly devoted to religious thinking. Nevertheless, no good purpose can be served by yielding to pessimism. Rather, knowing as we do what is at stake, we ought to be all the more eager to enhance the influence of the pulpit by rendering it more effective. Catholics, at least, do not wish preaching to become mere lecturing on natural morality or patriotism or hygiene ; they are quite alive to the inadequacy of these things as the ultimate interests of life, and their desire is to keep for religion its rightful place in their mental and moral education. Moreover, the power of the pulpit is not at so low an ebb as some report it to be. Preaching still exercises a very large influence upon religious people, and if more attention were given to it by preachers themselves, its power might be increased almost indefinitely. As long as human nature is what it is, the presence and the living voice of a speaker will be more inspiring than the thoughts of a writer set down in a book. Both education and politics continue to depend upon oral teaching and lecturing, and an efficient lecturer or platform orator can still be sure of an interested audience. Growing experience will convince a young priest given to pessimism that preaching *is* worth while ; for among other things, it will teach him how much harm comes from sheer ignorance.

Perhaps some of us despond because we expect too sudden a result from our words. We must not look for the harvest while we are sowing the seed. The slow, patient process of growth escapes us. If we seem to fail, we may remind ourselves that the Word, though in itself "living and effectual," does not always fall upon good ground. The parable of the sower is valid for all time; it was spoken as an antidote to unreasoning optimism and unjustified pessimism. We are too near our own work to judge it rightly—there is nothing to be done but to go on in manly faith and trust, and leave the results to God. "He is working His own purpose by us. We do not know to whom the message is sent. It often happens now that many years pass and we know for the first time that on such a day and in such a place some words of ours have stung a conscience, or stirred a heart, or moved a will, and brought a soul to God. But we shall never know in this world all that God may have done while we were unconscious. Therefore 'cast thy bread upon the running waters, for after a long time thou shalt find it again.'" [1] We who preach the merit of faith to others need to have faith ourselves in the efficacy of our own ministry. It is the ministry of the Apostles which we exercise, and the promise of the divine assistance descends to us with the duty of instructing the faithful in the law of Christ.

[1] Manning, *The Eternal Priesthood*, p. 187.

CHAPTER II

THE MAKING OF A PREACHER

ST BERNARD in one of his sermons on the Canticle makes use of an apt illustration to drive home the lesson that the instruction of others should be the overflow of one's own personal spirituality and knowledge.

" If then you are wise," he says, " you will show yourself rather as a reservoir than as a water-pipe. For a pipe spreads abroad water as it receives it, but a reservoir waits till it is filled to overflowing, and thus communicates, without loss to itself, its superabundant water.

" . . . In the Church at the present day we have many water-pipes, but few reservoirs. Those through whom the dew of heaven distils upon us are so great in charity that they wish to pour it forth before they are themselves filled with it ; they are more prepared to speak than to hear, are quick to teach what they have not learned, and long to preside over others while they do not as yet know how to govern themselves." [1]

It is especially during the years of an ecclesiastic's preparation—those spent in a seminary—that the reservoir of charity and knowledge is gradually filled with a supply which, later, is to be spread abroad for the good of souls. When we compare the length of time devoted to a priest's special training with that of most professional men, we are not surprised that a great deal is expected from us. Few men of the learned professions have so long a course of special studies as ourselves. Six years or thereabouts are given to a student, who has already finished his preparatory course of humanities, in which to prepare himself for his ministry. Apart altogether from the consecration of this

[1] *Sermons on the Canticle*, xviii.

system by the Council of Trent and the now almost universal custom of the Church, there is in the nature of things a complete justification of the wisdom of the seminary system. The exceptional vocation of the priest, his sacred character, the kind of knowledge requisite for his functions, demand a type of education altogether special, and one differing in many ways from that given to those aiming at a secular career. Hence he is removed from the agitation of worldly interests and dedicated by a particular preparation of mind and spirit to the duties of his state. The ecclesiastic needs to be something other than a cassocked layman ; he must receive a stamp which sets him apart from secular ambitions and creates in him a character fitted to uphold worthily and with dignity the sacred cause to which he has freely consecrated his talents and his whole being.

I

The influence of the seminary is perhaps the main factor in the formation of a priest's life and character. If the priest disappoints the expectation of laymen, there is much criticism of seminary methods and seminary studies. A superior of a seminary might not inappropriately address his student as one of Balzac's disreputable characters addresses his pupil, " I am the author, you are the drama ; if you fail, I shall be hissed."

As a matter of fact there are other elements into the formation of a priest anterior to his entrance into the life of a seminary. His vocation to the priesthood with its consolations and hesitations and panics has usually a long and inward history which reaches back to his early boyhood. Vocations have their dawn, not in calculation but in fervour or romance. They are the work of God in the soul, and it is a spiritual attraction which first draws a boy's heart towards the sanctuary. The duties and sacrifices entailed in the dedication are realized but gradually, and it is during his seminary course that they come to stand out before him plainly, as he learns in detail the manner of life that a priest is called to lead, and the responsibilities attached to the office of shepherding souls. What was in boyhood vague and idealistic slowly settles down into a concrete and clear ideal. The youth becomes conscious of a difference of outlook which he can contrast with the secular ambitions of the school companions whose ways have parted from his. Spiritual reading, meditations, retreats, the orderly ways of the house, the interchange of sentiments with those who have taken the same road as himself, the counsel of superiors in public and in private, impress upon him a sense of discipline of which he becomes more and more conscious. The years do not pass without leaving their effect in the depths of the spirit. The intelligence, especially, is re-shaped by the studies to which he is set. His faith is in a manner re-taught him, under forms that seem at first strangely technical. An abstract and intellectual aspect is put upon the truth upon which his soul has lived, the atmosphere about him is saturated with reasoning. Dogmas are examined, as under a microscope, and the world of mysteries is mapped out into treatises and then subdivided into questions and theses.

The religion of his childhood is poured into a new mould and takes upon itself an almost alien shape. Dogma, ethics, and even spirituality are reduced to orderly plans and form the object of continual disputation in the lecture-room. All this is a necessary process, for only thus can theology be set upon its seat of honour among the sciences and the intellect be given its commanding place in the hierarchy of the faculties. Sentiment and rhetoric would be but shifty foundations for a clear and intelligible system such as Catholic theology claims to be. "Every science," writes Huxley, "must consist of precise knowledge, and that knowledge must be co-ordinated into general propositions, otherwise it is not science." [1] The seminarist's mind is thus equipped for its contact with the thought of the world by the scientific study of theology; the revelation of God committed to the guardianship of the Church is presented as a cogent and well-articulated whole. He learns to distinguish what is comprehensible from what is mysterious, to penetrate the formulas in which the faith is enshrined,

[1] *Lay Sermons*, viii.

and to correlate his religious with his secular knowledge. In a world of confused ideas and fragmentary systems this is no small advantage. His spiritual perception of religion deepens, his intelligence calls upon faith, and his faith seeks intelligence. " He is fitting himself to grasp God's message to a perishing world ; to understand the great counsel of the Incarnation ; to penetrate Christ crucified. And he cannot but desire to study in God's sight—*coram Deo.* For he is in God's sight—the sight of the One who has chosen him and called him, who keeps his faith and provides him with every help, who watches his efforts and measures his progress, so that the good day may one day come when he may go out as a prophet and teach, guide and exhort those souls of men for whom the zeal of the Sacred Heart burns through all generations." [1]

I am here only concerned with seminary training in so far as it is a factor in the formation of a preacher. It is admitted on all hands that this equipment for preaching is but a part of the result that is to be looked for from the six years spent in a seminary and devoted to ecclesiastical training. A great deal of what is learnt in a seminary will have only an indirect influence on the preacher's art. But since preaching is one of the most important and essential duties included in the care of souls, it is but just both to the student and to the Church in general that preaching should be well taught ; it should not be left to chance, or come to be considered as a mere by-product of the process. The Professor of Sacred Eloquence has no unimportant post and no small responsibility. If priests are ordained, as some undoubtedly are, without having been taught how to preach, the Church suffers, and congregations become the *corpus vile* for the experiments in oratory by which a priest flounders into some sort of facility in public speaking. If the chair of sacred eloquence is merely a conventional and somewhat pompous designation of a professorship which entails no lectures and few duties of any kind, there need be no surprise at the discontent which laymen sometimes express at the way in which the office of preaching is dis

[1] Bishop Hedley, *Lex Levitarum*, chap. ix.

charged. It is small consolation to a layman to hear that his ecclesiastical torturer is a brilliant logician or an accomplished theologian, as familiar with the Porphyrian tree as if he had spent half his life among its gaunt and leafless branches ; the victim will be practical and perverse enough to answer that he has noticed that very few attend the services at which a sermon is preached, and that the people crowd in at Low Masses or trail in just in time for Benediction, after devoutly lurking in the church porch until the preacher has left the pulpit.

I have heard priests stalwartly defend the theory that no special training in preaching is necessary.

Their arguments were two : that if a man thinks clearly he will speak clearly and interestingly, and again, that not the language of the sermon but its subject-matter is all-important. Each of these fallacies contains, as most sophisms do, a measure of truth. Matter must always be the essential factor and style the accessory, and it is to be regretted that this truism is sometimes forgotten. In certain men the art of popular and clear discourse is a gift of nature, just as painting and music and mathematics appear to be in other men. But innate genius of this kind is obviously exceptional, and no one ever suggests that art schools and mathematical masters have no place in the universal scheme. It may be allowed that the man with clear ideas has gone a long way towards using clear language, for if his ideas were hazy his language could not possibly be clear. Still, when all is said, the faculty of arranging ideas and choosing suitable expressions is not inevitably included in the power of thinking clearly, and for this reason the art of preaching demands special training. The second fallacy—that style is of no importance —is a plain challenge thrown in the face of common experience. Here again there is some colour of reasonableness in the statement, for a subject may be in itself so enthralling that one scarcely cares how unsuitable may be the form in which it is communicated. Preachers, however, cannot assume that this intense interest exists in their audiences as a whole ; they have to deal with many who are listless and indifferent, and their first concern must be to awaken curiosity

and stimulate attention ; unless they can do this, they may
count their words as wasted upon many of their hearers.
The sum of the matter is this, that full justice is not done to
the seminarist, nor to the Church, unless close attention is
paid to direct and specific preparation of the priest for the
office of preaching.[1]

II

The Westminster Series already contains a book entitled
" The Priest's Studies," a guide to help priests to maintain
during their missionary life scholarly and ecclesiastical interests.   Any seminary that sends a considerable number of
its students forth at the end of their course without having
instilled into them a genuine taste for some form or other of
professional study must be held guilty of having failed in
one of the essential objects for which it exists.   Similarly any
student who has lived apart from the world for some six years,
without having imbibed an abiding curiosity and interest in
some department at least of sacred science, has reaped little
profit.   To recall St Bernard's figure of speech, he has become a water-pipe instead of a reservoir.   Nowhere will his
incompetence show itself more plainly than in the pulpit.   He
will preach, not because he has something to say, but because
he has to say something.   He will take over mechanically
the ideas of others, and even here he will usually choose the
most trite and conventional of these, and grind them out

---

[1] In a document sent to Rome in 1741 by Dr Thornburgh, the President of Douai, this passage follows the account of the course of the
Dogmatic and Moral Theology in vogue in the College :—
  " The superiors of the College, moreover, are fully persuaded that
the Christian commonwealth finds the greatest benefit from a frequent
and worthy preaching of the Word of God, and that innumerable
evils have resulted from its neglect.   Hence they strive by all means
in their power that each Alumnus should devote serious thought to
the apostolic duty of preaching, should practise it, and make it a
special object of his prayer, that he may be ' powerful in word and
in work,' preaching sound doctrine, and always suitably prepared
to refute by word and example those who assail the truth." E. H.
Burton, *The Life and Times of Bishop Challoner*, vol. i. p. 49.
The changes wrought by time in the state of Catholicism in England
have not diminished the actuality of this piece of sound good sense.

like a gramophone. The time spent at the seminary is the time for forming ecclesiastical interests if ever they are to be formed at all. And, if I may give a word of counsel to seminarists, I would ask them when they take up any hobby, to consider, besides their own inclinations, the needs of the souls who will be given into their charge. They are to shepherd the people of God, they are to enlighten and direct the faithful. In the ample province of sacred study which stretches before their gaze, is there not some small plot which they can cultivate both with pleasure to themselves and with benefit to those who will soon be committed to their keeping ? Since there are profitable and unselfish interests, why concentrate upon such as are futile and selfish ? The field is wide. Sacred Scripture is an inexhaustible mine which can be worked during a long life with interest and profit ; so is dogmatic theology, especially if some patristic study is included ; so also is that study of ever-increasing urgency, Apologetics ; and all these have a very intimate connection with preaching. They give direct help to the preacher, and preaching in turn gives an immediate and practical object to them. " Meditate upon these things," writes St Paul to Timothy, " be wholly in these things, that thy profiting may be manifest to all. Take heed to thyself and to doctrine : be earnest in them. For in doing this thou shalt both save thyself and them that hear thee." [1]

Later in this work will be found chapters devoted to special kinds of sermons—dogmatic, moral, etc. This, however, seems to be the fitting place to indicate the general bearings of the main branches of ecclesiastical study upon the office of preaching.

It is useful to note, first of all, that the scientific form in which knowledge comes to the student is not the one suited for its communication by the preacher to the faithful. The preacher's work is not to make good theologians of his people, but good Christians. As a student he has read many text-books and listened to many lectures. But his sermons, if they are going to be fruitful, will not take on the style of a

[1] Ep. to Timothy iv. 15, 16.

lecture or a manual. Theology must be stripped of its rigid intellectualism, and become transformed by meditation into a teaching accommodated to his hearers. This task is made specially difficult for us by the circumstance that many of our text-books and some of our lectures are in Latin. We are prone to get into a habit of laying up in our memory a number of succinct Latin terms, for which we never even attempt to get an equivalent in English. I mean such terms as *communicatio idiomatum, per accidens, per modum eminentiæ*, etc.; besides others which, though they have an English equivalent, do not when literally translated convey to a non-theological mind the clear notions which they do—or ought to do—to ourselves : for example—" the natural and supernatural order," " the hypostatic union." It is not at all easy to express the ideas underlying such terminology in plain current English, and yet it must be done, for what is normal technical language among experts is usually mere jargon when delivered in its crude state to laymen. We appreciate this ourselves when we deal with technicalities outside our own sphere, when we wade through a legal document for instance, or struggle to wring some precise meaning out of an Act of Parliament—let us then compassionately dilute our doses of theology before we offer them to our people. Preachers often take it for granted that their congregations understand the technical terms they introduce into their sermons. They would be surprised if they discovered the truth that the whole point of their discourse is sometimes missed because they have used certain terms which, though they are quite familiar in sound, are perfectly unintelligible to many of their hearers.

In addition to this necessity of accommodating or transforming the language of theology, there is that of avoiding whole questions, which, though essential to systematic completeness, are best kept out of the pulpit—such, for instance, as the controversy on the physical or moral causality of the sacraments, or again the theories which attempt to reconcile grace with free will. The shallowest student can, if he wishes, gain a reputation for portentous learning by employing learned tags or broaching difficult problems in sermons which appear magnificent merely because they are beyond the grasp of laymen. It is quite easy to be emptily impressive and pedantic, but it is not easy to cast grand conceptions into a mould of perspicuous but dignified language, and to transmute the technical language of theology into an idiom which is familiar without being hackneyed and commonplace. Only by the steady contemplation of the realities embodied in abstract forms is it possible to melt dry intellectual propositions into concrete images and to transpose rigid formulas into the modes of common speech. It need not be said that this process is possible only where there is knowledge both of the conceptions of theology and the genius of the English tongue. The exigencies of professional training demand a varied, even a crowded, curriculum, and leave little time for the cultivation of the medium through which the acquired knowledge must finally reach those for whose benefit the store is gathered ; so that the task of learning the secret of imparting technical knowledge in a popular guise has to be left in great measure to personal industry and initiative. A good preacher need not be " literary," still, inasmuch as his utterances are delivered in the English tongue, he is ill-equipped to deliver them effectively unless he has a fair facility in the use of sound, clear English.

III

Although the Church does not exact encyclopædic learning in her priests, she has often plainly intimated that the priesthood ought to be a learned body. Canon Law requires as a condition for ordination what it calls " competent knowledge "—which is interpreted by legislators and theologians to mean a sound, though not an exhaustive, knowledge of the sciences appertaining to his sacred ministry. As a confessor he must have a fair working knowledge of Moral Theology, such as would enable him to solve immediately the ordinary cases of conscience he would be likely to meet ; as the administrator of a parish he must have at least the " knowledge of the law " sufficient for the due discharge of his parochial duties. The Council of Trent decreed—in conformity with the preceding requirements already existing in Canon Law—that the order of the priesthood should be conferred only on those who were proved fit to instruct the people in whatever is necessary for salvation and to rightly administer the sacraments.[1] This is not a very exacting programme. Legislation of this general kind prescribes the minimum of requirements ; it demands what is essential ; and establishes what is of precept, not what is of counsel. Learning is not the only qualification demanded of a priest, it is not even the most essential ; a mere body of clerical scholars and bookworms, without zeal or piety, would quickly lose its hold on the faithful and involve the Church in serious loss. Nevertheless, a well-informed, intellectually eager clergy is necessary for the health of the Church, and in these times of widely diffused education it is perhaps more necessary than it ever was before. Hence the popes of the last and the present century have laid special emphasis on the intellectual preparation of the parochial clergy, and given to the requirements of Canon Law an interpretation conformable to the special needs of our age. That they have not neglected the important matter of preaching, the documents which will be found at the end of this work are. sufficient to show.

During his course at the seminary the candidate for Holy Orders will have surveyed the ground of sacred science with some minuteness. Before his ordination he will have received a solid training as a theologian. But, as we have already hinted, a preacher and a theologian are not the same thing. Theology is a science, preaching is an art —an art, it is true, inspired by science, always returning to science for its direction, yet not one with it. It seems to me that the main difficulty in preaching lies in the transformation of sacred science into an art, the adaptation of abstract knowledge to practical ends. This difficulty may be dealt with in two ways. The easy, but wrong way, to is evade it, the hard but profitable way is to master it.

If a young priest takes the easier road, he will leave his

[1] Session xxiii. 14.

theology alone after his ordination, it will remain shut up in his memory, and sharing the fate of all the unutilised contents of that "faculty which forgets." He will go to other sources for the material of his preaching, and chiefly he will run for help to books of ready-made sermons. On the other hand, he may determine that the knowledge he has acquired during his training shall be put to practical use, shall be transmuted into popular instruction, and completed by further researches. In the few paragraphs which follow, I assume that this is the method which will have commended itself to my reader.

Accepting this alternative, the task before the young preacher is in the main that of progressively making more concrete and popular what he has learned in a scientific and abstract fashion. The following hints may prove useful in this process:—

1. *Do not read and re-read text-books.* Text-books remain useful, and it would be a mistake to sell them —as some do—or to leave them untouched on one's bookshelves. We know our way about a text-book over which we have pored, and we shall go instinctively to it when our memory requires refreshing on some point which we intend to introduce into our discourse. A thesis from a manual will often provide the material and the orderly sequence of ideas, as well as the most useful way of treating our subject. Our text-book thus remains for us an almost indispensable work of reference. But to enlarge our view, to give it a more concrete and actual turn, it will be wise to give our attention to works having a more immediate bearing upon popular instruction. There is a wide choice of such books, and monographs are constantly appearing on special theological and moral subjects written in a freer style than that employed in most manuals—if these monographs are in English so much the closer are they to our immediate purpose. Gihr, *The Holy Sacrifice of the Mass*; Bishop Hedley, *The Holy Eucharist*; Rickaby, *The Lord my Light*; Allies, *St Peter, His Name and Office*, and books like them, supply a fund of ideas almost ready for use in the pulpit. I must not omit to make mention of one book which is commended to preachers by the highest authority—

the Roman Catechism, drawn up at the instance of the Fathers of Trent, a composite work in which many authors had a share. This is neither a theological manual nor a catechism intended for laymen, but a book of doctrine specially designed to supply theologians with prepared matter for the instruction of their people. Pope Leo XIII. had a high opinion of its utility: "Remarkable at once by the variety and the exactness of its doctrine and the elegance of its style, this catechism is a valuable epitome of dogmatic and moral instruction, and whoever has a thorough knowledge of it has always at his disposition resources by the aid of which a preacher is enabled to preach with fruit . . . and ꜱꜱe the objections of unbelievers."

2. *Read and re-read the Sacred Scriptures.* During his preparation for the priesthood the ecclesiastic has attended many lectures and read a considerable amount about the Old and New Testament. He has, in his course of Sacred Scripture, studied a General Introduction to the Old and New Testament, and in his course of Dogmatic Theology he has learnt the rules of Interpretation. Besides this he has attended lectures upon the exegesis of some books of the Bible. Much that he finds in his note-books will help his preaching but little—what concerns the history and authorship of the books, for example, and the formation of the Canon of Scripture. As a preacher he needs to use the Bible after another fashion; it is to be to him a storehouse of religious teaching, "a letter of Almighty God to His creature," as St Gregory expresses it. From its pages he will draw what is needful for the enlightenment and healing of souls.

Sermons illustrated by sacred Scripture have a spiritual unction that others lack, and it is almost literally true that all the great spiritual leaders in every period have drawn plentifully from the well of sacred Scripture. To steep oneself in the language of Holy Scripture, to investigate its depths, to quote it aptly and often, is the surest road to devout and fruitful preaching. I will, however, leave a fuller treatment of the homiletic use of Scripture to a later chapter.

3. *Take notes of anything you meet in your general read-*

ing which is likely to be of use in the pulpit. Hobbes's *Leviathan* is an example of the results of energetic note-taking. John Aubrey, Hobbes's admirer, tells us how it was written. " He walked much and contemplated, and he had in the head of his cane a pen and inkhorn, carried always a notebook in his pocket, and as soon as a thought darted, he presently entered it into his booke, or otherwise might have lost it. He had drawne the designe of the booke into chapters, and knew where about it would come in. Thus that booke was made." The children of light have still some wisdom to learn from the children of this world.

There are many ways of taking notes. The worst of all is to jot them down on an old envelope, which will almost in-evitably get lost. Another bad way (for most men at least) is to buy a large book and resolve to write down neatly what-ever strikes you in your reading as fit to be noted. This is not a bad method in itself, but usually it is frustrated by our want of perseverance. An easy, human scheme of note-taking is to copy what is not merely striking, but *very* striking, on one of a thousand or so pieces of plain white cardboard, place it in a drawer, and occasionally spend an hour in sorting out an accumulation of these detached notes. Each sheaf can then be kept apart in a small division of a drawer set aside for passages referring to a special subject. This may seem rather a useless process at first, but later on one is pleased to have a record of passages which in all probability would otherwise have slipped from memory. There is a still easier, though not so satisfactory a way—that of noting on the fly-leaf of any book we may be reading the number of the page in the volume on which a noteworthy passage occurred, together with a word or so descriptive of its drift. Each man knows what method best suits him, only let him be careful not to mark too many references, for that would defeat the end of the note-taking. Let him confine himself to marking passages that are likely to be really useful. In view of their purpose the notes most helpful will be those which contribute something actual, vivid, illuminating—not necessarily " purple patches " to be stitched on here and there, but penetrating views of religious truths, well-expressed illustrations, neat comparisons and analogies, pregnant maxims. Our purpose is not served by making a note of passages which can be met almost anywhere, and copying down truisms which we encounter in every manual. It would be difficult to describe in abstract terms the sort of passages I have in mind : my meaning will be clear if I give a few specimens. I find on the fly-leaf of a copy of Newman's *Idea of a University*—" p. 65 : God's witness of Himself." The passage is too long to quote, but what follows is characteristic: " Even where there is habitual rebellion against Him, or profound far-spreading social depravity, still the undercurrent, or the heroic outburst of natural virtue, as well as the yearnings of the heart after what it has not, and its presentiment of its true remedies, are to be ascribed to the Author of all good. Anticipations or reminiscences of His glory haunt the mind of the self-sufficient sage and of the pagan devotee ; His writing is on the wall, whether of the Indian fane or of the porticoes of Greece.

" He introduces Himself, He all but concurs, according to His good pleasure and in His selected season, in the issues of unbelief, superstition and false worship, and He changes the character of acts by His overruling operation. He condescends, though He gives no sanction, to the altars and shrines of imposture, and He makes His own fiat the substitute for its sorceries. He speaks amid the incantations of Baal, raises Samuel's spirit in the witch's cavern, prophesies of the Messias by the tongue of the Sybil, forces Python to recognize His ministers, and baptizes by the hand of the misbeliever. He is with the heathen dramatist in his denunciation of injustice and his auguries of Divine vengeance upon crime. Even on the unseemly legends of a popular mythology He casts His shadow, and is dimly discerned in the ode or the epic, as in troubled water or fantastic dreams. All that is good, all that is true, all that is beautiful, all that is beneficent, be it great or small, be it perfect or fragmentary, natural as well as supernatural, moral as well as material, comes from Him."

In *Civilization at the Cross Roads* (J. N. Figgis) the following is noted :—" The statecraft, the economics, the education, the literature, the social and family life of our day are organized on a basis frankly secular. So far as these things are concerned we might almost say that God does not count. Consequently it is the symbols of material possession that are alone striking in the world of to-day. For that very reason there is less of monumental expression, for men intent on money-making erect buildings only for utilitarian ends. If, however, any one such thing could represent our world of to-day to Macaulay's New Zealander, I suppose it would be the Stock Exchange. That is the true centre of the interests of the vast majority to-day, excepting small groups apart from the main current. To many others it would be the factory or the mill."

This passage was marked in Charles Meynell's *Sermons for the Spring Quarter*, under the rubric, "An Analogy: Time and Eternity":—" The traveller wends his way through the changeful country: and now, suppose the course of his journey lies along the windings of a river's margin, now through a weary expanse of heather; here he enters the noisy village street, there he is on the dusty highway; he enters a wood, he emerges again. And thus, while he keeps the level path, he only sees his journey piecemeal: as one scene appears in view another is hidden away from the sight. But suppose now that he climb up to some lofty mountain peak, then the whole country he has traversed in his journey is restored to the view in one scene. There again meanders the pleasant stream; here stretches the waste of heather; in yonder valley nestles the little village, and beneath his feet lies the sombre wood. And so shall it prove with the journey of life. In Time one scene succeeds to another; but in Eternity all the scenes of life shall be shown in one view. Then shall be to the wicked no Future in which to repent, but a state fixed and unalterable, and no Past, for alas! the Past is again present. The whole vista of the chequered life lies stretched out before the mind's eye. Here see again those idle, empty, unprofitable days—seasons of sowing wherein nothing has been sown save noxious weeds! Here see again those tainted moments of criminal indulgence. The soul is in Eternity and Eternity is the vision of life all in all."

Even in unlikely places a preacher sometimes encounters passages worth noting for use in the pulpit. I find a scene in Balzac's " Père Goriot " marked—the one which portrays the desolate end of Goriot, who in his agony excuses and imprecates by turns the ingratitude of his daughters, whom he has pampered, and who leave him to die unconsoled in his misery.

4. *Aim first at preaching simply*. Carefully prepared instructions on the great truths of religion and the plain duties of the Christian life are seldom dull. A young priest will probably fail if he devotes his first efforts to difficult, abstruse or delicate matters. Until he has taken the measure of his hearers it is wise to refrain from anything in the way of grandiloquence, and still more, of denunciation. He had better suppose them to be average Christians of average intelligence, and treat with them on that supposition. He will in time discover what are their strong and weak points, their temptations and their virtues—all, in fact, which gives to a group its moral personality. One hears sometimes remarks such as : " Father A. seems to think that we are on the point of losing our faith," or " Father B. must imagine that we are prodigiously intelligent people." The caution which Newman gave to University preachers fits all who have not had an opportunity of entering into the minds of their audience, and this is specially true of priests at the beginning of their missionary career.

" I need hardly say that a preacher should be quite sure that he understands the persons he is addressing before he ventures to aim at what he considers their ethical condition ; for, if he mistakes it, he will probably be doing harm rather than good. I have known consequences to occur very far from edifying, when strangers have fancied they knew their auditory when they did not, and have by implication imputed to them habits or motives which were not theirs. Better far would it be for a preacher to select one of those more general subjects which are safe than risk what is evidently ambitious if it is not successful." [1]

[1] Discourse on University Preaching in *The Idea of a University*, p. 418.

IV

All who pass through a seminary course make the acquaintance of the chief ecclesiastical writers and Fathers of the Church. Ecclesiastical History is full of their deeds and their teaching, dogmatic and moral and ascetical Theology draw largely upon their ancient treatises. Even the most rigid scholasticism, though quoting them but seldom, is steeped in their doctrine. Usually, however, it happens that, though much of their work is implicitly included in our seminary teaching, we are not brought to close quarters with them ; we do not make an intimate and first-hand study of what they have written—such, for instance, as we were compelled by schoolmasters to make of the actual texts of the Classics. It is not necessary to dwell on the reasons of this—the crowded curriculum, the urgency of laying broad foundations and of tracing well the outlines of complete theological science are the chief among them.

It is sufficient if we have made a beginning and know enough of the Fathers to have had our curiosity awakened for learning more of them. But here again there may be some difficulty. The more immediate claims on the time of a priest, the variety of his occupations and other reasons good or bad, may prevent priests on the mission from settling down to patristic study. After all, a priest knows that he may be very capable without having read a single work of the Fathers from end to end, and his preaching may be quite level with the average standard without his seeking help from patristic study. I venture, nevertheless, to plead for such an attention to this interesting branch of sacred study as is possible even to the busy parish priest.

As this book is concerned with preaching only, and not with the more general subject of ecclesiastical studies, I limit my plea to the study in the Fathers which anyone who is in earnest about improving his preaching may undertake without going beyond what is directly and immediately profitable. There is a " Preachers' corner " in patristic study, and anyone who finds time to visit it will be well

c

repaid. I will offer a few hints for the guidance of such a
one, and if they prove too slight for him he may go farther
and consult such admirable directors as Bardenhewer and
Tixeront.[1] For my purpose it is sufficient to indicate a centre
from which he can, if he wishes, work outwards over a wider
field.

A great deal of what the Fathers have left to us has no
close relation to preaching at all, and much even of their
homiletic work is unsuitable, as it stands, to modern audiences,
as a glance through a few of the excerpts in the Breviary
will clearly show. Our polemics, for instance, are not now
directed, as many of theirs were, against Jews; and though
heathenism is not dead, our modern heathens are not altogether of the same type as were theirs. Nor, again, are we
greatly interested nowadays in the mysticism of numbers
or in remote allegorical interpretations of the sacred text
of Scripture. Our modern preacher must make a choice,
and good sense suggests his beginning with what is plain
in itself and immediately pertinent to his actual duties.

Two models immediately suggest themselves—the two
great lights of the Roman Church, St Leo and St Gregory.
Posterity has bestowed the name of " the Great " on each
of these personifications of the practical genius of Rome,
both of them so distinguished by their power of government and their zeal for reform. Of the two, St Leo is the
more original, and his preoccupation with the Christological
controversies of his time led him to draw, with singular force
and with a splendour of language all his own, much sound moral
teaching from the theology of the Incarnation. The teaching
of St Gregory is less vivid; it was tempered to a mediocre age
and to a more commonplace, though very practical, scope.[2]

St Leo's Sermons are, in the form we have them, short;
they are mostly festal sermons preached on the greater
solemnities of Our Lord and the saints. They are brilliant
in style and abound in pregnant sayings and antitheses.
There is no fancifulness in his interpretation of Scripture;

---

[1] Bardenhewer, *The Fathers of the Church* (Eng. Trans.); Tixeront,
The History of Dogma (Eng. Trans.).
[2] Tixeront, *The History of Dogma*, vol. iii., chap. ix.

his speech is energetic, nervous and majestic; he is "the Roman prætor dictating the law, and delivering with authority the doctrine of the faith."

There are many extracts from St Leo in the Breviary which must have impressed us by the solemn majesty of their diction and their lucidity of thought. The doctrines of the Incarnation and of the Church were especially dear to him, and his sermons on the papal prerogatives are models of their kind. Several of them are contained in the small volumes of his selected sermons among the Opuscula of Hurter (vol. xiv.), and eighteen of them, all dealing with the doctrine of the Incarnation, have been translated into English, with an introduction by Dr Bright. There is perhaps no preacher among the Fathers who is the equal of St Leo in providing examples of short, substantial, doctrinal sermons. His moral discourses also are replete with suggestive thoughts, especially suitable for Lenten preaching. There is a good specimen of his manner of moral instruction in the lessons for the second Nocturn of the Office for the first Sunday in Lent.

We might begin our reading of *St Gregory* with the third part of his *Regula Pastoralis,* since this section deals with the pastoral duty of preaching. It was written to instruct preachers how to accommodate Christian teaching to different classes of men—to the rich and the poor, to the learned and to the dull, to the idle and the headstrong, the peaceable and the quarrelsome, and so on. The chapters are not ready-made sermons, but "hints to preachers." [1] As St Gregory's *Regula* was the standard work of Pastoral Theology during the Middle Ages, so his *Moralia* was the textbook of Moral Theology. This is an exposition of the Book of Job— historical, moral and allegorical. In our days the second part is of most immediate service. The writer, it will be seen, has not escaped some of the hard views attributed to St Augustine on predestination and on the lot of unbaptized children. There is no reason why we should adopt these from him.

[1] The text of the *Regula* is included in Bishop Hedley's *Lex Levitarum.*

Some of the "Opuscula" of *St Cyprian* deserve to be read as models. It is true they are not exactly sermons; they are probably sermons re-edited as pastoral instructions, but we can gather from them not only his views, but a fair notion of his preaching. Sacred Scripture was its framework. "Without the Bible he cannot speak or write, or scarcely even think." The skeleton of his discourse is formed by a number of Biblical texts, upon which he discourses; he uses them, not, as many do, to illustrate but rather to supply the different topics of his address. His style is polished, but it leaves his meaning clear; his tone is at once authoritative and familiarly persuasive. He is at his best when dealing as a bishop with some actual crisis in his city, or when giving his austere counsel in face of some public calamity endangering the spiritual interests of his flock. His treatise *De Mortalitate*, an instruction delivered to his people during the plague which ravaged Carthage in 253, is stamped with a high but natural eloquence. His moral exhortations on the Lord's Prayer, *De Dominica Oratione* might be read together with Tertullian's *De Oratione*, from which some of its ideas are borrowed. In *De Opere et Eleemosynis*, *De Bono Patientiæ* and *De Zelo et Livore* the ever practical subjects of almsgiving, resignation, and the vice of envy are admirably treated. St Cyprian's diction, as St Augustine remarked, is less ornate in his later than in his earlier works.

Father Chapman has observed that *St Augustine* is too personal to be reproduced successfully by more ordinary mortals.[1] A selection, however, might be made from his astounding abundance. We might begin with the *Enchiridion ad Laurentium*, a summary of religion written for a layman who had asked him to compile a short handbook of Christian doctrine and morals. The treatment of the three Theological Virtues (which form the divisions of the book) is brief, but the work is invaluable as an introduction to his theological thought. The simpler treatise, *De Agone Christiano*, contains chapters of practical instruction on the Christian's struggle against temptation.

[1] *Catholic Encyclopædia*, article "Fathers of the Church."

Though written to arm his people against Manachæan and other errors of his time, it has, almost everywhere, a general application. Special subjects are straightforwardly treated by St Augustine in *De Cura pro Mortuis gerenda* (questions concerning funerals and prayers for the dead), *De Bono Conjugali* (on the duties of married people), *De Fide Rerum quæ non videntur*, and *De Utilitate Credendi* (the reasonableness of submission in matters of faith). To pass to the actual preaching of the saint one might begin with one of his first collections, delivered by him when a priest. The two books *On the Sermon on the Mount* are an exposition based on St Matthew, chapters v. and vii., in which St Augustine sees the best abridgment of Our Lord's moral and spiritual teaching. The lessons read in the Breviary on the text, " You are the salt of the earth," in the Common of Doctors are a characteristic example of this suggestive spiritual work. Readers of St Augustine should be on the lookout not only for ideas and passages for quotation, but for the art of treating theology and morals before popular audiences.

A few words now on *St John Chrysostom*, for the sake of those who happily have not forgotten their Greek. Milman appreciates his merits as an orator in the following passage :— " Clear rather than profound, his dogmatic is essentially moulded upon his moral teaching. . . . His doctrines flow naturally from his subject or from the passage of Scripture under discussion ; his illustrations are copious and happy ; his style free and fluent ; while he is an unrivalled master in that rapid and forcible application of incidental occurences which gives such life and reality to eloquence. He is at times, in the highest sense, dramatic in manner." [1] St John Chrysostom had not the versatile genius of St Augustine, he was principally and almost exclusively a preacher. His life work was to elevate the morality of two great cities —Antioch and Constantinople. To this end he applied the teaching of the Scriptures to the actual problems, normal and extraordinary, of his place and time. He expounded sacred Scripture according to its literal sense, and usually

[1] *History of Christianity*, vol. iii., chap. ix.

in the form of the Homily. Realism is the note of his discourses, the most powerful of which were occasioned by dramatic events in the life of the two cities; the Homilies on the Statues and the discourses on the fall of Eutropius paint for all time two exciting crises in the cities where he ministered. The reading of a few of his Homilies on St Matthew and on St Paul's Epistle to the Romans would show a preacher how to use the New Testament in the moral instruction of his people. Those whose preaching suffers through over-compression or tameness or poverty of illustration will find in St John Chrysostom a good remedy for their failings, for his style is vivid, diffuse and highly coloured. The *Catecheses* of St Cyril of Jerusalem, "the ready champion of apostolic dogmas," are valuable rather to the historian of dogma than to the preacher, but the last five are worth consulting as models of dogmatic instruction. In Instruction XXI., chap. iii., the effects of the Sacrament of Confirmation are described, and XXII. and XXIII. contain useful exposition on the Real Presence and the Sacrifice of the Mass.

There is one province of instruction in which the Fathers are especially helpful. Priests exercising their ministry in centres of industrial life are at times obliged by their duty of preserving sound doctrine among their people to speak of economic and social questions from the pulpit. There is scarcely any class of subject so delicate or so likely to create trouble for a priest who dogmatises on these matters with superficial preparation and without clear and sound views. Some writings of the Fathers are invaluable to a priest saddled with the duty of treating the moral aspects of such questions, and it is all the more profitable for such a one to consult the Fathers, because they have already been exploited by agitators anxious to justify themselves in the eyes of religious people. Texts have been alleged which seem to convict some of the Fathers of revolutionary collectivism.[1] The true doctrine of the Fathers may be

---

[1] Some of the texts quoted are not genuine, as *e.g.* the opinion attributed to St Clement of Rome that everything is common property. This sentiment is not found in either St Clement's Epistle or the

separate and distinct in kind from the religion we preach to others.

Compassionate people, ready to excuse the human short-comings of their priests, sometimes construct a defence for them which we may well beware of accepting. A priest, they say, is an official, he stands for something so much greater than himself that the failures of his own life—be they what they may—concern no one save himself. The preacher is a signpost, and his sole function is to point the way. He obliterates his own personality when he assumes the vest-ments of his sacred office. There is something specious in this apology; in one sense, it is even true. The "ministry of reconciliation" has been committed to us, and it will be efficacious in some measure, though we be indifferent or positively unworthy. God may exhort by the mouth of a sinner, as He spoke by Caiphas "since he was the High Priest of that year." But, if there should be over-complais-ance in this generous theory, it is dissipated when a warning finger is laid upon another text. "The scribes and Pharisees have sitten on the chair of Moses. All things, therefore, whatsoever they shall say to you, observe and do; but according to their works do ye not; for they say, and do not. For they bind heavy and unsupportable burdens, and lay them on men's shoulders; but with a finger of their own they will not move them." [1]

Preachers who give themselves out as witnesses to supreme truths cannot escape that standard which men commonly use when they require that a man's creative work shall truly express himself. Statesmen, literary critics, artists, as well as many others who have no pretensions to be anything other than plain, common-sense men, are ever demanding sincerity in any workmanship on which they hold themselves to be competent judges. They look for the seal of personal conviction set upon the creation of the painter's or the writer's or the statesman's work, they seek in it the evident stamp of sincerity. Here, for example, is a passage from a recent little work on Style—and how naturally all its argu-ments fit the topic we are now discussing!

---

[1] Matt. xxiii. 2-4.

" In a general way we may take the claim of sincerity to mean that the author must stand behind what he asserts ; must have in his own person experienced or felt what he describes ; must share the convictions which he seeks to press upon others. We look to him for *choses vues* ; to which we may add *choses crues, choses senties,* and best of all, including all others, *choses vécues*. In Emerson's noble phrase, he must ' speak from within the veil, where the word is one with what it tells of.' Plainly this excludes not only wilful fraud and deception, but the pretence, artificiality, affectation or pose which presents the author as the thing he is not. There may not always be a conscious attempt to mislead ; if it be half-conscious and automatic, it points to a worse case still—that of inveterate and ingrained in- sincerity ; for just so far the result is to falsify and adulterate what is one of the most attractive and vivifying qualities of good work—the genuine *personal* element. . . . The author must not travel beyond the range of his experience— *choses vues, choses senties, choses vécues*—under a well-under- stood penalty in case of disobedience. The moment he does so we no longer feel in his utterance the unmistakable ' note of truth.' It is (if I may once more take a parallel from painting) like conventional ' studio work ' as com- pared with a life-like sketch that is done with the eye on the natural object." [1]

God's wisdom can bring good out of evil and bend even the sins of His creatures to His high purposes, but ex- perience shows that in this perplexing world evil bears its natural fruit of bitter consequences, even as good calls other good into being. At any rate, we must take it as the only safe hypothesis, that if we are unreal, the good we do will be small, and the evil we work will be proportionate to our shortcomings. St Paul throughout the pastoral epistles gives voice to general experience when he shows Titus and his beloved Timothy how they and the clergy chosen by them can secure an attentive hearing and disarm hostile criticism. The ministers of Christ must bear " the mystery of the faith in a pure conscience, they must be

[1] Prof. Hastings Crossley, *Style and Composition*, pp. 9 and 11.

irreproachable, temperate, prudent, hospitable, meek, above suspicion of avarice, free from duplicity and from arrogance." He tells Titus that conduct and preaching must be in accord. " In all things show thyself an example of good works—in doctrine, in integrity, in gravity ; the sound word which cannot be blamed ; that he who is on the contrary part, may be afraid having nothing evil to say of us." [1]

If a more theological declaration of the same truth is needed, it is supplied in a pregnant phrase of St Thomas Aquinas : " Preaching derives from the fullness of contemplation." There are many industries auxiliary to good preaching, intellectual, imaginative, literary ; but as the function is before all a spiritual and supernatural one, there is nothing so essential to the best forms of its exercise as the preparation of the soul by union with God and meditation on His law. It needs little observation to note a tendency in cynics and critics to treat preaching lightly as though it were a sort of religious play-acting. Even among the more light-minded of our own people there are traces of this sceptical estimate—there are faultfinders who think that preachers do not mean quite all they say. We have no means of combating this suspicion (evidently a dangerous one for those who entertain it) save that of rendering it utterly and manifestly untrue, by reconciling in ourselves, so far as human frailty allows, the ideals of our personal conduct and those of the Gospel we preach. This, indeed, is the hope expressed by the Church at the ordination of every priest : " Let your doctrine be the spiritual remedy to the people of God, and the fragrance of your life be the delight of the Church of Christ, so that by preaching and example you may build up the house, that is, the family of God." [2]

II

One of the diners who listened to one of Joseph Chamberlain's after-dinner political speeches tells how the orator converted a failure into a conspicuous success by a sudden change from one style of speaking to another.

[1] *Titus* ii. 1-8.   [2] *Roman Pontifical. The Ordination of Priests.*

Chamberlain began a well-prepared speech delivered from notes. There was no obvious fault in its delivery and it had evidently been well thought out, but somehow it was dull. The speaker looked round and read his ill-success in the faces of the guests, then he suddenly threw his notes on the table and launched into a passionate description of the sufferings of the poor of Birmingham. At once his hearers began to listen, as if a spell had been cast over them. Cannot we recall some similar change of attitude in ourselves as we have sat listening to sermons ? Sometimes sermons hold our interest throughout, at other times they never seize it at all; but does it not oftenest happen that they seem to find and lose touch with us in turn ? A preacher perhaps begins well, and is followed with attention, then he begins to travel on a line of thought which takes him, as it were, out of the range of his audience. There is no change in the style of language, no hesitation in manner, no symptom of failure of memory, but *something* has gone from the discourse, something has been lost. It may be that the preacher has made his way into a region unfamiliar to him, or not sufficiently explored, or perhaps he has entered a road of thought too steep for his audience to climb, or what is most likely, he has passed on from thoughts that are his own to something which he has borrowed, without assimilating, from somebody else. It is not easy to describe and much less easy to define the phenomenon that we so quickly recognize as unreality, and all that I can do is to indicate some of the causes from which it springs. I have already spoken of the unreality proceeding from conscious or unconscious insincerity, and will say something later about unreality of language ; the point I wish to speak of here is unreality in conception. Perhaps the commonest cause of this is a want of attention to the capacity or to the dispositions and interests of the audience one addresses. A subject, or the special treatment of a subject, may be real to me, but lacking in the least power of appealing to my people. Usually it is the manner of the treatment rather than the topic that is at fault. Most subjects about which we preach are sufficiently interesting not only in themselves, but actually to the people we address. Our audience would like to be told something more about them, but they are bored with what we actually tell them. In Washington Irving's " Sketch Book" there is a description, or perhaps a parody, of an old clergyman's Christmas sermon. " The parson gave us a most erudite sermon on the rites and cere-monies of Christmas, and the propriety of observing it not merely as a day of thanksgiving and rejoicing; supporting the correctness of his opinion by the earliest usages of the Church, and enforcing them by the authorities of Theophilus of Cæsarea, St Cyprian and a cloud more of saints and Fathers, from whom he made copious quotations. I was a little at a loss to perceive the necessity of such a mighty array of force to maintain a point which no one present seemed inclined to dispute ; and I soon found that the good man had a legion of ideal adversaries to contend with, having in the course of his researches on the subject of Christmas got completely embroiled in the sectarian con-troversies of the Revolution, when the Puritans made such a fierce assault upon the ceremonies of the Church, and poor old Christmas was driven out of the land by a proclamation of Parliament. The worthy parson lived entirely with the past and knew little of the present." All this was doubtless real to the clergyman, and if he had delivered the discourse as a lecture to other clergymen of his own kind he might have secured their passionate interest, but, as it was, every-body was glad when it was over, and on leaving the church " the congregation seemed one and all possessed with the gaiety of spirits enjoined by their pastor."

We avoid this sort of unreality by fitting our sermons to our audience, and by taking account of them, even before deciding what we are to say. A good sermon must be a human sermon, and its thought must move in the same plane as that of its hearers.[1] I cannot refrain from recommending Newman

[1] The contemporaries of St Bernard note this as a quality pre-eminent in his sermons. " His speech, whatever persons he spoke to for the edifying of souls, was adapted to his audience ; for he knew the intelligence, the habits and occupations of each and all. To country folk he spoke as if born and bred in the country ; and so to other classes as if he had always been occupied with their busi-

as a model of this good quality ; and though I am aware
that many are of another opinion, I think that the Parochial
and Plain sermons provide better instances for the ordinary
preacher's use than anything else he has written.[1] However
that may be, Newman points the way to that concreteness,
that contact with the thoughts of ordinary people which is
the groundwork of reality. Mr Birrell, in one of his racy
essays, emphasizes the very point, comparing him in this
respect with Burke. " Both men," he writes, " despite
their subtlety and learning and super-refinement, their love
of fine points and their splendid capacity for stating them
in language so apt as to make one's admiration breathless,
took very broad, common-sense, matter-of-fact views of
humanity, and ever had the ordinary man and woman in
mind as they spoke and wrote. Politics and Religion existed,
in their opinion, for the ben   of plain folk, for Richard
and for Jane, or, in other words, for living bundles of hopes
and fears, doubts and certainties, prejudices and passions.
. . . Dr Newman, recluse though he is, has always got the
world stretched out before him ; its unceasing roar sounds
in his ear as does the murmur of ocean in a far inland shell.
In one of his Catholic sermons, the sixth of his *Discourses
to Mixed Congregations*, there is a gorgeous piece of rhetoric

---

ness. He was learned with the erudite and simple with the simple,
and with spiritual men rich in illustrations of perfection and
wisdom. He adapted himself to all, desiring to gain all for Christ.
Vita Prima, iii. 3.

[1] The difference of the style in the Parochial and Plain sermons
from that of his later work was noted by the late Wilfrid Ward,
who thus described it :

" Their sure touch on the minds and motives of men, their frank
facing of the facts of life, impart to them a peculiar delicacy and
persuasiveness. They often bring the convincing surprise we experience when our thoughts are read truly. . . . But they evince
none of the richness of imaginative power, none of the rhetorical *élan*
of his later literary style. The magic of the preacher was not at the
time traced to oratorical eloquence. One of his finest critics—Dean
Church—points out their contrast in this respect to the sermons
of the great French preachers, Massillon and Bourdaloue. This
contrast could not be maintained in respect of the most eloquent
of the Birmingham discourses".—*Last Lectures*, pp. 55 and 56. It
seems to me, however, that there *is* a great deal of resemblance between
Newman in his earlier manner and Bourdaloue.

in which he describes the people looking in at the shop-
windows and reading advertisements in the newspapers.
Many of his pages positively glow with light and heat and
colour. One is at times reminded of Fielding." [1] Newman
sets us on the right track by teaching each of us how one's
own experience ought to be woven into our preaching. A
priest's pastoral experience can be converted into an immense
help in his preaching. His sphere may not be wide, but he
has exceptional opportunities of knowing his microcosm very
intimately. Enlarging observation improves preaching, provided it is an observation directed by intelligence; if it is
not, we live without learning, and see without observing,
and we may preach " even to old age and grey hairs " the
academic scholasticism of the lecture-room, or the impersonal
conventions of the sermon book.

There is another path leading to the same desirable end,
and this is to give our first attention to the matter of our
preaching rather than to the words. " I have finished the
preparation of my sermon," Bossuet is reported to have
said; "all that I have to do now is to find the words." Are
words then unimportant ? By no means, but the substance
is of greater moment than the form ; moreover, in meditating
the substance we are going far towards finding the words.
What is well conceived can be well expressed if one takes a
little trouble. Men speak of discourses as " empty," " thin,"
as " having very little in them." What does this common
parlance mean, if not that something more is required than
mere copiousness or even splendour of phrase ? A verbose
man is satisfied with his performance if only the words come
readily, but one with his mind primarily set upon things is
disappointed if he has not said all that he set out to say,
even though he has no reason to be dissatisfied with his
fluency of phrase.

Reality is mainly a matter of clear and definite ideas
as distinguished from half-conceived, vague, superficial
impressions. Clear notions must first be formed in the
mind by intent meditation, they must be gazed at, until the
mists clear away from them and their shape appears, precise

[1] A. Birrell, *Selected Essays*: " Cardinal Newman."

D

and definite. The language forms itself with the conception, though (usually) not quite adequately at first. To begin with words, in the hope of coming across ideas, is to reverse the natural process, though the polishing of the language will still further clarify the ideas. " I never," wrote Newman in one of his letters, " have been in the practice since I was a boy of attempting to write well, or to form an elegant style. I think I have never written for writing's sake ; but my one and single desire and aim has been to do what is so difficult, namely, to express clearly and accurately my meaning ; this has been the motive principle of all my corrections and rewritings. . . . I am as much obliged to correct and re-write as I was thirty years ago." [1]

III

" Be careful about words, but solicitous about things," says Quintillian to his pupils in oratory. Words have no value apart from ideas, yet inasmuch as they have the function of carrying ideas into the open, and setting them in the public view, it is unwise of a speaker to be so solicitous about the " things " of his discourse as to neglect to be even careful about the words that compose it. What is this care for words necessary for a speaker ? Evidently not the philologist's nor the linguist's nor even the literary purist's. In his aim at reality his chief preoccupation is to be intelligible, interesting, natural. This he can best achieve by the use of plain current English. Not dull or lifeless English ; a preacher can avoid that, without departing from the vocabulary and the level of diction customary in careful and deliberate conversation. Cicero has remarked that while in other departments of knowledge it is an advantage for a man to be well informed about things of which ordinary folk know nothing, this aloofness from common ways is not a virtue but a defect in oratory, since oratory loses in effectiveness in proportion as it departs from the common custom of speech.[2] The speaker should find his

[1] *Letters and Correspondence of J. H. Newman*, ii. p. 476.
[2] *De Oratore*, bk. i., chap. iii.

vocabulary in current idiom and avoid anything that savours of jargon. Jargon abounds; one can read a few columns of it every day in one's newspaper. Here, for instance, is an example in to-day's *Times*. " There was considerable activity in the opening (of the Stock Exchange) and heavy buying from all quarters resulted in the attainment of new high price levels in the industrial list of stocks. The chief influence was apparently the elimination of obnoxious features from the tax programme, which is having a nation-wide effect, but the enormous earnings of corporations and the brilliant trade outlook generally, also influenced buying." This is commercial jargon. Then there is the official style: " Your committee has the honour of presenting its quarterly report and begs to state," etc. Again, to take another instance, there is the jargon consecrated to certain social announcements: " The bride was led to Hymen's altar . . . the wedding presents were numerous and costly," and so on. All this sort of writing can be described as English, for all the words can be read in standard dictionaries; still, it is not the English either of literature or (thank Heaven !) of conversation. Its law is not that of nature, but of de-partmental convention; there is no spontaneity in it, it has no life of its own, it gives information, but appeals to no human feeling or passion. In a word, it is not current English, it is professional jargon.

But, it may be objected, " is not religious language itself rather remote and apart from the ordinary language of common life ? " It is true that there are some conceptions proper to religious writing, speaking and thinking; but after all they form but a small, almost negligible fraction of religious ideas. In the main, the language corresponding with the aims and function of preaching is the language of real life—nay more, the language of the preacher's own real life.

" A living form of speech is one which expresses real ideas and feelings and genuine convictions in a form suited to the audience and the occasion, springing from the mind of the speaker in the process of his thought, and revealing something at least of his personality. In order to arrest attention and compel interest, an utterance, whether it be a public oration or familiar discourse, must contain something more than the obvious truisms of a proposition in Euclid ; the style in which the thoughts are clothed must be personal to the speaker, and not the mere repetition of set phrases. The essentials of *living* utterance are then, reality of conviction and individuality of form and phrase." [1]

In that very useful book, *The King's English*, a few rules are given to guide speakers and writers in expressing their ideas simply and forcibly. They are not rigorous precepts, but rather counsels and warnings. They are of great service in the preacher's necessary task of self-criticism. I will mention them, together with instances which suggest themselves as being appropriate to our subject.

1. *Prefer the familiar word to the far-fetched.*

Thus it is often better to say "the greatness of our sins" rather than "the magnitude of our transgressions"; "heavenly home" rather than "celestial habitation"; "teach" rather than "inculcate" (inculcate by the way is a very favourite word with some) ; "good deeds left to our own free choice" rather than the more technical "works of supererogation" ; "unsuitable" rather than "incongruous."

2. *Prefer the concrete word to the abstract.*

When there is a choice between "luminosity" and "light," "glorification" and "glory," "limitation" and "limit," "obduracy" and "hardness," as a rule the concrete word will be more telling than the abstract.

3. *Prefer the single word to the circumlocution.*

Any striving after the "grand manner" as an end in itself involves us in long drawn out periods and gives an unreal air to what we say, especially when what we want to express is something obviously simple. I find in a sermon-book this form of asking people to send for a priest when some one is dangerously ill. "Those who are in attendance should see that the sick person neglects not to summon his spiritual guide, and to be fully reconciled with God and prepared for death, should there be any danger of a fatal termination of the disease." Let us hope that the orator's hearers were less leisurely in doing their duty, than he was in telling them

[1] Wild, *Historical Study of the Mother Tongue*, p. 349.

of it, otherwise the sick person might die before the priest got news that he was ill.

4. *Prefer the short word to the long.*

By this is not meant that words must be taken or left according to their size (as chimney-sweepers' boys used to be chosen), but that it is better to use a short word when it is as effective as its longer synonym.   There is such a thing as the simple enthusiasm for the long word for its own sake, as when one would always say " legitimate " instead of " lawful," " domination " instead of " rule," and so on.   Speeches made up of long words remind one of a heavy fall of hailstones; they represent, I suppose, the lapidary style in oratory.

5. *Prefer the Saxon word to the Romance.*

This advice is to be interpreted more broadly than that hitherto given ; to follow it with stiff uniformity would bring unreality instead of reality to sermons.   The English tongue is composite, for our language has been very hospitable to alien words, many of which have now an equal right of citizenship with words of Anglo-Saxon origin.   What words for example are better understood than " simplicity," " temptation," " strict," " pious," " chain," all of them Romance words ?   If then we tried to keep ourselves exclusively to words of Anglo-Saxon derivation, our idiom would lose its flexibility, and in fact there would arise instances in which our rule would have to give way.   Yet, rightly understood, the advice is worth attention.   The basis of English is Anglo-Saxon, which has supplied by far the greatest number of the most usual words.   If a discourse contains a good proportion of Anglo-Saxon words it will usually be found to be keeping close to the language and the ideas of ordinary life.   Much reading of text-books (often unrelieved by literary study of any kind) disposes seminarists towards a heavy, latinized style of writing.   They can do something towards correcting this natural tendency by cutting down, where it can be done without loss of force and clearness, the number of cumbersome words of Latin origin and putting Anglo-Saxon ones in their place.

These counsels were devised to simplify writing and speech, and relieve it of pedantry and bombast.   But bom-

bast is not the only source of unnatural language. The
advice of Polonius is not to be passed over lightly. " Be
thou familiar, but by no means vulgar." In his flight from
pretentiousness a preacher may run into the arms of meanness of diction. It is imagined by some that slang gives a
note of reality to speech, and that people who use slang
are delighted to hear it everywhere and from everybody.
This is not true. It is quite likely that the priest who uses
slang in the pulpit will be criticised more harshly by those
who use it habitually in common life, than by those who
never use it. It sounds unreal when it comes from him, and
savours both of affectation and condescension, as though he
is laboriously letting himself down to the level of those whom
he regards as his inferiors. To be real is to be natural, and
slang is unnatural when used by certain persons and on certain
occasions. One has heard of the contempt of schoolboys for
preachers who try to come down to their level by winding
out long allegories in language borrowed from schoolboy
customs or sports. That a topical reference can brighten
a discourse, no one would deny ; but the device must be
used sparingly, or it will fail. The worst of it is, that when
it does fail, its author may imagine that he has made a very
happy hit.

While I am speaking of this, I may allow myself a short
digression on the use of humorous language in the pulpit.
I shall not be accused of being puritanical if I suggest
caution to preachers who would be jocose. To flavour a
topic with a little quiet humour is no crime ; it is even a
virtue ; still, there are forms of wit which make the judicious
grieve and amuse only the stupid and frivolous. Besides, a
joke may be well enough if it is brought off successfully, but,
in the pulpit especially, it is a sorry performance when it misses
its mark. Even a good joke may not always be appropriate
or timely, but a poor joke that falls flat may well make any
preacher repent of his excursion into comedy.

To sum up : it is safer to use in the pulpit the sort of
language which we use when we converse privately upon
serious subjects, with a little—not too much—dignity added
in deference to the serious matter of our discourse and to

the sacred place in which we speak. Other kinds of speech may be employed as condiments, but sparingly, rarely, and appropriately, as condiments are meant to be used.

IV

To test the views of the last two sections it would be a good thing to read, or better still to listen to, two sermons— a good and a mediocre one, with the definite purpose in mind of discovering the reasons why one awakens and holds the attention and the other does not, why one hits the mark while the other misses it. It would take up too much space to print two sermons in full for the purpose of providing such a comparison, yet this matter of reality and unreality is of such moment that it needs to be illustrated by some actual example.

We will take two sermons then, and quote from each of them enough for our purpose. They were published about the same time; both treat the same subject and commend the same lesson, and both draw their materials from the same sources.

The author of one of them was Dr Meynell, of whom an account is given in a sympathetic preface written by Dr Ryder to introduce the posthumous book which contains the sermon.[1] Of the other preacher I know nothing except his name (which I shall not give) and the fact that he published several devotional books in America and in England about twenty-five or thirty years ago.

The topic of each of these discourses is the fall of Judas, and the object of each of the preachers is to show the special malice of the sin of the fallen apostle, to the end of exciting a horror of his crime and of every sin which resembles his in its meanness and ingratitude. Both sermons draw upon the same sources—the Gospel accounts of the Apostle's treason; and both naturally seek to throw into relief the figure of a man who basely sold and betrayed his Master and Friend. Let us take an extract from the unnamed preacher first.

[1] *Sermons for the Spring Quarter*, by C. Meynell, D.D.

" Several circumstances conspired to render the sin of
Judas so enormous, the first one of which was his exalted
position. He had been selected from among the millions
of men who had lived up to that period on earth and who
would live until the end of time, to be constantly in the
society of Jesus. Oh, what an honour ! In proportion to
it, therefore, his fall was immeasurably great. Another
serious aggravation of his crime was his abuse of the graces
bestowed on him to fit him for his vocation as one of the
twelve apostles—one of the favoured few, who for three years
and a half enjoyed the privilege of walking with the Saviour
of mankind. . . . Oh, what emptiness of heart ! What an
abuse of grace ! For his sin there was no excuse ! The
next aggravating circumstance was the terrible indifference
of Judas. . . . Thirdly, the sin of Judas was enormously
aggravated by his astonishing obduracy. Even though
already guilty of the basest treason, he dared to place himself
with the rest of the apostles, at the table of the Lord—the
Last Supper ! There Christ, elevating His voice, pronounced
those awful words : " One of you is about to betray me ! "
Awe-stricken, the disciples asked in trembling tones, " Is it I,
Lord ? " Judas remained obdurate. And again the Son of
God broke the deep silence saying : " The Son of Man indeed
goeth as it is written of Him : but woe to that man by whom
He shall be betrayed ; it were better for him if he had not been
born." Terrible sentence ! Mighty enough to move the
mountains to their very foundations, and to penetrate to the
inmost recesses of the ocean caves ! . . . Fourthly, the crime
of Judas was enormously aggravated by the incredible baseness of the treason. To betray his Lord and Master—his
Saviour who had given him such testimonials of His love—
for thirty pieces of silver, the price demanded for slaughtering
a head of cattle ! Can more unprecedented baseness be
imagined ? The enemies of Christ would gladly have paid
him ten, fifty, a hundred times more for his abominable
treason if he had but asked for it. . . . The last most terrible
characteristic of the crime of Judas was that hardness of heart
which, culminating in despair, condemned him on the very
day of redemption. . . . This miserable being, unable to

shall betray me.' And Judas reached forth his hand, ' Is it I, Rabbi ? ' he asks. ' Thou hast said it,' was the answer ; ' what thou dost, do quickly.' And so he vanished into the night, and quickly he did it, and thoroughly he acquitted himself, down to the signal kiss in the garden.''

Though it would have been more satisfactory to have placed these sermons in their completeness side by side, these extracts provide a sufficient basis for a comparison and a judgement. It will be agreed that the two are of very different quality, and that Dr Meynell's is by far the better sermon. But it is interesting to enquire on what grounds we judge it to be so. The sermon of the unnamed preacher is not an execrable sermon ; many who heard it probably considered, and considered rightly, that it was far better than many others that they had heard. Yet how mediocre it looks by the side of the other ! Why is this ? The literary superiority of Dr Meynell's sermon is beyond question ; its language is clear, and though restrained, is not frigid or heartless. The style of the other is grandiloquent and exclamatory. That however is not the only, or even the chief reason of the difference in quality. The radical difference is in the manner in which the two preachers conceive their subject. One of them apprehends it in its reality, he traces the external details of the story only in so far as they give him a clue to the essence of it. He brings his experience of life to bear upon the horrible perversion of a soul, and reconstructs its inner history. The other preacher flits over the surface of the story, he touches upon incidents without penetrating either their significance or their convergence upon the final tragedy. He vaguely enumerates circumstances, he mentions aspects, but he does not concentrate our thoughts upon that patch of evil in the soul of the traitor, which spread ever outwards, corrupting all that was sound in it until at last conscience was silent, and remorse was quenched and Satan entered as master into the spirit of the wrecked apostle. This is why his sermon is unreal.

CHAPTER IV

ST AUGUSTINE'S VIEWS ON PREACHING

THE fourth book of St Augustine's treatise, *De Doctrina Christiana*, can be read with profit by anyone who preaches or who is preparing to be a preacher. It is the conclusion of a work on the study of Sacred Scripture, but it stands separate from the part which precedes it, and deals exclusively with preaching. Though the treatise was begun in the early years of the Saint's episcopate, this book was not written until the closing years of his life, when, as he states in his " Retractations," he took stock of his writings and finding his " Christian Doctrine " unfinished, decided to complete it. A short explanation of the situation which called St Augustine to the task of writing it may give a more definite notion of its scope and purpose, and serve as an introduction to the statement of its main principles, which I wish to set forth in this chapter. It was written for the clergy, and would be not inaccurately described as a Preacher's Manual. The circumstances which called it forth were a consequence of the educational system then in vogue throughout the Empire. We have to remember as we read it, that it was addressed to ecclesiastics most of whom had been educated in public schools under a system designed for training men for a secular career.

Though the Empire was Christian in name, and becoming so in fact, education remained conservatively pagan. Scholastic customs, school manuals and text books were saturated with Græco-Roman mythology, and a large number of schoolmasters and professors were pagans. From these schools however came men like St Jerome, St Ambrose, Lactantius, St Hilary of Arles, and his namesake of Poitiers. To mention Christian writers of Africa alone, Arnobius,

Lactantius, and Augustine had been not only students but professors in the Imperial schools.

The aim of the Roman educational system was the making of orators. The methods of instruction varied from time to time in points of detail, but its object never varied, for the Roman's love of oratory was as wholehearted as his passion for military glory. St Augustine wrote his book to save Christian preaching from degeneration. The Italian Renaissance provides us with an instructive parallel of the situation at the time of the book's appearance : we know what preachers are capable of, when their interests are almost exclusively centred on pagan history, literature, and mythology.

The problem of the fourth book of the work on "Christian Doctrine" is the accommodation of the methods of secular oratory to those of preaching. Was preaching to be like secular oratory or was it to be altogether unlike it ? Was eloquence to be retained or was it to be cast out from the pulpit ? St Augustine's solution was a compromise, as we might expect from one who thought of Pagan education as he did. He rejoiced in the glory already given to the Church, by Christians who knew how to use the stores of Paganism aright,—"Cyprian, that most delightful teacher and most blessed martyr, and Lactantius and Victorinus, Optatus and Hilary, not to mention others still alive, coming up laden with gold and silver and splendid raiment they had brought from Egypt." [1]

In addressing himself to this problem of his time he might have written a book, so concentrated on an actual situation, that it would have been useful only as long as that situation lasted, or when it was repeated in an almost identical form. His book would then have been almost useless to us, precisely because he had narrowly confined his outlook to the needs of his own generation. Fortunately he did not treat his subject thus ; he did not content himself with abstract considerations on methods of education. He left that question aside, to deal with others of more universal interest—what should be the aim of preaching and what are the best means to be taken to make it effective. Because

[1] *De Doct. Christiana*, ii. c. 40.

of this radical treatment of his theme St Augustine's treatise, *De Doctrina Christiana*, will always read like a modern book ; it is a manual broad in its teaching, clear in its conceptions, practical in its scope.[1]

I

St Augustine in the " De Doctrina Christiana " shows a measured regard rather than an enthusiastic devotion towards the theory and art of formal rhetoric. His own experience probably counted more in producing this attitude than any detached investigation of the subject on its merits. From his boyhood until his conversion he had been either studying or teaching grammar or rhetoric. He had practised as a rhetorician successively at Carthage, Rome and Milan, and his confidences written in his *Confessions* make it clear that his experiences had been far from pleasant. At Carthage the students were wild and licentious, in Rome they abandoned their lecturer when his fees were becoming due. St Augustine's coolness towards his profession increased as the study of religious and philosophical problems claimed more and more of his attention and interest. Altogether his career as a teacher was uncongenial, if not bitter ; and it was without regret that he at last turned his back upon the " market of verbosity." When in his old age he finished the planned work on Christian doctrine, he was scarcely more sympathetic in his estimate of the value of rhetorical exercises.

The question he treats—namely, to what extent the study of rhetoric is useful in the making of a preacher—is not purely academic, it is really the same that exercises the seminarist and the young priest who asks himself whether Whateley or Blair or Bain can help him in his preaching.

[1] The text of the *De Doctrina Christiana* is to be found, of course, in Migne and in all the editions of the *Opera Omnia* of St Augustine. There is a Latin text with notes edited by W. Yorke Fausset (Methuen). An English translation of the fourth book and of the treatise on catechising (*De Catechizandis Rudibus*) is published by Mowbray. The translation and introduction are by the Rev. W. J. Vashon Baker and C. Bickersteth.

The saint begins by insisting that eloquence is not the most important asset for a preacher. There are some men who, try as they will, can never be eloquent. The most that is possible to them is to gain a moderate proficiency, and that by dint of Demosthenic discipline and perseverance. Can these hope to preach well? St Augustine maintains that they can, and advises them to apply themselves primarily and mainly to what he holds to be the first and essential attribute of good preaching—which is not eloquence but "wisdom." Do not, he says in effect, aim first at fine speaking or ornament or beauty of language; but meditate your message, study it until you possess it and it possesses you. You will not perhaps profit your hearers as much as you would if you were eloquent as well as wise, but then you will not be utterly unprofitable as they are who have eloquence but no wisdom.[1]

By this wisdom, of which he often speaks, St Augustine understands the maturity of spiritual knowledge that comes through continued and devout contemplation of the truths and principles of religion; he would therefore have a preacher assiduous in the study of the great religious teachers. "A man speaks with more or less wisdom just as he has made more or less progress in the knowledge of the Holy Scriptures; I do not mean in reading them much and committing them to memory, but in the thorough understanding and diligent investigation of their sense. For there are some who both read and neglect them—that is, they read them with a view of learning them by rote, and yet they neglect to probe their meaning. Far better, without any doubt, are those who have a less accurate memory of the words while with the eyes of their heart they contemplate the heart of the Scriptures; but he is better than either who can both quote them when he wishes and who understands them as he ought. It is, then, most needful for one who would say wisely what he cannot say eloquently to know the words of Scripture by heart; for the poorer he sees himself to be in his own words, the richer he ought to be in theirs, in order that he may prove from those words what he has said in his

[1] *IV. De Doct. Christiana*, v.

own, and that, though he is a man of no great eloquence, he may in a sense grow great through the greatness of those whom he quotes. For he who is not able to give pleasure by his language can do so by the truths that he proves." [1]

Thus he first gives to " wisdom " its supreme place in the utterance of the preacher. But eloquence is not to be neglected, and if the saint refuses it the first place, he is far from denying its value altogether.

The rules of rhetoric are in a great measure gathered inductively from the observant study of man and of language. In so far as they keep close to nature they are, he believes, commendable, but when they go astray from it and become purely artificial and conventional they are no longer worthy of study or even of respect, for then they choke up the stream of natural eloquence. He will not listen to the rhetorician who unduly magnifies his office ; he holds that whatever there is of good in rhetorical exer cises and theories can be learnt without such aids by anyone who has leisure, perseverance and good taste.

Still, "the devil should not have all the best tunes." " Since the art of rhetoric can be used for commending either truth or falsehood, no one would be so rash as to say that the defenders of truth ought to stand unarmed in the battle against falsehood ; so that those who uphold what is false should know how to predispose their hearers to be favourable, attentive and ready to learn, while the others (who teach the truth) are unable to secure attention. . . No ; eloquence, being a neutral faculty, is of very great power in enforcing what is bad and what is good alike ; ought it not, then, to be acquired by the zeal of good men, who will set it to fight for the truth, since bad men employ it for maintaining perverse and vain pleas to promote sin and error ? " [2]

Eloquence, then, is good in its own secondary and ancillary place, and therefore not to be neglected. He advises preachers, however, to learn it not from books but as a living art, exemplified in the teaching of those who are both eloquent and wise, from models rather than from rules.

[1] *Op. cit.*, v.   [2] *Op. cit.*, iii.

This was no novel theory : the best writers on oratory had insisted, before his time, on the advantage of an intelligent attention to the best models of eloquence. But St Augustine's view is original in the new application which he makes of this principle. While a pagan teacher of his day would direct his pupil to the Greek and Latin classics as examples of the best oratory, St Augustine sends his ecclesiastics to the Scriptures and to the best ecclesiastical writers—and this not for the primary end of gaining eloquence, but that they may appropriate the wisdom of the divine teaching. Yet, if they will follow his counsel, he promises them that by frequenting such company they will become not wise only but eloquent.

To prove and illustrate this, he selects passages from the Old and New Testaments and submits them to academic tests, pointing out, with the skill of the retired rhetorician that he was, the balance and harmony of the phrases, the appropriateness and splendour of the figures, which witness to the correct though untutored oratorical instinct of the sacred writers.[1] Here, he says, is natural eloquence not like that of the classics, indeed, yet admirably suited to the grave purpose of religious teaching. There is no parade of eloquence, for the writers did not seek the prizes of oratory ; yet their words do attain to eloquence, Providence having inspired them with a language worthy of the high wisdom they preached.

Other Christian writers, following in the footsteps of the authors of Scripture and striving solely after wisdom, received like them a second and unsought grace in the gift of eloquence. Let the preacher in his turn study and imitate these also. As children nurtured in cultivated households receive in their speech an impress of their polite surroundings even before they learn the laws of grammar from schoolmasters,

---

[1] As for instance : St Augustine cites the passage of St Paul, " We glory in our tribulations, knowing that tribulation worketh patience, and patience probation, and probation worketh hope," etc., and explains that though no one would maintain that the Apostle consciously followed the rules of eloquence, yet the passage is framed as a " Climax," he notes the rhetorical beauty of the short phrases (called by rhetoricians " membra," " cæsa "), followed by an ampler period (ambitus, circuitus, περίοδος).

E

so the preacher can, if he will, unconsciously assimilate a kind of speech appropriate to his message. If he will study wisdom at its sources, eloquent speech will come to him as it did to his models, as the natural expression of the sublime teaching which he handles. " Wisdom, coming forth from her house, which is the heart of the wise man, will not lack the company of Eloquence, her attendant handmaid." [1]

II

Referring to a passage from one of Cicero's treatises, and associating himself with its sentiment, St Augustine holds that the scope of the preacher is threefold—to teach, to give pleasure and to persuade.[2] It is on the basis of this classical analysis that he builds up his homiletic doctrine.

1. The first and essential qualification of a preacher is to be skilful in imparting instruction. Preaching in the primitive Church was mainly an exposition of sacred Scripture. Hence in the treatise on Christian doctrine the sacred text is assumed to be the principal source of the homilist's topics and language.[3]

The preacher must be clear, but the Scriptures are some-

[1] *Op. cit.*, vi. It may be of interest to notice how this principle is accepted by a modern writer. " Ponderable facts and external realities," writes de Quincey in his *Essay on Style*, "are intelligible in almost any language; they are self-explained and self-sustained. But the more closely any exercise of the mind is connected with what is internal and individual in the sensibilities—that is, with what is philosophically termed *subjective*—precisely in that degree does the style, or the embodying of the thoughts, cease to be a mere separate ornament, and, in fact, the more does *the manner* . . . *become confluent with the matter*. In saying this we do not vary the form of what we once heard on this subject from Mr Wordsworth. His remark was by far the weightiest thing we ever heard on the subject of Style ; and it was this—that it is in the highest degree unphilosophical to call language or diction ' the dress of thoughts,' he would call it the *incarnation* of thoughts. Never in one word was so profound a truth conveyed."

[2] " Ut doceat, ut delectet ut flectat—" See *De Oratore*, ii. 27 ; and *Brutus*, xlix. : " Tria sunt enim, ut quidem ego sentio, quæ sint efficienda dicendo : ut doceatur is apud quem dicitur, ut delectetur, ut moveatur vehementius."

[3] What St Augustine says of Scripture can be extended quite naturally to other sources of doctrine which we are accustomed to use in our own time.

times obscure ; what, then, is he to do when he meets difficult and subtle doctrine which his audience cannot be expected to understand ? St Augustine answers that he had better pass over what is difficult and employ himself on the clearer doctrine which abounds in the books of Scripture. " There are some things," he says, " which by their own nature cannot or can hardly be understood, however fully and with whatever skill of speech and clearness they are discussed ; such subjects ought never to be brought before a popular audience, or only very rarely, if there is some pressing need." [1] Further, the preacher must take account of the uneducated among his audience. They are more completely dependent upon preaching than the more educated, who have leisure for reading. St Augustine champions a certain chivalry in the preacher ; his congregation is, in a sense, at his mercy, and he should not take an unfair advantage by mystifying them into weariness. In church, he says, politeness and custom compel the assembled people to continue listening, whether they are bored or not, whether they understand or not ; they may not ask questions, nor call upon the preacher to explain again what they have not grasped, and " on this account the speaker's diligence ought to compensate the hearer for his silence." [2]

St Augustine, we see, insists on intelligibility as the groundwork of every other good quality in preaching; he advises his preacher to sacrifice everything else to it ; sublimity may go, and elegance, and even a correct vocabulary, whenever these very desirable qualities stand in the way of clearness.[3] The preacher is a teacher, and his object

---

[1] *Op. cit.*, ix.

[2] *Op. cit.*, iv. We may remark by the way that though this seems a very obvious point, it calls attention to a difference, not always noted, between the sermon and the written religious essay. Preachers, especially when they deal with difficult subjects, do not always sufficiently bear in mind that the style suitable to popular audiences allows of much more freedom, repetition, illustration than would be desirable or even endurable in a book. Men who write their sermons in full must make allowance for slowness of apprehension and occasional distractions on the part of some of their hearers.

[3] *Op. cit.*, iv. He defends the use of the incorrect " ossum " for " os " (a bone), because the Africans did not concern themselves with quantity and might confuse " ŏs " (bone) with " ōs " (mouth).

is " to bring to light what was formerly hidden." And of what use, the saint asks, is a golden key that cannot open the door, and what harm is there in a wooden one if it can, since our one aim is to open what was closed ? [1]

But, if one may express it so, St Augustine would not have preachers continue to push the door when it is already wide open. He advises a speaker who is extemporizing to keep watch on his hearers, and when he feels that he has amply discussed his subject, and that his listeners have thoroughly grasped it, he ought either to finish his discourse at once or to pass on to some other topic. " For as a man is acceptable who clears up what needs to be known, so he becomes a bore who insists on what is obvious." [2] People of ordinary patience and piety may forgive a preacher for saying the same thing twice during a sermon, but only the heroic can pardon him if he repeats it over and over again, after having made it perfectly clear.

2. On the second quality—that of pleasing—St Augustine's views may be thus summarized :—The average Christian is not so enamoured of wisdom as to seek it in its unadorned austerity. In condescension to this human imperfection, truth should (whenever the preacher's skill allows it) be embellished by attractive diction, " just as the very food by which we live has to be made tasty to please dainty palates." Besides being instructive, then, a discourse should be pleasant enough to awaken interest and sustain attention. But in bending to man's infirmity the preacher must be on his guard against deserting the more common-place aim of his preaching (*i.e.* instruction) in order to hunt after elegance. There will perhaps be some in his audience who are insatiable for ornate and delicate diction, and who believe that simplicity in exposition is a sign of poor capacity in speaking ; but such as these, St Augustine thinks, are not to be humoured overmuch. Evidently he has a repugnance for anything savouring of preciosity in a preacher, and dislikes it whenever he finds it. A passage in St Cyprian's early manner supplies him with an instance of the kind of speaking which he thinks unsuitable, as being too artificial ; he

---

[1] *Op. cit.*, xi. [2] *Op. cit.*, x.

accompanies the extract with the comment that St Cyprian outgrew this fashion of writing and brought himself in later life "within the limits of a graver and more modest style." [1]

3. For all his insistence upon clearness, and his cool and permissive yet genuine appreciation of elegance, our author was too observant to indulge the delusion that either the native force of truth or the embellishments of language are sufficient to beat down the resistance of an obstinate will. There are men who are well grounded in doctrine, and who take an æsthetic delight in elegantly spoken ethics, and who yet remain reluctant to take even a step towards living worthy lives. To rouse men of this stamp something other than clear ideas and well-chosen phrases is needed—the preacher's language must be impassioned and vehement.

The supreme achievement of eloquence, according to the classical rhetoricians, is to *move* men; according to St Augustine's Christian interpretation, it is to convert the heart. His own conviction of this empire of vehement speech over the heart and will give passion to his plea: "O eloquence, terrible in purity and vehement in strength! In very truth a hammer breaking the rocks! For to that did God Himself, speaking by the prophet, liken His word." [2] Knowledge of the law is vain, æsthetic appreciation of religion is vain unless the heart is stirred and the will is moved to right action. The crown of eloquence is gained only when the resistance of pride or passion is broken down, and the will—not the mind only—surrenders to the conquering power of truth.

---

[1] This is the passage; it is taken from Cyprian's letter to Donatus: "Let us seek this seat: the seclusion of the neighbourhood affords a retreat, where, while the straying sweeps of the vine-shoots creep with pendulous windings through the reeds that stoop beneath their weight, the leafy roof has made a vine-clad porch." St Augustine does not altogether disapprove of this style of writing, which he owns is not without an admirable fluency and richness of diction, but its artificiality offends his austerity of taste. He would not have preachers imitate its studied rhetoric.

[2] *Op. cit.*, xiv.

III

To the three aims of preaching which have just been enumerated—viz., instructing, pleasing, and urging—there correspond three styles of oratory. When we wish to be instructive we shall use a quiet and unadorned style, when to instruction we wish to add the graces of description, or what St Augustine calls " the judgments of praise and blame," our diction will become more ornate, and finally, when we seek to rouse our hearers to action, or to convert a reluctant will, we shall employ a passionate and vehement style.

Oratory moves in three planes, according to the object it aims at and the immediate purpose it pursues ; and in proportion as one or other aim predominates in any discourse, so will also the characteristics of one or other of these three styles. " The eloquent man," says Cicero, " will speak of small matters quietly that he may teach, of ordinary matters with elegance that he may charm, of great ones with grandeur that he may persuade." St Augustine modifies this principle, by explaining how in Christian preaching everything that is said is really great, since everything has a bearing upon the important business of salvation. Even the lighter precepts of the Christian law are dignified because they are related to the greatest of all things, which is Charity.

Yet, with admirable judgment, he goes on to say that this truth does not forbid variety of style. " Though our teacher ought to be a speaker of great subjects, he ought not always to speak of them with grandeur, but quietly when he is teaching anything, and with elegance or restraint when he is censuring or giving praise ; but when there is something to be done and we are speaking to those who ought to do it but will not, then something great should be said with grandeur and in a manner calculated to sway men's minds." [1]

1. *The Quiet Style.*—In most sermons there will be certain parts which give information, such, for instance, as the interpretation of a text or passage, the statement of a logical

[1] *Op. cit.*, xix.

argument, the citation of some authority, the explanation of some distinction the preacher wishes to note. In treating such matters, where the preacher's aim is to teach, it is not required of him to employ the ornate style of speaking ; all that is wanted is a straightforward, businesslike clearness. Attempts at elegance or passion are out of place here. It is enough if the preacher makes himself understood. This advice deserves to be pondered by those who preach as if they think that everything said in the pulpit ought to be invested with dignity and grandeur. Not so : information is best conveyed in a very simple form, and it usually leaves a blurred and vague impression if it is imparted in any other way. If a man asking his way is met by phrases about skirting immemorial oaks and golden corn-fields, he feels that, on such an occasion, his guide might with propriety have confined himself to prose. It is intolerably monotonous to listen to preachers who are bent on " trailing clouds of glory " everywhere. Eloquent figures of speech belong to the decorative elements of style ; they are not its groundwork, but its embroidery.

St Augustine exemplifies the quiet style by noting that the Epistle to the Galatians is written in the subdued manner, except in a very few passages. Another of his illustrations is from an argumentative epistle, in which St Cyprian discusses whether pure water or wine mixed with water should be used in the Holy Sacrifice. Instead of transcribing or translating it, I will quote a passage from an English author that exhibits the character of this style. Bishop Hedley, as a rule, wrote ornately, but the following extract is in the " quiet " manner :—

" The Poverty of Jesus and of His blessed Mother was extreme, and, we may say, excessive. That is, to all appearance, He carried it much further than was necessary in order to accomplish any visible purpose. He chose to be in want of the commonest necessaries. He was born, not in a house or a cottage, but in the stall of a beast. He laboured with His hands. He was often in want of sufficient food, as we gather from many passages of Scripture and from the words of the saints. To worldly prudence it would seem as if His work would have been better advanced had He chosen to possess more of the world's goods.   And let us further observe that He practised poverty not merely to edify others—that is, to enhance His character in the eyes of the Jews, or to attract souls to Him.   He practised it consistently from the Manger to Calvary in all things, in secret and in public, with an evident choice and preference.   This proves that Poverty has some Divine effect upon the acts of the heart. For the mere fact of being in need or want is no virtue, but often a temptation to sin.   Thousands of the poor are made worse by their poverty ; and the first step towards bringing them nearer to God is to lift them out of their sordid indigence. What, then, is the effect of Poverty such as Jesus prac- tised ? " [1]   Here the words are chosen simply with a view of making a matter plain ; there is no attempt to do more than that.

2. *The Ornate Style.*—We pass now to the middle style, which holds its place between quietness and vehemence.   The characteristic property of this is a beauty of language, " which consists in the harmonious balancing of appropriate words, each as it were rendering to each its due."   In this kind the diction is more highly coloured, and it has a certain warmth about it which is, however, kept in check and not allowed to rise to the heat of unrestrained passion.   Cicero called it the " tempered style."   The passages which St Augustine selects to illustrate it are taken from the 1st Epistle to Timothy and from Romans xii. and xiii., and include one which is now usually considered to be a hymn used in the earliest Christian assemblies.   " Charity is patient, is kind ; charity envieth not, dealeth not perversely ; is not puffed up, is not ambitious, seeketh not her own.   It is not provoked to anger, it thinketh no evil.   It rejoices not in iniquity, but rejoices in the truth.   It beareth all things, believeth all things, endureth all things," and the rest.[2]   Here again an English example will make the point more clear, so I will sub- stitute an illustration from Bishop Hedley for St Augustine's citation from St Cyprian's *De Habitu Virginum* : " But the servant of God knows how, in Office and Liturgy, to sanctify

---

[1] *Retreat*, chap. xx.   [2] 1 Cor. xiii. 4 and foll.

the Lord Christ in his heart. His heart seizes every word that sounds forth, every rite, every detail of ritual, of place, of posture, and lifts itself to its Lord, as a little bird flies swiftly up towards the sky when it has found its morsel of food upon the lower earth. From choir to choir, in the sight of the Angels, the psalm passes, and the sound of holy words makes sweet melody ; but sweeter far is the melody of the heart which transposes the sacred sounds into acts of worship, of adhesion and of petition—which pass, not from one choir to another, but to the very roof of the firmament, to the gates of heaven, even to the throne of God." [1]

St Augustine counsels preachers to use the ornate style sparingly, and to avoid a certain artificiality which is liable to insinuate itself, much to its detriment. The preacher must avoid all that savours of vanity and affectation. " Thus we use even the elegant style of speaking not vaingloriously but wisely, not contenting ourselves with its own end, the mere pleasure of the hearer ; but rather endeavouring to help him on even by it to the good which we desire to establish in him." And again, " We should aim at all these points—to make our hearers intelligent, pleased and obedient, even in this kind in which the giving of pleasure holds the first place." [2]

3. *The Vehement Style.*—If grace of diction is not sufficient to persuade the hearer effectively, another weapon is at hand. The preacher must now appeal, not through beauty but through vehemence of language. Strong feeling is the characteristic mark of this third style. The speaker surrenders himself to the impetuosity of his emotion, words do not seem so much to be chosen by him as to spring of their own accord from the heart of the passions that master him. There may be beauty in his language, but even if it is lacking its absence will not diminish an effectiveness which relies little upon so tame an emotion as æsthetic appreciation.

No lengthy speech should ever be conceived wholly upon this plane, for long-drawn-out vehemence is mere rant. The great emotions lift a speaker above himself, and carry him

[1] *Retreat*, chap. xxv.
[2] *IV. De Doct. Christiana*, xxv., xxvi.

along for a short space upon a mighty wave of passion ; and the mode in which the preacher utters himself in these great moments is, in St Augustine's phrase, " the grand " or " the impassioned " style. He exemplifies it by scriptural passages from 2 Corinthians and Romans (2 Cor. vi. 2 and foll., Romans viii. 28 and foll.), and notes a sudden occurrence of it in the Epistle to Galatians (iv. 10-20), where the Apostle interpolates the quiet style with ten verses glowing with passion and pathos. From ecclesiastical writing St Augustine chooses as examples diatribes of St Cyprian and St Ambrose against the feminine custom of painting the face. A better illustration in an English sermon could scarcely be found than that terrible passage in Newman, describing the fate of a Catholic's soul rejected by its Judge [1]: " Oh what a moment for the poor soul, when it comes to itself, and finds itself suddenly before the judgment-seat of Christ ! Oh what a moment, when, breathless with the journey and dizzy with the brightness and overwhelmed with the strangeness of what is happening to him, and unable to realize where he is, the sinner hears the voice of the accusing spirit, bringing up all the sins of his past life, which he has forgotten, or which he has explained away, which he would not allow to be sins, though he suspected that they were, when he hears him detailing all the mercies of God which he has despised, all His warnings which he has set at naught, all His judgments which he has outlived ; when that evil one follows out into detail the growth and progress of a lost soul—how it expanded and was confirmed in sin—how it budded forth into leaves and flowers, grew into branches, and ripened into fruit—till nothing was wanting for its complete condemnation. And oh, still more terrible, still more distracting, when the Judge speaks and consigns it to the jailers, till it shall pay the endless debt which lies against it. ' Impossible ! I a lost soul ! I separated from hope and from peace for ever ! It is not I of whom the Judge so spake ! There is a mistake somewhere ; Christ, Saviour, hold Thy hand—one minute to explain it ! My name is Demas : I am but Demas, not

---

[1] *Discourses to Mixed Congregations* : " Neglect of Divine Calls and Warnings."

Judas or Nicholas, or Alexander or Philetus or Diotrephes. What ? hopeless pain ! for me ! impossible, it shall not be ! ' And the poor soul struggles and wrestles in the grasp of the mighty demon which has hold of it, and whose touch is torment. ' Oh, atrocious ! ' it shrieks in agony, and in anger too, as if the very keenness of the affliction were a proof of its injustice. ' A second ! and a third ! I can bear no more ! stop, horrible fiend, give over ; I am a man, and not such as thou ! I am not food for thee, or sport for thee ! I never was in hell as thou, and I have not on me the smell of fire, nor the taint of the charnel-house ! I know what human feelings are ; I have been taught religion ; I have had a conscience ; I have a cultivated mind ; I am well versed in science and in art ; I have been refined by literature ; I have had an eye for the beauties of nature ; I am a philosopher or a poet, or a shrewd observer of men, or a hero or a states- man or an orator or a man of wit and humour. Nay—I am a Catholic : I am not an unregenerate Protestant ; I have received the grace of the Redeemer ; I have attended the Sacraments for years ; I have been a Catholic from a child ; I am a son of the saints ; I died in communion with the Church ; nothing, nothing which I have ever been, which I have ever seen, bears any resemblance to thee and to the flame and stench which exhale from thee ; so I defy thee and abjure thee, O enemy of man ! ' " Then the sermon drops at once into the quiet manner : " Alas, poor soul, and while it thus fights with that destiny which it has brought upon itself and with those companions whom it has chosen, the man's name perhaps is solemnly chanted forth, and his memory is deeply cherished by his friends on earth," and so on.

As a last quotation I will cite a very wise passage in which the author of the book *On Christian Teaching* suggests the variation of the three styles as an antidote to the bane of monotony. " Let it not be thought that it is against the laws of composition to intermingle these styles ; on the contrary, so far as the subject allows, all the styles should be employed for the sake of variety ; for too long a continuance of one style fails to keep the hearers' attention ; but by passing from one style to another a speech may run a pleasant enough course, even if somewhat long. Good speakers can, moreover, introduce variety into each one of the various styles, and thus avoid allowing their hearers to become cold and dull. But it is less irksome to listen to a long speech in the restrained style only than one in the grand style only, for the stronger the feeling which needs to be excited . . . the shorter the time it can be maintained. And therefore we should be careful lest, while we are trying to rouse to a higher pitch feelings already aroused, they should actually fall back from that pitch to which they have been already brought. But if we insert matter which demands the more restrained manner, we can then return with good effect to that which requires vehement diction, in order that our eloquence may ebb and flow like the tide. Accordingly, if we have to speak at any considerable length in the grand style, we must not confine ourselves to that, but pass now and then to the other styles for variety's sake : still, the speech as a whole will take its character from the style that most prevails in it." [1]

This chapter has given a summary of the principal points touched upon by St Augustine in his book. There are minor details, well worth attention ; but these I have passed over, because the introduction of them into a condensed sketch would overcrowd the limited canvas. The book should be read in its entirety, for it contains the essence of our traditional doctrine, and has been drawn upon directly or indirectly by nearly all our writers of homiletic treatises. Within its short compass is contained the substance of what is most useful and practical in modern guides to preaching.

[1] *IV. De Doct. Christiana*, xxii.

CHAPTER V

THE PREPARATION OF A SERMON

FOR a young priest to take kindly to the duty of preaching is the exception, not the rule. Usually a newly-ordained priest finds more difficulty in this duty than in any other that falls to his lot. But if from the beginning he will resolutely devote time and care to the preparation of his sermons, many difficulties which at first seem insuperable will gradually melt away. Anxiety and nervousness are at the root of most of his trouble, for he has a distressing sense of the novelty of his situation and of his inexperience.

The sermons he has preached before his professors and fellow-students at the seminary were an ordeal, but they were, after all—and this was a consolation—academic exercises and nothing more. Besides, they were composed at a leisurely pace and with the help and counsel of others. But now he has to stand before an audience of strangers and to address them as their teacher. Even before he has learnt their dispositions, their needs and temptations, their tastes and habits, he appears before them as their spiritual guide and leader.

Fortunate is the young priest whose rector takes compassion on him and sympathetically encourages him in this new and terrifying duty, inspires him with courage, suggests suitable topics, looks over his manuscript, and offers friendly criticism of the matter and manner of those first sermons. Help of this kind is invaluable, and is welcomed by any young priest who is wise enough to recognize that his seminary training has not made him infallible and omniscient.

It is sometimes from the lack of this brotherly charity, or at least thoughtfulness, in older priests that the habit

of depending on books of ready-made sermons is formed.
Help is needed, and, failing a friendly critic and guide, the
sermon-book presents itself as the providential way of escape
from the drudgery of original composition. The criticism
of an older priest would have been a tonic, but this remedy
is a dangerous sedative. *Dormi secure* was the title
chosen for a book of ready-made sermons by a mediæval
author who understood the symptoms of his patients and the
nature of his drug.

St Augustine sets forth a very sound, tolerant view concerning the use of the sermons of others in the *De Doctrina
Christiana*.[1] His view is that those who cannot compose
sermons are justified in taking over bodily the sermons
written by others and preaching them word for word. This,
in his opinion, is not piracy, as some might call it, since
the doctrine contained in the sermon is a sort of universal
gift and therefore, in a sense, public property. It is to be
observed, however, that he suggests a very restricted employment of this innocent plagiarism. The men to whom
he allows it are those who cannot compose sermons
of their own, and the work they appropriate should

---

[1] *De Doct. Christiana*, lib. iv. 19. Addison, in the *Spectator*,
genially portrays the country chaplain of Sir Roger de Coverley.
The patron had presented the clergyman with all the good sermons
that had been printed in English, begging him in return to " pronounce " one of them every Sunday from the pulpit. Addison
approved of this proceeding: " I could heartily wish that more of
our country clergy would follow his example, and instead of wasting
their spirits in laborious compositions of their own, would endeavour
after a handsome elocution and all those other talents that are proper
to enforce what has been penned by greater masters. This would not
only be more easy to themselves, but more edifying to the people "
(*Spectator*, No. 106). This layman's view is interesting and even, within
certain limits, just. It is but reasonable in any layman to prefer a good
borrowed sermon, well delivered, to a poor but original sermon badly
preached. Nevertheless, his statement of the case is not complimentary to the capacity of the clergy. Less complimentary still
to the efficiency and, one may add, to the training of the clergy of
our time is the profusion of modern books of mediocre sermons
which are evidently considered good enough to serve as substitutes
for original compositions. One would not wish all sermon books
to be abolished, but the less a young priest accustoms himself to
depend upon them, the better his preaching is likely to be or, at any
rate, to become.

be "eloquently and wisely written." It is doubtful whether he would have encouraged the habit even to this restricted extent in men if they had been trained for their career by years of special study; from such as these he would certainly have expected original sermons. And whether he would have considered the ordinary sermon-book to be "wise and eloquent" is quite as doubtful. How few are there of these books, issued in such torrential abundance, and advertised as "of immense service to the hard-worked clergy," which deserve to become the sources and models of Catholic preaching!

In the mass these books have been described, not unjustly, as "aids to idleness and nests of platitudes." How some of them manage to get written and published is a mystery—so pitifully wanting are they both in matter and style. Their appearance answers no reasonable demand, for there are too many of their kind already. The "baser sort" of these productions might be classified in two main categories—the first containing those which are utterly uninspiring and commonplace, and the second, those which constitute the homiletic department of sensational and pretentious journalism. Removed by a whole universe from these are the printed sermons of genuine masters—the classical models of preaching. It is these which deserve to set the standard and to become our examples. Yet to study even these should be part of the remote rather than of the proximate preparation of sermons, for it is their spirit and their craftsmanship and not their paragraphs that we should endeavour to make our own.

I

How are we to set about the composition of a sermon? The first thing to be done is evidently to choose a subject; we must definitely decide what we purpose to speak about before we begin our composition. It is highly important to do this in good time. Tuesday of this week is quite late enough for choosing the subject of next Sunday's discourse. The first and most obvious reason for beginning early is that the composition of a sermon takes time, and if it is to be done well it ought not to be left till the last moment and then done in a hurry. There is a second reason also. The invention of ideas and their development are subject to processes of complex nature and irregular action to which psychologists have given a synthetic name, " the law of the association of ideas." Ideas proceed from a starting-point and collect themselves about it by this inherent law of the mind. The subject of our discourse is the focus round which we wish its development to accumulate.

This accumulation requires time, and study does not by any means count for everything in the apparently irregular and haphazard process of growth. The seed, once set, spontaneously assimilates whatever connatural elements it can seize on. The theme develops, even while the mind is occupied with other things. It is superfluous to labour this point ; every preacher knows, whatever his practice may happen to be, that he cannot reasonably look for good results if he delays the choice of his subject until he is driven by sheer necessity to make it.

Whateley's counsel for the choice of workable themes is excellent : " The first step is to lay down the proposition to be maintained, clearly and in a suitable form. He who makes a point of observing this rule, and who is thus brought to view steadily the point he is aiming at, will be kept clear, to a great degree, of some common faults of young writers, viz., of entering on too wide a field of discussion, and introducing many propositions not sufficiently connected, an error which destroys the unity of the composition. This last error those are apt to fall into who place before themselves a term instead of a proposition, and imagine that because they are treating of *one thing* they are *discussing one question*. Nearly akin to this fault is the other just mentioned, that of entering on too wide a field for the length of the work, by which means the writer is confined to barren and uninteresting generalities, as, *e.g.*, general exhortations to virtue (conveyed of course in very general terms) in the space of a discourse only of sufficient length to give a characteristic description of some one branch of duty or of some one particular motive to the practice of it.

Unpractised composers are apt to fancy that they shall have the greater abundance of matter the wider extent of subject they comprehend ; but experience shows that the reverse is the fact ; the more general and extensive view will often suggest nothing to the mind but vague and trite remarks, when upon narrowing the field of discussion, many interesting questions of detail will present themselves." [1]

If we follow this advice we shall not definitely fix upon a subject until we have, in a general fashion at least, appraised what may be called its virtuality. We must have some notion of what we can draw out of it in the short time that is allowed us by the conventions of preaching. A definite sermon is usually a good sermon ; and a definite sermon requires as its first condition a well-limited proposition for its subject. Choosing the theme is not merely fixing upon a text or a topic, it is also defining the direction that the treatment of it is to take. This demands good judgment, since the sermon ought to be nothing more nor less than this proposition set before the people with all the clearness at our command—an exploration of this one topic, conducted it may be with some freedom, yet never losing contact with the truth which it aims at illustrating. A masterpiece and example of judicious selection of topics is at hand in the *Summa Theologica*. The thoroughness that is such a remarkable feature in it results not only from the theological acuteness of its author, but from the sure judgment with which he arranged and distributed the vast material with which he dealt. The *Summa* never leaves the impression either of diffuseness or of over-crowding : its arrangement is both leisurely and compact, and so naturally is the distribution managed that the correspondence between the topics and the length assigned to their treatment seems to be produced not so much by the adroitness of art as by the inevitability of nature.

II

" In the spacious halls of memory there are laid up treasures of innumerable images, drawn from all manner of things

[1] *Rhetoric*, chap. i.

F

which have been presented to the senses. . . . I demand
the production of whatever I will, and some things come forth
at once, some need longer search, and are dragged out as
it were from more remote receptacles, and some rush out
tumultuously ; and when something else is being asked and
sought, these leap forward as if crying ' Do you not want
us ? ' Others present themselves in an orderly sequence
as they are wanted, as happens when I tell a story that I
know by heart." Thus St Augustine, in the tenth book of
the "Confessions," describes the capricious surrender of the
stores of the memory at the demand of the will.

What do I know already of the subject we have chosen ?
is the question one should put to himself as soon as he has
marked out his theme. It is much better to put and answer
this question than that other which often starts up, "What
books shall I go to for matter for the sermon ?" Let us fish
first in our own pond—there is more to be taken there
probably, than we are inclined to think. If our search does
not yield all we require, then we go to books, taking care
to note in full or in abridgment what we want to keep
This we add to such contribution as our memory may
have made, which we have also noted down in writing
When at last enough material has been gathered, the
accumulated hoard has to be examined and sifted. What
is alien to the subject we reject, though it may be with
a qualm. It may be useful at some other time, but it is
a hindrance now, for "no train of thought is strengthened
by the addition of those arguments that, like camp-followers
swell the number and the noise, without bearing a part in
the organization." [1]

From the material emerge some few main topics which
provide the rubrics or "points" under which sections may
be grouped. The matter is then distributed in its due order
and the plan of the sermon is complete.

There are many kinds of plan, and each preacher will find
by experience which kind helps him most. Some will sketch
out a few short indications of divisions and subdivisions
others will favour a full synopsis. Provided that the plan

[1] *Style*, Sir Walter Raleigh, p. 96.

does what is asked of it, any kind will serve. Its object is to register the distribution of matter, to fix the order of the composition, and so secure for it a vertebrate and organic unity. It is to stand before the mind and eye of the writer as a reminder of his purpose, and a warning against wavering and aimless digression from it. If difficulties are experienced in following out the design that has been traced, it is far better to grapple with them and overcome them than to turn aside and modify the scheme. Departure from the plan during the course of composition endangers the coherence of the work—for one change leads to another, and the discourse insensibly drifts from its bearings, and straggles along without the guidance of any controlling aim.

III

One matter connected with the distribution of the different parts of sermons needs to be touched upon, especially as there is a difference of opinion about it. All agree that unity is not a mere superfluity, but an essential quality in any set discourse.[1] Unity demands orderly construction, as a building requires a framework. But, to pursue this comparison a little further, just as in a building some parts of the framework are hidden and others displayed, so the question arises as to the degree in which the plan of the sermon should, as it were, show through the completed work. Opinions, or perhaps we had better say tastes, are divided. As some men like flat ceilings with all the rafters hidden from view, and others admire the adorned or unadorned carpentry of open timbered roofs, so preferences are divided between an implicit and an expressed plan in sermon.

It has been remarked, sometimes with exaggeration, that sermons were quite lacking in any evident plan, until the time of the mediæval scholastics, who imported from the theological

---

[1] I say *set* discourse—since the homily, being of the nature of a commentary, does not demand this unity of idea; its essential qualities, as we shall see later, lie elsewhere.

schools to the churches that tendency to divide and subdivide
which was a feature of their academical methods.[1] This much
is certainly true, that scholasticism did in fact influence the
construction of sacred oratory very appreciably, and introduced a more orderly and formal style, which lessened its
spontaneity, but, by way of compensation, bound it more
closely to the laws of natural logic. The tendency to division
was carried to its height by the great French orators who
flourished under Louis XIV., and if one wishes to see oratorical
division in its most unadulterated form it is to these that
he naturally turns.

A specimen lies before me—Massillon's court-sermon on
" The virtues and the vices of the great." [2] What one first
remarks in it is its extraordinary length ; in this edition it
occupies over forty pages, and could not be preached in less
than an hour and a half. First comes the introduction, in
which the preacher divides the subject under two main
headings. After that, he passes to the first of these, and
subdivides that again into two divisions. There are no less
than six subsidiary divisions introduced into the treatment
Then follows the second main point which he had indicated
at the beginning of the discourse. Two more divisions are
made, under which are grouped nine subdivisions. The
sermon is brought to an end in a long peroration.

Throughout this sermon, which is typical of a large class
the preacher makes no concealment of his divisions and sub
divisions ; he expressly enumerates them, and, we might say
parades them.

Fénelon criticized the whole conception of sermon-making
of this kind in his Dialogues on Eloquence ; its schematic
form seemed to him intolerably artificial.

Bishop Hedley, in one of the conferences in his Lex
Levitarum, ranged himself on the side of Fénelon, and
doubtless there are many who think with him. Lest in
attempting to condense I might unwittingly disturb the
balance of his statement, I had better quote the passage
in full. " To achieve order is the first step to seizing on

[1] Dargan, A History of Preaching, p. 232.
[2] Œuvres, vol. vi. (Paris, 1822).

onception and impressing the minds of others. But it is
step further when the writer attempts to discard mere
uccession or, as we call it, division. I will here content
nyself with saying two things. First, divide, if you do
ivide, a small field and not a large one. Divide a field and
ot a county or a canton. Divide vain-glory and not pride ;
he prayer of petition and not prayer in general ; Bethlehem
nd not the Incarnation. Large subjects cannot be treated
n divisions ; because with large subjects each division
ends to become an independent subject. This is what
ou meet in many of the French orators of the classical
eriod. As Fénelon expresses it, they frequently fire off
hree epigrams rather than divisions, apparently to dazzle
he hearer from the beginning. Secondly, lean rather to
he side of suppressing formal division, and of substituting
or it logical and emotional order. Experience shows that
ew things more inevitably dispose an audience to that kind
f disaffection which arises from anticipated tedium than
ormal divisions. If, as may happen, the unregenerate
earer grows tired of the very first of the stages before him,
is irritation is indefinitely increased by the reflection that
here are still more to come. The best kind of order is that
vhich is clearly in the preacher's mind, but only reveals
tself in effective sequence, in growing clearness and increas-
ng warmth. Fénelon describes the process very well, ' The
ncients,' he says, ' did not divide a discourse ; but you
nd three things in their discourses ; first, things that had
o be made distinct were carefully distinguished ; next,
verything had its proper place ; and thirdly, it was a
natter of the most careful consideration to put everything
ust in the place where it would be the most effective.'
here are no better rules for dividing and arranging a sermon
han these." [1]

Here is the case against formal divisions, stated clearly
y one who had special competence in such matters, one
rom whom it may seem presumptuous to dissent. Neverthe-

---

[1] *Lex Levitarum*, pp. 116-7. Bishop Hedley's reference is to the
econd of the *Dialogues sur l'Eloquence*. This short work of Fénelon
ell deserves to be read by preachers.

less some may feel that there is something to be said on the
other side, and that an arrest of judgment may be pleaded
for until that other side has been heard.

It will be allowed that a great deal of the ineffectiveness of
preaching comes from its want of definiteness, and that the
indefiniteness is caused by confusion in the treatment. The
topics, in such sermons, run into one another and get into
one another's way. A second argument is begun before the
first has been well hammered in, a second train of thought
jumps up suddenly in the middle of the first. The commonest
of all criticisms is that a speaker did not " keep to his point,"
and that a speech or sermon was " hard to follow."

Now, a rigid division goes far to preclude this difficulty. It
keeps the speaker from drifting away from his proposition
and sets the proposition well in front of his audience, so that
they too know exactly what is being spoken about. Its very
formality makes the necessary transitions plain and business-
like. Fénelon's complaint that the French classical preachers
" fired off epigrams " is scarcely just. It is true that the
three or four sections of this sort of sermon do seem like
distinct little sermons, but, in the best preachers at least
each section contributed a real and logical development to
the subject of the discourse ; the preacher explained their
connection with his subject in his exordium and gathered
up the cumulative doctrine in his peroration. The whole
scheme tended to clearness, to explicit order, and therefore
to definiteness. It would be hard to believe that any who
heard Massillon's sermons went away without knowing what
the preacher meant to say.

Further, it may be urged that Bishop Hedley's " unregenerate " listener might be even more weary of a sermon
without divisions than of one with divisions. Confused
thinking is often accompanied by long-windedness, and the
dreariest sermons not only appear, but often actually are
the longest. Perhaps his " unregenerate " listener might be
consoled rather than exasperated by knowing that there
were two points yet to be treated—after all there might
have been three or four, whereas there are only two—and
the end is in sight. No such consolation is granted in a

poor sermon the points of which are not formally divided.[1]
I will not labour the controversy further. In practice it
may be a good thing to experiment with both methods and
to use each of them on occasion; according as the nature
of the subject and the manner in which we apprehend it
may suggest which method is most suitable.

Naturally, a sermon of, say, twenty minutes' length should
not luxuriate with divisions, like the plan of Massillon which
I have just sketched, otherwise it promises more than it
can possibly perform. In a sermon of ordinary length,
when division is used, two, three, or four points are quite
enough, and every one of them should have an obvious and
logical connection with the subject. We must be on our
guard against multiplying subdivisions, which, when too
many, confuse rather than assist a hearer. Many published
"schemes," "plans," "skeletons" are over-divided, so when
we use sketches of this sort we do well in making a selection.[2]
At the end, it is advisable to bring the points together and
focus them on the conclusion we wish to draw or the application we wish to make, not forgetting Cicero's admirable
counsel to do it in such a way that "not the discourse, but
the memory is renewed."

IV

Quintilian describes extemporary speech as the acme of
the rhetorician's art. It may be taken for granted,
that there are very few young priests capable of speaking
well in public without having chosen not the topics only,
but the very phrases of their discourse. The qualities

[1] A passage in Quintilian confirms this view. "Partitio orationi
plurimum lucis et gratiæ confert. Neque enim solum id efficit
ut clariora fiant quæ dicuntur, rebus velut ex turbâ extractis; sed
reficit quoque audientem certo singularum partium fine, non aliter
quam facientibus iter, multum detrahunt fatigationis notata insculptis
lapidibus spatia. *Nam et exhausti laboris nosse mensuram voluptati
est, et hortatur ad reliqua fortius exequenda scire quantum supersit.*"—
Inst. Orat., lib. iv. 5.

[2] The "Aids" of Fr. Schouppe, S.J., are very suggestive. Dr
Beecher of Maynooth has translated his *Adjumenta Oratoris Sacri*
under the title *Pulpit Themes* (Gill & Son, Dublin).

necessary for the success of extemporary speech are so various and so rare, that it would be sheer folly and presumption for every speaker to attempt it. Without a thorough grasp of the subject, a copious vocabulary, and a ready, instinctive skill in using it, alertness of mind, and prompt imagination, there is little chance of success ; and self-assurance is a poor substitute for even the least of these gifts. The talent for extemporary speech is comparatively rare ; it is something quite different from what is sometimes called " a good flow of language," which is often nothing better than facility in continuous and ample talking. A priest's supernatural humility and natural good sense ought to reveal to him the source and quality of his fluency of speech—if he happens to possess it. Something will be said presently about extempore preaching, for the moment I may presume—what will be true except in very rare instances—that a priest inexperienced and unpractised in preaching takes the only wise course when he makes it his habit to write, not a plan only, but the full text of his sermon. " The emptiness, barrenness and commonness of sermons come almost wholly from a refusal to take the trouble to write. Without writing, practice in preaching is merely the growing more and more confirmed in weak and irritating trivialities." [1]

Yet, I must hasten to add, there are some evident disadvantages in the practice of sermon-writing. The sermon which has been written cannot have the freshness, the spontaneity of good extemporary oratory. It has to be delivered *sub aliá specie*, as an improvised effort, and not as a written discourse. Writing, in view of public speaking, is after all an artificial expedient, forced upon a man by the limitations of his oratorical talent. We write because we cannot trust ourselves to clothe our thoughts with fitting words on the spur of the moment. Besides this drawback there is another that detracts from the naturalness of written discourses. The very act of writing puts many people into a thoroughly artificial mood, and brings to the surface all that is heavy and laborious and uninteresting in them. Though their

[1] Bishop Hedley, *Lex Levitarum*, chap. viii.

language in conversation is quite graphic and vivid, it takes
upon itself, when they come to write, a strange and alien
pomposity, or shapes itself into neutral and colourless prose.
In the pulpit such men " talk like a book," and a very
dull book; their speech sheds all the swiftness and strength
that they display in familiar conversation. Nevertheless.
it is better (exceptions being allowed) that priests should
begin by writing their sermons. The benefits so outweigh
the disadvantages that there seems no room for doubt that
writing is normally the safest way to success. Writing
stimulates the mental faculties, helps originality and order,
clarifies expression and gives to speech greater precision and
exactness.[1] And are the defects which I have mentioned as
incidental to writing so inherent in it that attention and
practice are powerless to correct them ? Not only is it
possible, but it soon becomes easy, to keep before us, while
we are writing, the simple truth that we mean to speak what
we write. An Anglican lecturer on Homiletics tentatively
recommended clergymen to place a photograph of an
" average parishioner " on their desks when they wrote their
sermons. If we do not practise this counsel literally we
might profitably follow its spirit, by keeping in mind the
people for whom we are working, and attending to the sound
as well as the sense of our sentences as we write them.

When the sermon is drafted, it is advisable—if circumstances permit—to lay it aside for a day or so, and try
to forget its existence. Unless we take an enthusiastic
pleasure in writing, we find the company of our manuscript
rather tedious by the time we have finished it, if not before.
When we return to revise it let it be with a fresh mind.
During the revision everything academic—not to say pompous
or pedantic—should be unrelentingly cut away. Long
sentences must be broken up, abstract expressions made
concrete, proportion between the different numbers of the *members*
discourse rectified by compression here and amplification
there. Before we have finished with it it should have
acquired the character, hard to describe, but easily felt—of
a popular discourse : clear, without being arid, persuasive

[1] See Newman on *University Preaching*, p. 423.

without dropping to the level of sentimentality, fervent without being declamatory. Who shall say that this is an easy ideal and yet who shall say that it is wholly beyond the reach of the average man ? It must be confessed that it seldom comes without effort, without obstinate effort even. Yet it is worth the labour.

I am thinking now of a priest, dead only a few years, who preached two sermons every Sunday. He had the sole charge of the same parish for over twenty years. Before he was appointed to his only parish, he had been an assistant priest at a very busy city church. During these first ten years he found time to write in full every sermon that he preached. He was not a studious man, but what study he found time for he put into his sermons. F 's style was not oratorical, nor his voice or manner exceptionally attractive. He was a preacher of well-prepared, interesting plain sermons. I was shown some of his manuscripts. He had written them carefully amidst the many claims that are made on the time of a priest working in a large city, and which are supposed generally to make the careful preparation of sermons an impossibility. He managed to write them, however, and laid by a good store for the future. Later, he used them again, improving them by the additions and corrections which I saw noted in his manuscript. Though his sermons never appeared in the newspapers, or made any great stir, it was commonly said of him that he never preached a sermon that was not well worth hearing. The same people listened to him Sunday after Sunday without weariness. I always think of him when I hear it said—as it is often said—that in these days of strenuous work priests are much too hard driven to find time for the careful preparation of sermons.

CHAPTER VI

EXTEMPORARY PREACHING

WHOEVER reads sermons published a century or so ago will at once notice how different they are in style from those to which he is accustomed. He feels at once that they are "old-fashioned" and represent a taste both in preachers and hearers that is not of our time. They are conceived in "a grand manner," the sentences are long and elaborate, there is a care for the dignity of the discourse which too often gives an air of pomposity and remoteness from common language. Frequently the preacher seems to have avoided plain and short words, and studiously chosen those that were sublime and sonorous. This sort of writing was customary at that time, and sermons followed the fashion closely inasmuch as they were usually written out in full and read from the pulpit.

Their type seems to have been that of the great French preachers, and the custom of reading was probably borrowed from the Anglican fashion of those years. Nowadays it is but rarely that one hears a sermon read from a Catholic pulpit. The fashion has changed, and the traditional manner of preaching, which suffered eclipse for a period, has come back.

The style of contemporary preaching is more familiar and natural. In this respect we follow the taste of our age, for the same change is noticeable in literature, especially in journalism and in political oratory. Parliamentary speaking is more colloquial and business-like than it was even twenty years ago. Everyday speech now sets the standard both of writing and public speaking, whereas formerly the written composition dominated the whole field.

There is no reason to regret the change; and even if now

and then one hears complaints of the slipshod performances of public speakers and preachers, few would seriously suggest a return to the older fashion. Audiences nowadays want those who address them rather to talk to them than to deliver essays before them. Of course they expect more dignity in a sermon than in conversation, for there is something more formal in monologue than in dialogue; and in speech addressed to a number of people than in that directed to one or two people only.

All this is a question of art and convention. What lies at the root of the matter is that in public speaking, just as in writing, just as in conversation, one ought to have something worth saying and to say it plainly and clearly and appropriately. Whatever method we choose to employ, this should be the aim ; the process that brings it about is dictated by the special nature of our talents and capacity, and the matter of which we treat. In our education as preachers, talent and taste count for much. Even in such exercises as those of a school debating society there is a great difference between one boy and another. Some of the members speak readily and logically, others can scarcely put two clear sentences together. Naturally the discipline required for one type will have to be much more exacting than for the other, and years of effort will scarcely gain for the one what nature has freely tossed over to the other.

When a man wishes to take a choice of the method of preparing his sermons, the first thing that has to be done is something analogous to making a general examination of conscience. He must first of all understand himself. What is the proportion of each talent in the mixture of those faculties which nature and education have supplied to him ? Has he a reliable memory, a vivid imagination, a ready command of language ? And which of these gifts predominates ? Is his thinking instinctively clear, or does he find that his second thoughts are nearly always the best ? Where is he weak and where is he strong ? This is of the first importance, for the instrument that he is to use most constantly is his own personality. In the last resort, it is this self-knowledge that should solve this problem of method.

Having premised so much, I shall be safe when I say, that good extemporary speaking is very much more effective than any other. Unless some essential defect in him puts it out of the question for this or that particular man, it is the kind of speaking to be aimed at. What was said in the last chapter in commendation of writing was chiefly for the guidance of beginners, who might be tempted to take to extempore preaching before they were capable or ready. The opinion to which I incline (which, moreover, is that of the greater number of authorities I have consulted) is in brief this : let the preacher begin by writing his sermons, then, as time goes on and his powers develop, let him gradually emancipate himself and accustom himself to preach, not indeed without preparation, but without that special sort of preparation that involves the writing of the whole discourse.

I

" Extempore preaching " is a phrase used by different writers in different senses. Some contrast it with a speech which is read to an audience. To their mind a speech, however prepared, is extemporary provided it is not read from a manuscript. Others take the literal sense of the word, and regard it as synonymous with impromptu. For them an extemporary speech is one delivered without any proximate preparation either of matter or style. The special sense in which I shall use the word is that which considers as extemporary any discourse of which the matter is prepared, but not the form. The sermon which I call extemporary is not an unprepared sermon. It is one for which the material has been collected and set in order beforehand, but of which the actual phrases are chosen at the time of its delivery.

This way of preaching commends itself to many, for the reason that they hold it to be an easier way. It does indeed demand less time and labour for its immediate preparation, but on the other hand we must bear in mind that it is not at all exempt from difficulties proper to itself. The chief of these are worth considering.

1. In the first place, extempore sermons demand a full measure of knowledge. Preachers are saved the time and trouble of writing and correcting a manuscript, but they are thrown back more upon the fund of information which they have acquired by their general education and reading. A man speaks fluently and interestingly and securely only on topics which he knows thoroughly ; and his mind must be well stored with the facts of a subject and able to move easily among them before he can trust himself to explain himself in words which he chooses (or rather which come to him) on the spur of the moment. He must have so made the subject his own as to possess it and to be possessed by it. A mechanic or a plumber can pour out interesting information if he can be got to speak freely about the things of his trade. He can instruct others about objects which they have seen a thousand times without reflecting upon their use. We feel this, for instance, when we are being shown over some large factory by an intelligent workman. The machinery, the material, the processes of manufacture are to him " as familiar as his pocket." How different is the impression he creates from that which we get when a caretaker or verger expounds architecture and history as he shows a party of visitors round his domain. Our guide has learnt his formula, which may be quite interesting, yet his description strikes one as something in which his own intelligence has but little part. He never improvises. He always says exactly the same thing about this tomb or that window, and everybody knows that he is repeating something that he has got off by rote. The boundary of his knowledge is precisely that of his formula, and outside the ring of his crowded information there is sheer ignorance. No one is surprised at these limitations, for he is a verger and not an artist or an archæologist. He is not like the plumber, who has got not words only but realities to declare—things which he knows well, among which he lives and works. It is the thoroughness of his knowledge that permits the workman to extemporize.

If a preacher would extemporize he must know his subject well. He must not be content with " reading it up " in a casual and superficial way; he must "read round it" and "think it out," otherwise he will be brought up, unexpectedly, by the boundary wall of his knowledge. Had he learnt his sermon by heart, he would have known exactly what he had to say, but as it is, should he by any chance venture into a region of thought which had not entered into his calculations, he is liable to lose his way hopelessly. He strays from the road and gets rapidly entangled. He may escape—but with what little glory—by means of a few trite generalities that occur to him and open a path from his bewilderment.

If, then, we are to extemporize, we must lay hold of our facts tightly—to glance at them merely is not enough. Ideas have to be mastered and comprehended, arguments must appear before the mind in their logical clearness, quotations or texts have to be studied not in isolation, but in their context. If we intend to employ figurative language its appositeness and relevance ought to stand out plainly before us. To use an expression of Whateley, we must look at the elements of our theme through a microscope. We hear of sermons that are over the heads of the people, but sometimes it happens that they are over the head of a preacher, his knowledge of ~~his Maker~~ *the matter* is so hazy and "factless."

Fortunately we are at liberty to choose our own subjects, and are not compelled to venture often upon subtle themes, considering the need our people have of plain preaching. If we elect to speak extempore let it be about matters that we understand well and of which we can speak not merely out of a bare sufficiency, but out of an abundance of information. No man who has almost completely given up theological reading can sustain this burden. It means study, for it means that the wastage has to be made good. How quickly our original store of knowledge, which (perhaps with undue pride) we brought from the seminary, is dissipated and exhausted! A great deal of it went to the making of a theologian and not directly to the formation of a preacher. Much again was soon lost through the natural limitations of memory or was crowded out by more immediate interests thrust upon us in parochial work.

There is an unwatched but continuous evaporation going on year by year, as well as the loss of our original store which is drained away by preaching itself. Our sermons cannot be fresh unless our knowledge is being continually renewed and extended. Even studious men, if they preach often, must repeat old ideas; but they manage to save themselves by mixing something new with what is old. The reiteration of the same ideas in the same language (inevitable in preachers who never renew their stock of thought) sends our people to the empty excitements of pulpit orators who manage to please without either instructing or converting, or else keeps them away from religious instruction altogether. Clerical bookworms are not held in great esteem by their parishioners, but a clergy with an unslaked curiosity for sacred learning is needed in every country and in every parish. When its number diminishes, stagnation sets in and religion languishes. The first movements of ecclesiastical reform in all periods of Christian history have been in the direction of a revival of clear, instructive preaching. How can it be otherwise, since " faith comes by hearing and hearing by the Word of God ? "

2. The second difficulty in extempore preaching comes from the circumstance that words are sometimes hard to find when they are most urgently wanted. Philosophers have often mooted the question whether or not we think by the medium of words. The problem may be important to that speculative tribe, but it is too abstract to detain us here. In practice it is only too evident that words are sometimes very slow in coming, especially the right words. Many men seem to be incapable of finding words when they most need them. This trouble is not confined to superficial people, who have no clear vocabulary because they have no clear ideas ; it is felt even more painfully by some who, with a large range of ideas at their command, are afflicted with a sort of intellectual or æsthetic scrupulosity. They are so anxious to get the one right word that nothing inferior to the best will satisfy them. John Bright, who was almost without a rival as an extempore speaker, sometimes kept his hearers waiting quite a long time while he was ransacking his mind for the phrase he wanted.

It need scarcely be said that there exists no ready-made and infallible method of finding at once and upon demand the very best possible words for expressing what is in the mind. Only a special talent can secure promptness in speech. Many cultivated men never acquire it, many uneducated men possess it without effort. Still, every one who can speak at all must have at least the rudiments of self-expression. When the child acquires his simple vocabulary he is put into possession of the means of communicating such thoughts as he has to others. As he grows up he learns more words, and his powers of self-expression expand. But though the capacity of self-expression grows with the acquisition of a wider vocabulary, readiness in the use of words does not necessarily grow in the same proportion. Here, then, is the crux of extemporary speech—the thoughts are there, the words are there, but they are not inevitably conceived together. The question is, Can anything be done towards mitigating the difficulty that some experience in finding words ready for use ?

The answer to the question is that facility can only be obtained indirectly. Three habits are recommended for securing it—reading much, translating from foreign languages, and lastly and chiefly, writing. Of the first I need only say that many orators have been wide and yet judicious readers, and of the second that many of them—the younger Pitt is an instance—attributed their facility of speech to constant practice in translating the classical authors.

As for writing, Cicero laid great emphasis on it as a means to oratorical excellence. It is a labour, he confesses, and we often shirk it in consequence, but it is the best way open to us of gaining a ready use of words.[1] By writing we are forced to deal with words, and, moreover, to deal with them *actively* and not passively, for the words are our own, by title of discovery. Many priests have no time for writing. With seminarists it is different, and they may be advised to make the best of their opportunity while they still have time. They can write as a literary exercise the substance of their lectures and reading ; and their

[1] *De Oratore*, i. 33. The whole chapter is very suggestive.

G

preaching, later, will be all the better for it. And besides this, there is usually in any large seminary a number of clubs and debating societies in which essays are read. Superiors encourage a moderate indulgence in extra-professional hobbies of this kind, and they do still better when they lay aside their learned aloofness and place their wider experience and maturer judgment at the disposal of the students who are energetic enough to keep such societies afloat. Many a priest in after life realizes the abiding good that has come to him from these modest gatherings; the memory of those eager discussions clings to him longer and more tightly than his recollections of the lecture-room. It is likely that they have helped him, more than he foresaw then, or perhaps realizes now, to discharge better his office of preacher.

3. There is yet another difficulty—that of making an extemporary speech orderly and consequent. In conversation men are apt to take up and lay down topics as their whim leads them. This is no matter for regret, for it saves us from becoming a race of pedants and bores. The desultoriness, however, which is no small part of the charm of informal conversation, easily becomes a bad defect in public speaking, of which the purpose is not entertainment but instruction. A speech must have an orderly progress if it is to leave a clear impression. It must have unity and coherence. If these qualities are absent, those who listen feel that they are constantly set upon new scents, instead of being helped to run an idea to earth. The result of a shaky plan is a vague and blurred impression.

Quintilian compares an oration without a plan to an army without leadership and to a traveller groping his way about a strange place in the dark. The plan opens a straight road to the speaker, and marks his course by fixed points which guide him through each separate part from beginning to end. It does away with his chief trouble—that of " not knowing what to say next." That the labour of speaking is lightened by the simple expedient of travelling forward from one clearly fixed point to another is so evident that it would be sheer waste of words to argue about it. Anyone who has skill in constructing a well-knit, logical plan has gone a long distance on the road of sound extempore preaching.

II

The idea at the root of a sermon—both the word and the thing—is that of speech, a free and spontaneous address of a pastor to his people. It is felt that even the learning of the very words of a sermon detracts from the personal and familiar character which should belong to really effective preaching. On this point the taste of the laity coincides with the main current of tradition, which is on the side of extemporary preaching. It is sometimes thought that the number of complete sermons which have come down from earlier times is an evident proof that preachers of primitive and mediæval days used to write their sermons in full before delivering them. An examination of the facts does not justify this inference.

The sermons of the Fathers and of mediæval preachers have been preserved in the form in which they were taken down by shorthand writers, or else in that in which they were written down by the preacher, not before but shortly after he had spoken them, for the benefit of those who were not present when they were preached.[1] Many of the Latin mediæval sermons which we have were not preached in Latin at all, but in the vernacular, though their authors wrote their preparatory notes and published their sermons in the current ecclesiastical language.[2]

[1] St Bernard, for instance, though he prepared (he called it "cooked") his sermons, left much to the inspiration of the moment, and accommodated his discourse to the attitude of his hearers. In Sermon IX. on the Canticles we find, "Another sense also occurs to me which I had not thought of before, but which I cannot pass over." In Sermon XXXVI. he makes an unprepared reference to some monks who were yawning and dozing. A remark in Sermon LXXVII. shows that he preached extempore: "Even though what I say were perchance put into writing, they would disdain to read it." See Preface of Mabillon in the *Works of St Bernard*, vol. iv., edited by S. J. Eales.

[2] See Dargan, *A History of Preaching*, pp. 164 and foll., for a discussion of this matter. Also, as an example, see *The Life of*

If extempore preaching is the most effective as well as being the traditional method, it may be asked how it comes about that writers on homiletics are so insistent upon the utility of the fully-written manuscript. Many answers might be given to this natural inquiry, but it suffices to say that observation has led them to believe that the writing of sermons is the best possible preparation for extempore preaching. They usually recommend it as a temporary and educational discipline. And it may be added that many of them recommend it with some reservation—as something which will prove useful to many, but not to all. If this man or that honestly believes that he is being hindered instead of helped by writing his sermon, he is at liberty to begin extemporizing as soon as he begins to preach. But I think that if we look about us and investigate the methods by which any good preachers we happen to know have attained to ease and readiness of speech, we shall find that, in most instances, those who excel in extempore speaking have in the first years of their preaching written their sermons. We shall find also that many a young priest who gave early promise of natural and spontaneous eloquence has become in a few years nothing better than a voluble talker because he too early ventured to preach without having prepared himself by setting his thoughts down in writing. Writing would have given solidity to his natural gift; the deliberation entailed would have helped him to mature it; and his growing experience would have been more carefully and soberly registered if the discipline of writing had sifted and classified his impressions.

If failure may come to a man of talent in this way, what is to happen to one who has no talent worthy of the name but merely a rudimentary capacity for expressing his

St Bernardine of Siena, Thureau-Dangin (Eng. Trans. by the Baroness von Hügel). Chap. iv. gives an account of the saint's preparation and preaching which is of historical interest. He preached in Italian, but, following a contemporary custom, published and probably prepared in Latin. This practice (a common one in past times) has led many to believe, unwarrantably, that there was very little vernacular preaching during the Middle Ages.

thoughts ? The ineffective preacher—with his hesitation, his interminable repetitions, his constraint and stiffness, his pitiful instinct for feeble phraseology, his pathetic attempts to bring his discourse to a fitting end—is the butt of our critics and satirists and an object of compassion to sympathetic hearers. It may well be doubted whether defects of this kind are inevitable and irremediable. To compose the whole discourse and to master it beforehand appears to be the most rational way of improving these first inexperienced efforts and opening the way to a freer treatment later on. Facility will come in time, but neither nature nor art do their work hurriedly. Prudence suggests that aids ought to be used in the first stages which can be discarded when they have achieved their purpose. Let us examine this matter, and observe how a preacher may travel from his early to his later method of preparation.

We suppose him to begin by writing out his sermon in full and committing it to memory. As to the writing, enough has already been said; but what of learning sermons by heart ? Some men of experience hold that it is a mistake, even at the beginning of a preacher's career. Canon Keatinge's advice is categorical. " Do not attempt to learn your sermon off by heart," he writes in a useful chapter on Preaching, in his well-known and practical book.[1] I would not contest this point too hotly with so wise a guide, but I think some reservation ought to be made in accepting this view. For a man with a good memory, learning by heart is quite an easy matter; it is, in fact, the best way he has of getting hold of his sermon. To other men, those with an imperfect and treacherous memory, the labour is exhausting and the result by no means safe; and these might be persuaded to learn their sermons substantially by heart from the beginning. They might read their composition over repeatedly and attentively, until they are familiar with its order, its ideas and many of its phrases. An illustrative passage will show what the phrase " substantially by heart " stands for.

A preacher has written, let us suppose, these sentences :

[1] *The Priest, his Character and Work*, chap. xi.

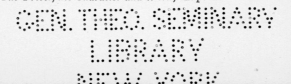

" While the multitude was making a rout with music and singing, our Lord remained outside the house. He entered only after the crowd had been cast forth." If he has learnt this substantially by heart, he might render it in some such shape as this : " So long as the crowd inside the house played and sang within the house Jesus remained outside. It was not until the death chamber was left empty and quiet that He entered."

Here the general drift of the narrative and the order of its conception and some of the phrases have been kept, but there has been a freedom in the use of the words of the manuscript. This freedom may be allowed more and more scope, as use gives greater confidence and dexterity in the management of language. The preacher will emancipate himself gradually from the text of his manuscript and render it with greater liberty as he finds himself more and more able to improvise. At the same stage he will begin to write something less than the whole sermon. Later, when he discovers that, when preaching, he can safely depart from the text of his manuscript, and amplify, condense, and modify his treatment of his topics, he may make a further change.

When he can thus treat his matter with ease and freedom, introduce illustrations and enter upon digressions, it is time —if he wishes—to leave some of the less delicate points in his discourse to be put into words at the time the sermon is delivered. In preparing, he merely notes them down and meditates them thoroughly.

Little by little his manuscript assumes the shape rather of a plan than of a finished composition, and at length a mere sketch will be all that he need write. But it will be wise for him to bring about this transformation patiently and without haste ; for so long as he is writing his sermons or the chief parts of them he is accumulating well thought out idioms and images, of which practice gives him a ready and instinctive use.

I may suggest here that he makes good employment of what opportunity he gets of preaching those familiar and less formal kinds of sermon which are customary in many

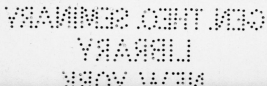

parishes—such as addresses to confraternities, or to week-day congregations, or the five-minutes instructions at Low Mass on Sunday. These give him occasion to experiment rather more freely than he would venture to do in more formal discourses, since the subjects will be simpler and the occasion less embarrassing. Nor will he despise the opportunities of improvisation afforded by the publication of the " Notices " Sunday by Sunday—though there is no need for him to waste so much eloquence as is sometimes expended in lengthy pronouncements about collections and parochial tea-parties.

These are in general the lines on which progress can be made towards good extempore preaching. The following two quotations from the life of the Curé of Ars, written by a relative of the saint, shows the process at work.[1] His biographer first describes his method of preparation at the beginning of his priestly life :

" Convinced as he was of the importance of instruction, he devoted all the time which was not taken up in prayer or parochial visitation to the preparation of his Sunday discourses. Having chosen his subject, he would take down some of the favourite volumes from the library he had inherited from M. Balley, such as the ' Familiar Instructions of Bonnaudel,' Curé of Semur-en-Brionnais ; the Homilies of Messire Claude Joly, Bishop and Count of Agen ; the Sermons of Père Lajeune ; ' Christian Perfection,' by Rodriguez, or the ' Lives of the Saints,' by Ribadeneira. When his reading was finished, then the tortures of composition began ; whether he contented himself with simply adapting a sermon or putting the borrowed doctrine into a new frame, the labour was the same, for he did not want to say anything that could not be thoroughly understood : he desired to adapt to these uneducated rustics that which had been written for cultivated minds, he wished also that his preaching should profit by all that he had learnt from his own experience of life. . . . Seated before his modest table, the poor orator wrote, erased, corrected ; saw the hours pass without any percep-

[1] *The Blessed John Vianney*, by Joseph Vianney (Eng. Trans. by C. W. W. " The Saints " Series. Duckworth).

tible result ; sometimes he spent seven hours pen in hand, sometimes the whole night.

" If in the end he was able to preach not only every Sunday but every day, if he succeeded in giving his daily instruction without any preparation whatever and with astonishing facility, it was no doubt because grace supplied what was wanting to nature ; still, one can understand that such assiduous toil had already transformed nature.

" All those young priests who feel they have not the gift of public speaking, and who dread having to preach, should make a pilgrimage to Ars. They would be shown M. Vianney's books, they would see those worn leaves, they might count the markers left in the pages and the passages underscored. Before these proofs of ardent labour they might calculate the time which a man, to whom study was a real martyrdom, must have spent in reading. They would be inspired with zeal for the salvation of souls, by recognizing the trouble which the curé of a village of only two hundred souls took for his modest audience ; above all, they would own that no one has any right to be discouraged seeing that one of the greatest of extempore preachers was obliged to devote several days each week to composing a sermon of three-quarters of an hour's duration." [1]

The other quotation refers to the later phase of Blessed John Vianney's preaching. It will be noted how the trying preparation of his early days had a real and direct influence on the preaching of his later years, when he preached daily to crowds of pilgrims without any immediate preparation at all.

" The present Curé of Ars recently (1895) asked an old inhabitant of the parish what his predecessor's preaching was like. ' His preaching,' answered the other, ' was full of comparisons.' Among these metaphors there were some which are familiar and even trivial, but others which are charming ; there were certainly many which he had gathered during the time of his laborious preparation, and which may be found in the sermons of certain preachers of the beginning of the seventeenth century ; again, there are

[1] Pp. 40 and 41.

others which are happy memories of his life as shepherd and peasant, and which he had stored up during the course of his conversations and meditations." [1]

It may be said that little can be inferred from this for our present purpose, because English parochial sermons are so different from the fervid exhortations of a French curé to a crowd of pilgrims, and because the exceptional sanctity of the venerable priest counted for so much in the effect produced by his words. There is some force in the objection. Yet this remains true : that grace did not obliterate nature, and that the plodding industry of the early days of his priesthood prepared him for that spontaneous outpouring of spiritual wisdom which raised an obscure parish church to the dignity of a shrine of pilgrimage, and drew Lacordaire from the most famous pulpit in the world to listen to the unstudied eloquence of a village priest.

III

There are sure to be some among my readers who feel that the methods I have recommended in this and the previous chapter are not suitable to them. This difference of view is inevitable from the very nature of things, since it arises from the evident fact that men's minds are not created according to an unvarying type. The memory, for instance, as I have hinted already, is not uniform in its working ; in some men it is reliable and in others it is the most unsafe of the powers and the most untrustworthy. And not only that, but the faculty itself operates in specifically different ways. Some memories attach themselves to words, others to ideas, others to images. You find men saying, " I have no memory for names, or no memory for faces, or no memory for dates and numbers." These simple confessions really point to a whole world of difference that exists between one mind and another. On account of this variety in mental outfit, no system of preparation can claim to be universally valid. It is but just

[1] P. 110.

that I should point this out plainly, and suggest some aids to those who feel, who know, that they can speak more clearly, more naturally, more effectively, by plunging at once into extemporary speaking.

I have come into possession of a lithographed copy of some hints for preaching in which Mgr. Benson briefly describes his own method, which is almost the direct opposite of the one for which I have been pleading. It may be found of use to those who are naturally of his own turn of mind; and some of his suggestions may help them to improve or perfect the method which best suits themselves. I give them here as he wrote them, at the request of some theological students.

" How to write a Sermon." By R. H. Benson.

" This is my own system."

I. Preach or lecture on *Subjects*, not texts; choose text last, and get the subject in mind so clear that it is possible to state it in one sentence.

E.g. " To Produce Contrition."
" To Explain such and such a Dogma."
" To rebut such and such a charge."

II. Construct sermon on organic system—head, body, tail —thus :

Introduction
Points I—
II—
III—
IV—
Conclusion.

These " points " are the most important part, and should be done first (not less than two, or more than four)—they are the backbone. Each should be capable of statement in one sentence.

III. Construct notes deliberately and slowly, in form the eye can take in at a glance, with small neat handwriting.

Use underlining a good deal, and capital letters—and, at first, coloured inks or pencils. I believe that the memory works much more easily, visually, than intellectually or logically. Use other symbols or devices that catch the eye, and when chosen, use the same in all sermons, *e.g.* square brackets for illustrations.

IV. Write out the last sentence in full, or nearly : and *never* in preaching attempt to develop this last sentence, however much tempted.

V. Do all this a day or two at least before preaching ; and then, *just before preaching*, sit down in an easy position with notes before you and get the thing, with a phantom photograph, into your head. *If possible, doze or sleep a little then*—that keeps a clear memory extraordinarily. I invariably do this. (Never talk before preaching.)

VI. Let the introduction be *interesting*—and, apparently, rather disconnected from main subject. (This catches and fixes the attention.)

VII. Don't bother about words *at all* beforehand, unless on a *very* thorny or difficult point or definition. This will mean slowness and halting at first (one must not mind that), but absolute safeness in a few months.

VIII. Never learn a sermon by heart. Know what you want to convey, absolutely clearly, but not the words. (Unless one is a born actor, to learn by heart means mechanicalness and dullness.)

IX. In speaking take care of the consonants, and the vowels will take care of themselves.

SPECIMEN.

(Idea to be Conveyed : That the Holiness and the Scandals of the Catholic Church both support her claim to be Divine.) Texts : Isaias vi. 3. Holy, Holy, Holy, and 1 Tim. i. 15. *Introduction. Our Lord was hated for two Reasons.*

1. *Personal Holiness* (Woman in adultery. " They went out one by one ").
Teaching—Demands He made, *e.g.* " Be you Perfect."
2. " Friend of Sinners " (Zaccheus . . . Magdalene).

I. Two Accusations against Catholic Church.

1. Too holy. Her teaching on sin. Friday fast. Lives of Saints. Religious Life.
2. Too unholy. She tolerates outcasts. Statistics of crime (Sacrament of Penance).

II. Explanation. She, like Jesus Christ, is human and divine.

1. *Divine.* Always desires and inculcates perfection. (A collector of silver keeps it spotless.)
2. *Human.* Tolerates anything (she is more human than man).
Because (*a*) Human nature plus sacraments is capable of sanctity.
(*b*) She can save, even if not sanctify entirely.

Conclusion. Her extremes, then, show her Largeness. She is the Incarnation of the love of God. She stands with her head in Heaven ; her feet at the gates of Hell.

(Last Sentence.) " Holy, Holy Holy, is Her Name : and to save sinners is her work."

IV

I would give a short development to one excellent piece of advice given in Mgr. Benson's document. Point IV recommends that the last sentence, even in an extemporary sermon, should be written out in full, and be spoken as it is written. This is done, of course, to save the preacher from over-long sermons and from uneasy and straggling endings. How many sermons would be appreciably more forcible if only they ended at the right time, and in the right way ! A vain young clergyman tried to wring a compliment from Rowland Hill by pestering him with the question, " What passage in the sermon pleased you most ? "

The answer he got at last was, "Your passage from the pulpit to the vestry."

Many a discourse, though good in all its parts, is unsatisfactory as a whole because it is too long—the preacher does not know *when* to bring it to an end. Obviously, it is impossible to lay down any hard and fast rule as to the length of sermons. An hour is allowed as a maximum in the Body of Rules drawn up for the guidance of Jesuit preachers.[1] St Francis of Sales, in his letter to the Bishop of Bourges, judiciously says that it is almost better for the sermon to be too short than too long; "in that matter," he adds, "I have so far been at fault and I want to correct myself, for, providing the sermon has lasted half an hour, that is enough." Many would say, nowadays, that half an hour is more than enough, and that a sermon of twenty minutes or so will be more beneficial to the people than a longer one. Really, much depends upon the sermon. If it is thoroughly interesting a long sermon appears all too short; if it is dull a short one is tedious. In a popular mediæval hand-book for preachers, the *Speculum Ecclesiæ* of Honorius of Autun, directions are given to the preacher to omit certain points in winter when the church is too cold and in summer when it is too hot. As to the length, that is wisely left to his good sense. "Here make an end if you wish: but if time permits, continue thus." Common sense must in the end decide the question of length. The worst of it is that even the wisest of us are not good judges in our own case, and congregations sometimes have to suffer for our miscalculation. If our sermons are too long, the best remedy is to prepare them more carefully; usually an over-long sermon can be reduced to a decent brevity if the feeble passages and the irrelevances are cut out of it.

Besides ending at the right time, the sermon ought to end *in the right way*. A traditional habit still lingers of finishing a sermon with the pious wish that all the congregation may find their way to Heaven; and particularly that they may at their life's end hear the words, "Well done, thou good and faithful servant," etc. I have no wish to carp

[1] *Corpus Institutorum Societatis Jesu*, Regula 23.

at this custom ; but clearly it is sometimes responsible for a very awkward conclusion. The preacher who is addicted to it feels that, come what may, he must remove himself from the pulpit by the aid of the good and faithful servant. The result is that that overworked domestic does not merely come in ; he has to be dragged in. Evidently all sermons do not end like this naturally, why then should they be forced to do so ? There have always been conventional endings, to sermons as to letters ; we meet them constantly in the discourses of the Fathers : in St John Chrysostom and St Leo, for example. But such preachers as these introduce them skilfully and bind them neatly to the body of the discourse. St Augustine's endings are worth noting. Frequently he employs a doxology, at other times he finishes abruptly, often again some incisive text from Sacred Scripture, or some pithy reflexion of his own brings about the close. There is no groping about in search of an elegant ending. Having said what he intended to say, he clinches his point by a suggestive and vigorous phrase, and the sermon is finished.

CHAPTER VII

IN THE PULPIT

SERMONS are composed in order to be preached, and a great deal of their effectiveness depends on how they are preached. Delivery in itself cannot make a wretched sermon into an excellent one ; but if it is good it can compensate in some degree for deficiencies, and if it is bad, it can spoil even a well-prepared and instructive discourse. No one who has listened to many sermons can doubt the truth of this, and many would claim that this view is too moderate ; they would argue that a good delivery has the power of turning a mediocre sermon into an effective one. St Francis of Sales, for one, seems to maintain this opinion in his well-known letter on preaching written to Monseigneur Frémiot.

At the very least, it is certain that more attention to delivery would vastly improve a great many sermons, and that all of us would be wise if we honestly examined ourselves on the point. Is there not, must there not be, a great deal of self deception regarding it in very many preachers ? Some priests go on for years without seeming to realize that there is anything wrong with their delivery, while every one who listens to them knows perfectly well that they have glaring faults of manner which a very little attention and care would mend ; yet these mistakes are never set right, nay, more frequently than not, they harden into habits. When, then, we take stock of our preaching, this important matter should not be missed. If we are unable to get to the bottom of it unaided, why should we not consult some of our hearers—our fellow priests, if they form part of our auditory, or some sensible lay-people not given to flattery—and profit by their judgment ? But even we ourselves, unaided, may discover a great deal, if we will but assume that we have faults, and look about for indications of their presence and their kind. If we consider the attitude of our listeners closely, it is not unlikely that we may be set upon the track of our misdoings. Perhaps our people are fidgety while we are in the pulpit. We have assumed that this comes from their restlessness or from uncomfortable benches : may it not be that the real reason of it is that we are too dull and long-winded ? We notice that after they have heard a certain amount from us they show signs of drowsiness. We have thought that they must be tired after their week's work, but perhaps it is that they are tired of us because we do not know when to stop. Or, again, we notice that a number of people at the far end of the church lean forward with strained faces, evidently because they cannot hear all we say. We have put this down to the perversity of deaf people, who seem always to crowd into back benches—but these people may not be deaf : it is not impossible that they find it hard to hear us because we are too sparing of our lungs.

We owe it to our congregation, whom we set out to teach, to discover our defects in delivery and do our best to correct them. Very often a slight effort will suffice to put matters right, but of course we must find out what is wrong before we are in a position to search about for remedies. The advice which we so frequently give when we speak of spiritual diseases and their cure is applicable here also: the remedy must be specific and not general, and it must be applied perseveringly until first the habit and then the tendency is destroyed.

I

A good delivery is not an accomplishment to be acquired merely by attending to technical rules ; it has its roots in nature, in a speaker's mental and moral attitude towards his audience, and in a true conception of his own aims. It begins and ends, in one sense, in the pulpit ; in another sense its conditions are to be sought elsewhere ; in his own personality. This is a truism, but it is one worthy of being explored, for it has wide and important implications. We must have heard many criticisms touching the delivery of sermons, and we cannot have failed to observe the diversity of standpoint inspiring them. We discover the same differences of view in the assumptions of writers who claim to supply technical rules for the guidance of speakers. Writers of " Hints for Preachers " and similar aids appear to form very different practical ideals of the " Complete Preacher," though they start from the same premises. They all assume that the preacher bears a message from God to His creatures. But differences show themselves when they begin to define and illustrate their conception. Some compare the preacher to an ambassador, a plenipotentiary even, delivering his sovereign's message, with all the dignity that attaches to its import, and to his own function ; and from this they are naturally led to speak much of the " dignity of the pulpit." Others think of the preacher as a lowly instrument, " the least of the Apostles," who should feel that he is unworthy of being called an Apostle, and these emphasize the humility, the self-forgetfulness of a man who effaces himself in order that his message may shine forth the more. Can we reconcile these diversities in some higher unity ? Theoretically, I cannot see how it can be done, but in practice it is not impossible. In practice the preacher can turn away from himself and concentrate his mind upon the lessons he teaches, and upon the object he has in view, which is the instruction and the sanctification of his hearers. He steeps himself in his subject, and endeavours to communicate it to his people. He leaves the question of manner almost in the shade, for his chief thought is elsewhere. By this I do not mean that he neglects delivery, but rather that he gives it from first to last a secondary place in his interest ; he shapes it, he embellishes it not as a personal accomplishment, but as if it were rather an attribute of his message than of himself. To use a comparison of St Augustine, he will be like a soldier who in the stress of battle thinks nothing of the jewelled hilt of his weapon, but only of the tempered keenness of its blade. He will make his manner,

H

like his language, lean upon his subject ; for matter and not manner is paramount.

Do we not know from experience, both as speakers and listeners, that a message loses much if its exponent thrusts himself between it and its hearers ? The great rhetoricians of antiquity felt how true this is in the sphere of secular oratory. Aristotle says that men are suspicious of oratorical devices " as they are of doctored wines." Quintilian warns orators against ambition, because it is likely to lessen the power of their pleading ; " above all," he says, " one should strive to escape a risk which is often run, when the desire of praise spoils the effectiveness of the plea." Nothing good can be added to our delivery by artificial mannerisms, and if we cultivate them they are sure to excite quite as much ridicule as admiration. I do not wish to depreciate attention to delivery, that were both harmful and inconsistent, but something must be said in commendation of a " natural manner." Whateley, in his enthusiasm for it, fell into the exaggeration of maintaining that if a good de- livery does not come spontaneously, it is useless to attempt to produce it, or to mend it by attending to rules. Obviously we *can* improve our delivery, partly by taking Whateley's own advice, and gaining a better grip upon our subject by seizing it more tightly with our mind and imagination, but partly also by correcting mannerisms bred by slovenliness or pomposity, by rusticity or affectation. Those who have studiously but mistakenly learnt mannerisms are surely capable of unlearning them, and a man can retrieve by care a dignity of manner that he has lost by carelessness.

As to the means to be taken, three especially may be recommended as the most effective even as they are the most obvious. The first is to use our observation and judgment profitably ; the second is to listen to and take advantage of enlightening criticism, whether directed at ourselves or others, whether kindly or captious ; and the third is to consult some sound treatise on elocution. But let us beware of this last ! Many books written by rhetoricians have a bad habit of magnifying the artificial at the expense of the natural. They suggest complicated methods and exercises where simple ones are sufficient. Yet they may be of use, of great use even, if we study them critically. Hidden under a luxuriance of meticulous precept, and obscured by a professional enthusiasm for rigid mechanical systems, a residue of good sense and profitable suggestion will be found by the discriminating reader of these tiresome manuals.

II

The young priest, coming from the seminary into the midst of the activities of parish life, though he may be competent and well forward with his studies, lacks the thing which only a longer contact with life can give—maturity of experience. He quickly discovers this, and if he happens to be a man who is easily depressed, the knowledge of it causes him some alarm. The weekly sermon, to such a one, is a trying duty ; he finds it hard to choose a subject, hard to find material, hard to compose, but hardest to deliver. He mounts the pulpit with terror in his heart, as the defendant climbs the steps of the dock, he spends a wretched, bewildering half-hour there, and can only breathe freely when he realizes that seven days must pass before he has to face the ordeal again. He is shy in his new position, he knows it himself, and he knows that everybody present knows it too. If we are to tender him some scraps of consolation, we must first search out the causes of his nervousness—for there may be definite causes for it, besides the vague terror that defies definition and description.

First there is the natural diffidence of speaking of such an intimate subject as religion to a number of unknown people. So far he has kept the best of his thoughts on that matter to himself. Then he feels keenly his inexperience of the technique, so to speak, of his new duty, and again he has the obscure feeling that what he has got ready is not worth saying ; he is like a nervous guest at a dinner-party, who is too shy to be silent, yet who dreads to speak a word lest the others turn to glare at him reproachfully for breaking a long silence by a commonplace remark.

He stands with his elbows chained to his sides, and his

hands glued to the pulpit. His words come rapidly, treading too swiftly on each other's heels, and now and then ceasing in a long and uncomfortable pause. Sometimes he loses the thread of his discourse, and after groping about, picks it up awkwardly. Sometimes he may break down altogether. Can any help be given, or any consolation to this Child of Despair ? I remember one piece of comfort given to me in the sacristy by the best of rectors on an occasion when I felt mortally nervous. He said, " Why are you in such a state ? There is A in the church, and B and C (he mentioned some unformidable names) and two or three hundred like them. Surely you are not afraid to talk a little theology to them for half an hour." The words were a great consolation, they seemed to separate the sticks of a big bundle, and I knew that it was easy to break each one of the sticks taken separately ; though bound together they looked a tough sheaf. I would pass on this sound counsel to anyone who is awed by a fear of mere numbers.

If one is afraid of the vagaries of an unreliable memory, he may counter his difficulty by taking a few notes into the pulpit—a few suggestive words to prompt him if he forgets the order of his plan.

But, above all, it will help him if he will realize that congregations do not exact, nay, do not even desire, an exceptionally original sermon every Sunday. Too much eloquence fatigues them ; what they want much more than continuous sublimity is variety, a pleasing change of subject and style of treatment. I sometimes think, by the way, that if travelling pulpit-orators were fixed to one church, they might, unless they preached more simply, empty their church as regularly as they now fill the churches of others.

But to return to our nervous preacher. What a young preacher often fails to grasp is the difference between the sermon as it appears to him and the sermon as it appears to his hearers. He has had the trouble of composing it, and through dwelling long upon it he becomes tired of it. He has written it out, or at least parts of it, and he has changed and corrected it. This occupation brings a sense of lassitude and staleness to the brain. But the people who listen are making the acquaintance of the sermon for the first time. He must not imagine that they share his dissatisfaction or that they are aware, as he is, that his achievement is far below his ideal. Further, there are faults and slips which he notices and they do not. He may lose the thread of his discourse, yet no one in the church, besides himself, notices his lapse ; his pauses appear much longer to him than they do to the people, and so on. He is a harsh critic of his own performance, while they make benevolent and generous allowances for his inexperience. It is certain that a congregation is much more sympathetic towards this Child of Despair than it is towards the Son of Presumption—the preacher who, through self-sufficiency or through an unfortunate cocksureness of manner has the air of being too much at his ease. Nervousness, uncomfortable though it be, has, except in its extreme and paralysing form, very definite compensations ; it " wears yet a precious jewel in its head." It stimulates effort, and keeps facile mediocrity at a distance. It may persist for quite a long time, for months or even years ; and when it disappears totally, anxiety to do one's best is liable to slacken, and in consequence the standard of a man's preaching is lowered. It is analogous in its effects to the sobering " virtue of Holy Fear."

There is one eventuality for which a nervous preacher, or in fact any preacher, ought to be prepared. It creates a very trying situation, and hence calls for mention here. The memory sometimes fails completely and leaves the speaker in the unenviable position of having to continue his discourse without knowing what to say. What is he to do ? The best way out of his difficulty seems to be to continue his sermon in some fashion or other ; if he makes a long pause it is only too possible that the darkness will deepen. Usually the blankness is only momentary, like the sudden blinking of an electric lamp. If only he can keep his head, and say something—anything at all appropriate will serve—his memory will get to work again and lead him back to his plan.

I leave this subject with a sincere regret that I cannot

altogether banish the fears or annihilate the difficulties of
the nervous preacher. I would advise such a one to take
St Augustine as his wise and tender counsellor, and glance
through the treatise, *De Catechizandis Rudibus*, by which he
comforted a zealous but diffident deacon of Carthage, who
had been made wretched by nervousness and scrupulosity
concerning his preaching and catechizing.

III

Accepting Buffon's well-worn aphorism, " The style is the
man," we immediately infer that as there are many preachers
so there must be many styles of preaching. Unless the
" pulpit manner " is to be something hopelessly uniform
and conventional, it must, from the nature of things, be
different in different men. " One good custom," and much
more emphatically one bad custom, should not be allowed
to set the tune to all the pulpits of Christendom ; every
preacher must be given liberty to cultivate his own manner.
I say *cultivate*, for we must not make the mistake of believing
that manner is incapable of improvement, or imagining that
nature is so perfect in its primitive forms as to forbid the
possibility of progress. The direction of progress, however,
should be determined by one's own personal character and
gifts. It is nothing but reasonable in us to recognize that
we can improve our delivery without interfering with its
basic qualities. If it is over-exuberant, it should be tempered
and brought under discipline ; if it is too dull and lamb-like,
it should be enlivened ; and these changes for the better
need not destroy its essential qualities or substitute an
altogether different sort of delivery in its place. It is a
grave mistake for one preacher slavishly to copy another ;
let him but attempt it and, as likely as not, he will lose
what is sound and effective in his delivery without managing
to get possession of the perfections of his model—the experiment will be no more successful than that of a man who
decks himself in somebody else's clothes.

Traditions in preaching start up now and then and become
fashions with very deplorable effect. They usually have

their origin in the performances of some exceptional man, who awakens wonder and creates a vogue ; demand creates supply, he gains imitators, and the fashion spreads. Frenchmen sometimes say that Lacordaire was the disaster of the modern French pulpit, inasmuch as he raised hosts of feeble imitators who wedded their prosaic language to his vehement manner, with incongruous and sometimes comic effect. The worst of it is, that unintelligent imitation usually chooses for itself uncommon, exotic models, and thus the reign of imitative eccentricity is established. In our time and country its most visible manifestations (outside the sermons themselves) are the outlandish advertisements one reads in newspapers and upon flamboyant posters exhibited in front of churches and chapels.[1] We Catholics are not so prone to be led away by these fashions as some religious bodies in which sermons appear to be the central acts of worship, but I would not say that we escape the tendency completely. As I am writing for the average preacher, it is safe to assume that a moderate and quiet style of delivery will be more natural to him than any other. However that may be, he cannot go far wrong if he sets his face against adopting any mannerisms that would make him a pinchbeck imitation of some other man. What we can naturally assimilate of the good qualities in others is all to our good, but we ought not to urge our nature by violence to adopt a style of preaching which, natural though it may be in another, looks artificial and affected in ourselves. Good preaching, preaching which may well serve as an ideal to the best of us, which will have as deep and as durable an effect upon others as we can possibly desire, can find all the outward expression that it needs in a simple and almost conversational delivery, as the accounts left of Newman's Catholic preaching convince us.[2] Even if this or that extra-

[1] I will not go so far as to say that out-of-the-way titles are infallible signs of out-of-the-way sermons. The clergyman who advertised as his title " Three days in a submarine " preached quite an unexciting sermon on the prophet Jonas.

[2] See the Introduction to *Sermon Notes to J. H. Newman*, 1849-1878, edited by the Fathers of the Birmingham Oratory. Longmans.

ordinary style may be better than our own, as it is assuredly more striking, it does not follow that we are to try to make it the rule, instead of leaving it to astonish the world by its unique impressiveness. We may, if we are so minded, be mightily rejoiced that there are preachers of that kind, without desiring their amazing manner to oust more normal styles or rob more modest ways of the good repute which their solid and well-tested qualities have gained for them.

A passage in a modern author, though it is concerned with writing and not with speaking, confirms and epitomizes the view I have been trying to commend. This is the passage ; it is taken from a course of lectures given at Cambridge in 1915 : " I grant you, to be sure that the claim to possess a Style must be conceded to many writers—Carlyle is one—who take no care to put listeners at their ease, but rely rather on native force of genius to shock and astound. Nor will I grudge them your admiration. But I do say that, as more and more you grow to value truth and the modest grace of truth, it is less and less to such writers that you will turn ; and I say even more confidently that the qualities of Style we allow them are not the qualities we should seek as a norm, for they one and all offend against Art's true maxim of avoiding excess." [1]

IV

The immediate object of the priest in the pulpit is to make an impression on his audience. Lest this statement should suggest what it does not logically and literally imply, it may be well to explain that making an impression is not making a sensation. The very word " impression " calls up a natural, and perhaps not inappropriate, illustration. The purpose of a seal is evident ; it was designed, and cut and fitted to its handle that it might leave a definite mark upon little bits of hot wax. When a man takes up the seal and brings it down on the wax, and not till then, has this purpose been brought into effect. His action from the point

[1] Quiller-Couch, *The Art of Writing*, pp. 245-6.

of view of art is negligible, it is not on the same plane with that of the designer or the engraver of the seal; nevertheless it is necessary, it puts the finishing touch on the work already done; and if it is done amiss, the work of others is frustrated, for the wax does not receive the figure cut upon the seal. The delivery of the sermon is the application of its thoughts and language to the minds and consciences of the people. It belongs to the essence of preaching, and though it is not its noblest, it is its most decisive function.

Like most comparisons, this one of the seal fails if it is too closely examined. To bring down the seal upon the wax is a simple matter; the delivery of a sermon is not at all simple, for it consists in the appropriate fusion of a number of miscellaneous elements. The effect, of course, should be simple, yet the means bringing it about are complex. It would be long to enumerate the means brought into play; voice, attitude, gesture, facial expression are the chief among them, and each one stands for something almost infinitely various. To organize these means effectively, so that they are made to converge upon the object intended by the preacher, is no mean accomplishment, especially when, as often happens, the instruments themselves are not perfect. As I do not purpose to enter into great detail, one general recommendation must suffice; and after making it, I will go on to make a few suggestions on the proper use of the two principal elements in delivery—action and enunciation.

The remark which applies to all the means at the speaker's disposal is this—that they must, if they are to be effective, give the impression of rising naturally, inevitably even, out of the sermon itself. It must not appear that their use is factitious, that they are conceived separately and, so to say, fitted on as an afterthought. The sermon has to be presented as a unity, and delivery must hold its place in it, not as something contingent and separable, but as something essential and natural. To put it more simply, the preacher must not look as if he were doing a number of things at the same time, such as remembering his phrases, choosing his tones of voice and his expression of countenance, arranging his attitudes.   No, he must obviously be doing one duty, that is, communicating his thoughts to his people.   If he has arranged any of his effects beforehand, this should not appear ; there should be no smell of the lamp about the discourse.   And really, the best of our resources are those which we have from nature ; we should employ ourselves principally in the elimination of flaws and the correction of awkwardness, in the discipline and not the manufacture of our manner and delivery.

We pass now to gesture.   The first condition of correct gesture is a correct attitude in the pulpit.   One has often read, somewhat unsympathetically, adjurations to cultivate a dignified, or even a majestic, manner.   Whatever this may mean, it cannot mean that a priest is to ascend the pulpit with the conscious intention of taking a majestic attitude. It will surely be sufficient if he remembers what he is going to do.   He is going to reveal God's truths and God's counsels to his flock, not as a mystagogue declaring an oracle, but as an apostle announcing a message.   " When I came to you," wrote St Paul to his Corinthians, " I came not in loftiness of speech or of wisdom, declaring unto you the testimony of Christ. . . .   And my speech and my preaching was not in the persuasive words of human wisdom, but in showing of the Spirit and in power : that your faith might not stand on the wisdom of men, but on the power of God,"[1] and who can doubt that his manner corresponded to his conception of his sacred office ?   If, then, we must think of dignity, let it be

[1] 1 Cor. ii.   It was this text which Pope Benedict XV. quoted in an exhortation to the Lenten preachers in Rome when speaking to them of artificial fashions of delivery.   His Holiness spoke strongly against certain preachers who in their oratorical affectation succeeded only too completely in absolutely concealing from the people the Word of God they were entrusted to reveal.   "Preachers should guard themselves against that excited delivery, those wild looks, that frenzied speech, those insane gestures that would be out of place even on the stage.   It has been a sorrow to us recently to learn that such preachers do exist who defend themselves by saying that the people like it.   And even if this be true, such taste should be condemned and not fostered by those who, with us all, should remember those words of St Paul, the great master of preaching, 'And my speech and my preaching, etc.' "—*The Tablet*, 3rd March 1917.

of the dignity of the truth we preach ; that thought will invest us with all the "majesty" of manner that we need.

To descend now to prosaic details. The preacher should stand firm and erect, without rigidity and without slovenliness. He should keep from swaying, from leaning to this side or to that, and from sprawling over the ledge of the pulpit. In most churches there is a point towards which it is best to direct the voice, so as to be heard easily by all in the church. If he faces this point, with his eyes looking towards it, his glance passing just over the heads of the people, his hands resting naturally on the pulpit, his body held without stiffness, he will be in a position suitable to any gesture he may make. But if his attitude is unnatural, his gesture will be unnatural also.

A chapter in St Charles Borromeo's pastoral instructions touches upon the chief points to be observed when gesture is used. I take the liberty of treating them freely here.[1]

1. Gestures should be *natural*. They should not be immoderate nor studiously graceful, but such as manliness and good taste demand. We should avoid what comedians describe as " business," a would-be-impressive manipulation of cuffs or handkerchief, and similar " devices of oratory." I cannot understand how these tricks can be considered natural in anybody, nor how they come to be admired. There are, of course, mannerisms which become natural to affected people, and are admired by folks who like affectations, but good sense and good taste will have none of them.

2. *Restraint* heightens the effectiveness of gesture. If action is overdone, or employed continuously, it stultifies instead of intensifying the emotions of the speaker. The commonest purpose of action is to add emphasis, but what is more wearying than long drawn out or uncontrolled emphasis ? Perpetual motion has the effect of over-heating the preacher while it freezes the audience. As a rule the background of a speech or sermon should be calm and only the " great moments " brought into relief by movement.

---

[1] *Pastorum Instructiones*, Pars I. cap. xxvi.

Then gesture is quite in its place, " with this special observance that you overstep not the modesty of nature." [1]

3. *Meaningless* action should be avoided. This is doubtless what St Charles wishes to be understood when he warns the preacher against stretching out his arm immoderately " like a gladiator." In England we use other metaphors, and speak of " sawing the air " and the " pump handle " action as characteristic of their Englishman's delivery. At their best these gestures are not graceful, and if they are used indiscriminately they can only be appropriate by a lucky accident. Why should one sprinkle them about a speech on the remote chance of their being appropriate now and then ? We may note in this place that an action which follows the emphatic word is always feeble ; even Whately, who will have it that Rhetoric can supply no rules for gesture, cannot refrain from calling attention to this. Gesture should either synchronize with the emphatic phrase or precede it by an almost infinitesimal point of time.

4. *Feeble, apologetic gesture* detracts from a sermon. Our custom in these countries is to employ gesture sparingly, and it is not deemed remarkable if none is used. But action ought to be used with courage, if at all. Speakers sometimes make slight and timid movements with the forearm— from the elbow outwards. This gesture appears to be a mannerism special to the pulpit, for it is never employed in private life, even by nervous men. It means nothing and looks both weak and awkward.

V

The sins of schoolmasters are visited upon their pupils, as many a preacher has found by painful experience. Youth is the time when foundations of accomplishments and habits are laid, when those elementary industries which support the whole fabric of adult knowledge—correct taste and right judgment—are learnt or neglected with lifelong results.

---

[1] *Hamlet*, Act IV. Sc. 2. The counsels given by Hamlet to the players in this scene are quite worth a preacher's study.

At school a child can be methodically taught to read correctly and intelligently and to speak distinctly and unaffectedly, and if his pedagogue, backed by despotic authority and armed with the goads of love and fear, will look to this, he will be responsible as no one else can be for his pupil's later achievements in elocution. If he neglects this duty he leaves to his charges a trying task in which success is difficult and failures are many. The neglect of schoolmasters in this branch of their craft must be my excuse for venturing to write these few paragraphs on such an elementary theme as the one to which I now apply myself—the right use of the voice in public speaking.

We speak in order to be heard, and, moreover, to be heard easily. We all have a voice of some kind, most of us of the kind that requires some little management. I wish to mention here some special points in which care is necessary in our management of it. Speakers sometimes appear to believe that loudness is everything, or almost everything, in public speaking. A speaker hears that some of his sentences are missed. Some one tells him in private that he could not be heard in some parts of the building; or, if he happens to be speaking in circumstances that allow interruptions, discontented and impatient people call upon him to "Speak up." We are prone to take the view that "speaking up" is all that is needed. But, really, it is much more important to attend to the *rate* of speaking than to volume. Our normal pace should be what musicians call *andante*, literally an ordinary walking pace, neither lagging nor hurrying. Choose this, then, as the normal pace; it may be quickened or retarded according to the demands of the subject, but get back to it frequently; it is a steady rate, like that of the regular walk of the worldly-wise man of business from his home to his railway station.

Attention to the right pace is good in itself, but it has the further use of helping *clear articulation*—one of the most necessary qualities in public speaking. Deliberate pronunciation, the clear utterance of every syllable, will atone for many defects—it diminishes, for instance, the trouble arising from weakness of voice. A speech is built up of words, and words are built up of syllables, and hence, though the unit of speech is grammatically the word, vocally it is the single syllable. If I mumble one poor syllable when I take a railway ticket, I may find the wrong ticket handed to me by the clerk. In preaching, then, when every syllable is clear, every word is clear, and the whole sermon has a good chance of being heard from the text to the last word. Especially, attend to the last syllable of a sentence ; when the voice is dropped, the last syllable runs risks of being unheard unless it is clearly uttered.

Clearness is assisted by our hitting the consonants well, especially *b*, *v*, *t* and *d* ; the vowels scarcely need any care at all, they are so unlike among themselves that there is little danger of their being confused with one another. One word of caution, however : do not run to extremes and pronounce syllables as though they are in every sense complete in themselves. It is intolerably dreary to listen to a sermon delivered *staccato* ; to preach in this unnatural fashion is to show an excess of reverence, a slavish obsequiousness towards the single syllable. Elocutionists often recommend it, but plain people would, I think, prefer even gabbling to this absurd and unnatural performance.

Next let us consider the *pitch* of the voice. This varies in different speakers, of course, for a voice may be high or low in pitch. The compass of a speaking voice is, let us say, five or six tones. According as it has a tenor or a bass quality this group of notes will occur in different sections of the musical scale. Within this compass we can speak without strain ; if we go beyond it our voice becomes unnatural, and sounds either too high or too low. Find your own particular compass then, and take the middle note (how much the " golden mean " counts in preaching !) between the two extremes. We shall always do right to take this as the dominant note in our sermon. We shall, of course, go below this middle note for the more solemn passages and above it when we need to enliven the tone of our discourse. There must be no idolizing of the single note, any more than of the single syllable, otherwise we shall fall headlong into the pit of monotony, our harp will have but one string. On a high note monotony is nerve-racking, on a low one it is soporific.

There is another fault kindred to this one of monotony; it is called *isotony*, or, more descriptively, sing-song. This is, as every one knows, the regular recurrence of one simple change of tone. Here our harp has two strings—but the twanging of two strings, at fixed intervals, can be as wearisome as the twanging of one.

The *volume* of a voice determines its capacity for loudness and softness: its throne is in the lungs. Too much importance is sometimes conceded to volume; people speak of it as though it were the one quality necessary for making a speech audible, especially in a large building. It would be truer to say that it is the quality necessary for filling a large building with sound. But sound is not everything; it is not, for instance, a word. A muffled tempest of sound is not a speech, and yet it is all that can be created by mere loudness. No one would wish to defame a strong voice; it is patently a good weapon in any speaker's armoury; but it is not his chief, nor his best. It must be wielded sparingly and at the right moment. What would be the effect, for instance, if a preacher bellowed out the Beatitudes at the top of his voice? Yet, notwithstanding its limitations, the usefulness, and in some circumstances the necessity, of volume is not to be minimized. Preachers who have strong voices are apt to take it for granted that they are exempt from the lowly duty of taking trouble to use them well. Instead of directing their sermon to the further end of the church, they may be content if what they say can be heard distinctly by those sitting near the pulpit. A man who has the voice to do it, ought to speak loudly enough not only to be heard, but to be heard easily and without strain by every soul in the church. It is more irritating to hear by dint of strain a portion of the sermon and miss the rest than it is to miss the whole. When the sermon is totally inaudible the layman in his pew can say his prayers in peace, and wait, with what patience he has, until the preacher has finished; whereas, if he catches some words and misses others, he can neither attend fully to the sermon nor to his own thoughts.

We will pass now to consider some of the means we have at our disposal of improving our speaking. Those who are conscious that their voice is not all they would wish it to be may be consoled by the thought that an extraordinary perfection of elocution is not exacted in a preacher. A resonant, flexible, sympathetic voice is a boon, but should it happen that such a voice is out of the question for this or that person, on account of some organic defect, there is still room for hope of his attaining a passable delivery. It is remarkable how many of our great orators have been handicapped by serious defects of utterance. Burke's voice was harsh when he spoke calmly, and hoarse when he became excited. Hooker's was weak; Curran stuttered; yet weighted though these men were by these drawbacks, they made their good qualities compensate for these defects. We, like them, must make good use of what gifts we have, and remedy such faults as are susceptible of amendment. A man handicapped by defects should first of all make good use of what voice he has, for it is rare that a voice fails in every respect. If he has, for instance, a weak voice, can he not restore the balance by more careful articulation ? If he articulates badly, let him moderate his pace. If he has a nasal intonation, he can do much to counteract the defect by practising reading or speaking, taking special pains to use his mouth and lips in speaking, thus ousting his nose from its undue interferences.

The other way of meeting difficulties of this kind is by a frontal attack upon one's shortcomings. A man's voice is monotonous, a little practice in singing ought to make it less so; he emphasizes the wrong words, he can unlearn this habit by reading passages, underlined so as to indicate the right words to emphasize. I admit readily that this sort of exercise seems rather unfitting in any adult, and indeed it should have been finished with years ago, but then, since it was not done then, it must be done now, unless one is to abandon all efforts at becoming a tolerable preacher. Men of the world submit to much lowlier processes than this in pursuit of their aims; ought we to count even such efforts mean and undignified when their final object is nothing less than the glory of God and the instruction of Christians in His Law? [1]

[1] I would refer such readers as this matter concerns to two chapters in Fr. Lockington's book, *Bodily Health and Spiritual Vigour*, chapter viii. in Part I. and chapter viii. in Part II. The second of these gives straightforwardly, without unnecessary philosophizing, a plan of exercises for the use of preachers in quest of a better voice.

CHAPTER VIII

THE USE OF SCRIPTURE IN PREACHING

SACRED Scripture is not merely one of the sources of preaching ; it is the principal source. Such is the common doctrine developed insistently and emphatically in almost every treatise on homiletics. To prove it to be sound would be to repeat once again arguments and testimonies with which all are familiar.

Yet, in this matter, theory and practice are greatly at variance, as anyone can see for himself if he glances through any half-dozen sermon-books, chosen at random, and notes the use of Scripture that is made in them. For lack of any better criterion of estimating the style of our modern preaching, the indications furnished by this ready test may, by revealing a deficiency, point the way to an improvement in our way of preparing sermons. What, then, do we observe in these printed sermons ? Chiefly this : that preachers have adopted a very conventional way of using Scripture, and that the sacred text appears to have dropped from a primary to a secondary source. The passages of Scripture that are cited in most sermon books seem to have filtered into the sermons through the theological middleman, the writer of manuals and textbooks. The similarity that exists in the demonstrations contained in different theological manuals is reflected in the narrow and conventional use of Scripture in the sermons. Passages which have become " classical " are sprinkled about in greater or less profusion, and beyond them there is little Scripture at all. Even the liturgy, with which preachers must be familiar, supplies but a negligible fraction of the scriptural content of sermons, although the liturgy is mainly a mosaic of Biblical citations. Whole books of Scripture seem to be almost passed over. The sapiential books, for instance, though they abound in practical teaching and illustration, are seldom quoted ; and the employment of St Paul's epistles is remarkably restricted. The Gospels themselves are represented by conventionally chosen citations, taken chiefly from the pericopes used in the Sunday liturgy.

How seldom, for example, do we find a sermon upon a parable such as that of the " Prodigal Son," though nothing could be more consoling and fruitful than its teaching on penance ; or upon the incident in St John's Gospel (chap. v.) on the cure of the lame man, though it illustrates so vividly the reluctance of many to accept the supernatural ; or again, upon the story of the importunate friend, read on Rogation Days, which teaches, in so homely and intelligible a way, the reward of persevering prayer.

The difference between modern sermons and those of the Fathers in this respect is striking—it is not so much a difference as a contrast. When we reflect that these ancient sermons, so replete with scriptural quotation and allusion, were composed with so little aid such as we receive from introductions, concordances, commentaries, Biblical dictionaries and so on, we wonder as we realize how familiar the text of Scripture was to these writers, and how naturally the words of Scripture leapt to their lips. Their knowledge was neither indirect nor haphazard ; no one can for a moment doubt that their intelligence and their memory were habitually occupied with the contents of books which they unceasingly studied. It was no question with them of " getting up " a number of texts when they prepared to preach ; the whole Bible lay before them, and its thoughts and expressions were woven into the fabric of their knowledge and speech. " The monk," writes a mediæval Carthusian, " must get time for reading at fixed hours and of a fixed character. Casual and scattered reading, taken up as it were by chance, does not edify, but makes the mind unstable. Things lightly acquired lightly depart from the memory. We must dwell upon the Scriptures with fixed minds, with fixed intelligence, and train our

minds to it.   The Scriptures should be read in the same spirit
as that in which they are written ; for it is thus that they
must be understood.   You will never understand the meaning of St Paul till, by the use of a good intention in reading
him, and the effort of continual meditation, you imbibe
his spirit.   You will never understand David until by actual
experience of your own you make the emotions of the Psalms
your own." [1]

In a former chapter we have briefly sketched the homiletic
theories of the greatest of the Fathers, and it is well to
recall here what place he assigned to Holy Scripture in popular
preaching.   He who, more than any other man since the
apostolic times, directed the course of Christian thought and
inaugurated vast developments in Christian theology points
to the Scriptures as the all-important study of the preacher.
Do we wish our teaching to be theological, to be fresh and
original ?   St Augustine, whose doctrine glows with personal
insight, directs us to the most traditional of sources—the Old
and the New Testaments.   In recent times, Pope Leo XIII.,
who was far from being indifferent to systematic theology,
insisted that the sacred Scriptures should be the first study
of a preacher.[2]   And it is within the experience of us all, that
here is the best remedy against arid emptiness of substance
and unreal routine in exposition.   To know something *about*
Scripture is not enough ; a preacher must have a direct and
first-hand knowledge of the text of Scripture itself ; for it is
in the Bible and especially in the New Testament that he will
find the germ and often the full fruit of the doctrine upon
which the souls need to be continually nourished.   In
this chapter it will be presupposed that the preacher
possesses a practically adequate, though not necessarily
academic, knowledge of the text of the written tradition of
the Church.

[1] Appendix in Benedictine edition of the Works of St Bernard.
[2] Leo XIII., *Providentissimus Deus.*

I

Holy Scripture, according to Catholic teaching, does not stand by itself nor carry with it its own interpretation. It is part of a greater scheme of supernatural enlightenment, and is one of the organs of ecclesiastical tradition, of which it performs a function side by side with the spoken word. Hence, the hermeneutical principles by the aid of which it is interpreted, have been gradually established by tradition, which has based them mainly on a close observation of the manner in which inspired writers have interpreted the teaching of the sacred authors who wrote before them, and on the homiletic methods customarily employed by Fathers and exegetes. "All Scripture, divinely inspired," St Paul wrote to Timothy, "is profitable for teaching, for reproving, for correcting, for instructing in justice: that the man of God may be perfect, furnished to every good work."[1]

The adaptation of sacred Scripture to the uses indicated by the Apostle in this passage has led to the formulation of certain distinctions in the "senses" of the sacred writing, and so it happens that preachers are not only supplied by the Church with the Bible as their religious manual, but also with rules for its due interpretation. At the base of these rules is the principle asserted by Catholic tradition, that the Scriptures, besides their primary, literal, or historical sense, present also, in parts of them at least, a secondary or mediate sense variously described as typical, spiritual, or mystical.

In addition to these senses, strictly so called, there is a usage of the words of Scripture called "accommodatious," which is not, properly speaking, a "sense" of Scripture at all, but is an allusive or quasi-literary use of phrases contained in the Scriptures. Since preachers are also exegetes, a few paragraphs may profitably be given here to each of these different uses of the sacred text.

I. *The literal sense.*—As the sacred writers employed words, and each word has a meaning, there is in Scripture as in all literature a signification immediately intended by the

[1] 2 Tim. iii. 16, 17.

writer. He wishes to convey through his writing ideas existent in his own mind. The language he uses may be plain or it may be figurative, it may express his thought in the shape of a maxim, or an historical incident, or an allegory or a parable; but, whatever be the medium of expressing it, there is a thought to be conveyed, an idea to be signified. When a reader finds what this idea is of the sacred writer —which he will usually do without much pains if he has a correct text before him and reads the passage in its context —he is in possession of the literal sense.

Every passage of Scripture must have a literal sense; and the literal is always the true sense, since it is the one which the sacred author directly had in view when he wrote under the inspiration of the Holy Spirit. Moreover, this sense of a passage, whenever it is ascertained with certainty, has always the value of a theological proof. It is, then, of the first importance that the literal sense should be the primary object of investigation both on account of its intrinsic authority and because it is the only safe foundation for any spiritual sense that may be discovered. When interpretations are not firmly based upon this primary sense they are apt to degenerate into error and futility, whereas if the literal sense is well grasped, it may be made a starting-point for natural and edifying development of the spiritual truths that lie hidden beneath the letter of Holy Scripture.

II. *The spiritual sense.*—The facts and personages of the Bible may be treated as being typical of something over and beyond what is said of them in the text. They may be brought forward as dramatically presenting the spiritual teaching of the Bible and the Church. Theologians usually enumerate three ways in which the letter of Scripture may yield a spiritual sense:—(*a*) It may allegorically represent some truth or principle of faith (hence *the allegorical sense*), (*b*) or it may be seen to contain and enforce some moral lesson (*the tropological sense*), (*c*) or it may typically point to the realization of Christian hope in the glory of heaven (*the anagogical sense.*)[1]

Dante, in his dedication of the " *Paradiso* " to Can Grande,

[1] See St Thomas, *Summa Theologica*, Pt. I., q. i. art. x

explains the verse, " *In exitu Israel de Egypto, domus Jacob de populo barbaro,*" according to the various senses. In its first and literal signification the words apply to the exodus of the Hebrews from the Egyptian captivity. Allegorically this fact symbolizes the redemption of mankind from the servitude of Satan ; according to its moral sense it is applicable to the sinner's conversion from vice to virtue ; and anagogically it represents the soul's escape from the labours of this present life and its entrance into the reward of the just.[1]

Catholic homiletical tradition favours the employment of the spiritual senses of Scripture, and in this it can plead wide precedents in Scripture itself and in the writings of the Fathers. What, for instance, is more natural for a preacher than to interpret Our Lord's prophesy of the impending ruin of Jerusalem, as a warning to those who reject God's calls to repentance, or to draw the comparison between leprosy and sin when he treats the gospel relating the cure of the ten lepers ? Good sense recognizes that restraint and caution have to be observed in this usage of Scripture, and especially so when a preacher ventures into original and recondite interpretations. He should make it clear that his personal exegesis, when it leads him to suggest spiritual interpretations, is not to be received as if it were the literal and primary meaning. Except where secondary senses have been fully authenticated (as, for instance, where a New Testament

---

[1] The following homiletic examples will illustrate the three typical senses :—(1) *Allegorical* : " Jesus is the good Samaritan ; when mankind had been despoiled of the supernatural robe of innocence, and lay wounded and helpless, Christ came to his aid. Neither priest nor Levite, neither sacrifice nor the law of the Old Covenant could help him. But the Son of God came down from heaven : He healed his wounds, pouring upon them the wine of His precious blood and the oil of His grace and bringing him to the refuge of His Church." (2) *Tropological* : " Jacob's journey to Egypt recalls the truth that God's servants are strangers and pilgrims on this earth. They, like him, are buffeted by pain and encompassed by dangers. They, like him, look with hope for the day of rest and deliverance." (3) *Anagogical* : " The life of our first parents in Eden suggests the life of the blessed in heaven. They were happy in Paradise. Peace reigned within and about them, for they were the friends of God. They knew no pain nor want. They gazed upon God, who walked with them in the Garden and shared His thoughts and His life. But now comes the difference. Heaven is for ever, the earthly paradise was but for a time."

writer gives a spiritual interpretation to some incident of the Old Testament) the spiritual sense has no force of strict theological proof.[1]

Proof, however, is not the only function of preaching, and, provided the preacher keeps well within the bounds set by scriptural and ecclesiastical analogy, he is free to explore the text of Scripture and draw from it all the edification and instruction he may. For example, though the author of the Epistle to the Hebrews does not explicitly refer to bread and wine in the sacrifice of Melchisedech as an anticipated type of the elements of the Holy Eucharist, the fact that he compares Melchisedech's priesthood with that of Christ is sufficient ground for an extended application of the idea of the Epistle to the use of bread and wine in the Eucharistic rite. Similarly the comparison of Solomon with Our Lord in the same Epistle (i. 5) may be drawn out by a preacher's attributing certain of the characteristics of Solomon—for instance, his wisdom and justice and zeal for God's worship—to Our Lord. There occurs a passage in Bishop Hedley's sermon on " Sanctification " which I will quote as an actual and modern instance of the homiletic use of the spiritual sense. It will be noticed how the preacher disclaims for his interpretation the authority which attaches to the primary sense of Scripture and how he keeps himself well within the limits of permissible analogy in his mystical interpretation of the Old Testament story.

" There is a story in the fourth book of Kings which has always appeared to me to be meant as an instruction to some who see difficulties in the dispensation of an ordained ministry of grace. The child of the Sunamitess had been struck by a stroke of the sun, and had died on her knee at the noontide hour. After Giezi had carried the staff of Eliseus and laid it upon the face of the dead child and ' there was no voice nor sense,' then Eliseus came in person, and going in, he shut the door upon him and upon the child and prayed to the Lord. And then he went up and lay upon the child ; and he put his mouth upon his mouth and his eyes upon his

[1] *Cf.* St Jerome on Matt. xiii. 33.

eyes, and his hands upon his hands ; and he bowed himself upon him ; and the child's flesh grew warm. Then he returned, and walked in the house, once to and fro ; and he went up and lay upon him ; and the child gaped seven times, and opened his eyes (4 Kings iv. 32.) He was raised to life again. This is a strange history. But a reverent reader of God's Word will ponder over it. Ancient saints have meditated upon it, and seen the ' instruction ' it was meant to convey. It was a figure of the Incarnation. It would have been no greater effort of God's power had Eliseus stood at the door, or stood afar off, and raised the dead child with a word. So it would have been perfectly easy to the Infinite Creator and Lord of all things to save the world by an act of His will, and to Jesus Christ to have dispensed altogether with ministers and priests. But the Word became Flesh. The Infinite bowed Himself down to our littleness. The invisible God became visible and tangible to the senses of man's body. And so it was to be to the end. The mouth to the mouth, the eye to the eye, the hand to the hand ; thus was to be carried *on* the dispensation of Life eternal ; man was to announce the Truth to his fellow-man ; man's Law was to regenerate, man's voice was to consecrate and sanctify, to bind and to loose." [1]

III. St Bernard, in Sermon LI. on the Canticle, rebukes the strictness of those who would confine preachers to the literal sense. The scriptural text, he declares, is one of the common gifts of God to the souls of men, as water is to their bodies, and, like water, it is rightfully applied to many uses. " In like fashion let every rendering of the divine speech be used, provided it gives a diversified understanding suitable to the varied need and profit of different souls." Accommodation is one of these " renderings " ; it is an allusive or devotional application of the words of Scripture to matters outside the original scope of the writers. The liturgy abounds in such " accommodations." Thus, for example, in the Gospel read on the Feast of the Assumption, the words spoken by Our Lord to Mary, the sister of Lazarus, are adapted by the Church to Our Lady : " Mary hath chosen the better part

[1] Hedley, *Our Divine Saviour*, pp. 84-86.

which shall not be taken from her." Again, the Gospel for
the Feast of St Monica is taken from St Luke's description
of the raising of the widow's son—a beautiful adaptation of
the scriptural story of Christ's compassion on a mother's
grief, to the widow whose tears brought her son Augustine to
the life of grace. So too in the Breviary, many of the passages
for the Feast of a Confessor are devotionally borrowed from
praises rendered to Old Testament saints. What the Church
does for a priest in the Breviary he may do for his people
by his sermons. There is something very attractive in
sermons which employ Scripture in this way.

No point of doctrine can be validly proved from Scripture
used in an accommodated sense. It would not, for
instance, be permissible to introduce those parts of the
sapiential books read in the Lessons of the Office of
Our Lady to establish a scriptural argument in favour
of her special privileges. One could not say, "The Holy
Scripture says of Mary that God 'possessed her from
the beginning of her days.'" But one might say that
the Church applies to Mary the words spoken by the
Holy Ghost concerning the Divine Wisdom. It is scarcely
necessary to add that all irreverent or jocose applications of
scriptural language should be avoided.[1] These are unfitting
the pulpit and are, moreover, expressly forbidden by the
Council of Trent.

II

True and right opinions often seek support from arguments
which are hopelessly at fault. This general observation is
at times exemplified when scriptural passages are adduced
in confirmation of religious doctrine. A well-known instance
is given by Camus in his *Spirit of St Francis of Sales*.
Once when he was preaching in presence of St Francis, he
was led by his subject to speak of the contagion of evil
company. In scriptural support of his view he quoted the

[1] Such, for instance, is a jocular application of the text, " I was
a stranger and you took me in," to a man whose simplicity is
traded upon by a cunning rogue ; or again, such is the irreverent
witticism of Caramuel, who pointed out the easy moralist Diana with
the remark, " *Ecce qui tollit peccata mundi.*"

verse, "With the holy thou shalt be holy and with the wicked thou shalt be perverted." When they were next alone the Bishop asked him why he had used that text in such a sense. The preacher answered that usage justified the application of the passage to his topic. This did not satisfy St Francis, who maintained that at least he should have mentioned that he was not quoting according to the literal meaning, which refers solely to God, who is in that passage said to be merciful to good men and stern towards the evil.[1]

There are a number of texts commonly used in this inaccurate way ; and a few years ago a French theologian gathered about a hundred and fifty of them from French books of sermons.[2] A number of the specimens he adduces are not used thus, so far as I know, by English preachers. This circumstance need not be for us a temptation to pride ourselves on our greater accuracy ; probably the reason of the difference is that there is a much less ample use of Scripture in English sermons than in French ones ; we make less mistakes because we employ less Scripture. Among the collection there are some which we do use in the same inaccurate sense as our neighbours across the Channel ; and I will make a short list of these, in the hope that it may prove useful to English preachers.

"*Let us make man to our image and likeness*" (Genesis i. 26). Some theologians, as well as many preachers, cite these words as an indication of a plurality of Persons in God, and also adduce it in confirmation of God's creation of the natural order (His Image) and the supernatural (His Likeness). In doing so they follow patristic custom. The text, though it may be used to illustrate these doctrines, has little authority as a decisive theological proof."[3]

"*Give me souls, and take the rest for thyself*" (Gen. xiv.

[1] *Spirit of St Francis of Sales*, Pt. III., ch. iii. (Eng. Trans.).
[2] *Les Contresens Bibliques des prédicateurs*, J. B. Bainvel. Lethielleux.
[3] See concerning this passage and others in the Old Testament sometimes adduced as proofs of the Blessed Trinity : The three guests of Abraham (Gen. xviii.) ; the Trisagion of Isaias (Isa. vi. 3) ; the words of Psalm lxvii.—Lebreton, *Origines du Dogme de la Trinité* pp. 441 and foll.

21). This passage is frequently cited as witnessing to the value of the soul and the comparative unimportance of all else. But "soul" here is not "soul" in the Christian sense. The context shows that in the division of the booty taken by Abraham and himself, the King of Sodom claimed the captive men (souls), allowing Abraham to take the rest. English preachers use the text in the same way as French, quoting from the Vulgate, *Da mihi animas*, though, in the Douai Bible, everything is quite clear, and the passage runs, " Give me the persons."

" *I am thy protector and thy reward exceeding great* " (Gen. xv. 1). The Beatific vision of God is the reward of the just, but this text is no proof of it, although a devotional consequence may be drawn from the passage by accommodation. The true sense is, " I am thy shield ; thy reward is very great."

" *Joseph is a growing son, a growing son and comely to behold ; the daughters run to and fro upon the wall* " (Gen. xlix. 22). The text is often applied to St Joseph, typified by the Joseph of the Old Testament. Hebraists find this a difficult passage and give as the probable meaning, " Joseph is the son (a figure for *an offshoot*) of a fertile tree near a river, the daughters (*i.e.* the branches) run along the length of the wall."

" *The light of thy countenance is signed upon us, O Lord, thou hast given gladness to my heart* " (Psalm iv. 7). The text as it is in the Vulgate seems to tell of the light of God shining by reflection in the intelligence of man. In the Hebrew the first part of the verse is a prayer for protection, " Spread over us, O Lord, the light of thy face."

" *I said to the Lord, Thou art my God, because Thou hast no need of my goods* " (Psalm xv. 2). This is not, as it might seem, an equivalent to the saying which Our Lord puts into the mouth of the humble, " We are useless servants " (Luke xvii. 7-10). It means literally, " Thou art my God, and in Thee I find all that is good for me." St Jerome translated it, " *Bene mihi non est sine te.*"

" *O Lord, make me know my end . . . that I may know what is wanting to me* " (Ps. xxxviii. 5). Preachers cite these words as a prayer for light to understand one's moral shortcomings. Its meaning is, " O God, teach me the shortness of life, that I may know that I am but the creature of a day."

" *Man shall come to a deep heart, and God shall be exalted* " (Psalm lxiii. 7, 8). Some Biblical theologians consider the application of these words to the Sacred Heart as nothing short of a material sin of blasphemy. The " deep heart " spoken of is the malicious heart of the sinner. The passage is not clear in the Vulgate ; though even there the context suggests that it refers to the scheming of the sinner and to his punishment by the " arrows of God."

" *God is wonderful in His saints* " (Psalm lxvii. 36). *Sanctis* in the Vulgate is neuter and refers to the sanctuary, or the places where the ark rested before being deposited in its permanent shelter. The passage may be so treated as to be applicable to the saints, but its direct reference is to places and not to people.

" *My soul is continually in my hands* " (Psalm cxviii. 109). For a man to have his soul in his hands is a Hebrew fashion of saying that he is in danger of death (see Job xiii. 14). Ascetical writers found upon this passage many beautiful thoughts on the practice of our being always watchful over our spiritual interests and ready to give an account to God of the state of our souls ; and preachers follow them in this interpretation.

" *Thy eyes did see my imperfect being* " (Psalm cxxxviii. 16). This is not equivalent to " Thy eyes saw my imperfections " : it means, " Thy eyes saw me whilst I was yet in the womb."

" *I have hated them with a perfect hatred* " (*ibid.*, verse 22). " Perfect " is not here a synonym for " innocent," and hence no argument can be framed from these words to justify the ascetical principle that we can blamelessly hate sin in a person, while we love the sinner. It simply means that the Psalmist hates God's enemies with a complete and absolute hatred.[1]

[1] Psalm cxxxviii. is very difficult to interpret in many of its verses. See Fillion, *Les psaumes commentés*, p. 616. This learned book

"*The Lord is sweet to all; and his tender mercies are over all his works*" (Psalm cxliv. 9). The mercy of God extends to all His creatures ; this is the correct interpretation of the verse, and not that which represents the Psalmist as praising the Mercy of God as the chief among all His attributes.

"*The Kingdom of heaven suffers violence, and the violent bear it away*" (Matt. xi. 12). This saying of Our Lord is enigmatical, but the true explanation is not that the Kingdom of heaven is only obtained at the price of violent mortification. Two interpretations are suggested—the first, that Our Lord was pointing to the storming of the citadel of the new Kingdom by sinners and publicans ; and the second, that He was alluding to the persecution begun by the scribes and Pharisees, who were attempting to destroy the new Kingdom of God from the face of the earth.

"*Your reasonable service*" (Romans xii. 1) means, "your spiritual (as distinct from legal and formal) worship of God." Preachers frequently use the expression as if it gave apostolic sanction to the doctrine (which, of course, is true) that reasonable motives of credibility should accompany the exercise of faith.

"*The sensual man perceiveth not these things which are of the Spirit of God*" (1 Cor. ii. 14). "Sensual" does not give the true meaning, nor that best suited to the context, which is concerned not with the impure but with the worldly. The word translated sensual is ψυχικός, the man who uses natural reasoning.

"*No one can say the Lord Jesus, save by the Holy Ghost*" (1 Cor. xii. 3). Grace is required to perform any supernaturally meritorious action. "Without Me," Our Lord says, "you can do nothing." But in our passage the Apostle deals with another subject—the rules for the discernment of spirits. When read together with its context the signification of the words is plain : the surest way to test whether a doctrine is from the Holy Ghost is to examine whether it

is of great service to priests, both for preaching and for interpreting the difficult psalms occurring in the Divine Office. It is published by Letouzey et Ané, Paris.

corresponds with the true Christian doctrine concerning the Person of Jesus Christ (See 1 Ep. of St John iv. 1 and foll.).

The general observation suggested by the list is, that from the doctrinal point of view the preachers' use of them is harmless ; the inexactitude is wholly in the attribution to sacred Scripture of a sense it does not bear.

But has it not been said in this chapter that accommodated senses are admissible ? Certainly, but it should be remembered that care is needful when the authority of Scripture is invoked as *demonstrating* a truth. When there is question of directly establishing or confirming a doctrine by a scriptural argument, a verbal accommodation does not do so as a consequence of the inspiration of Scripture. There is a wide liberty allowable to preachers in the use of Biblical language, but it is not legitimate to give as inspired truth, what is, after all, something other than the authoritative teaching of sacred Scripture.

III

The Homily is the scriptural sermon *par excellence.* In the early Church homiletic preaching was the almost universal form in which the pastor addressed his people, and it was not until the Middle Ages that the subject-sermon disputed the field with the more ancient expository discourse. Nowadays the set sermon, in which a subject is chosen for development, appears to have in great measure superseded the homily, but the custom is still followed in some places of retaining the form of the homily for the morning sermon and preaching a set sermon at the evening service. This arrangement provides a variety in the style of preaching which is usually welcome to the people, and it has the further advantage of preventing scriptural exposition from falling into disuse.

The homily, as its name denotes, is a familiar address of the priest to the people ; it is freer than the set sermon, inasmuch as it is not confined to the unity of a regular plan, nor to the orderly development of one single theme.[1]

---

[1] The use of the word ὁμιλία (intercourse, then instruction) to signify a familiar expository discourse dates from the time of Origen. It contrasts with λόγος (*oratio*), in which there is methodical order and unity of theme.

The matter of the homily, as it is now preached, is the pericope, or portion of sacred Scripture appointed to be read in the Sunday Mass ; sometimes the Epistle is chosen, but more frequently the Gospel. The custom of commenting upon a scriptural book from beginning to end, taking some small portion of it at a time, seems to have become entirely obsolete, though now and then a voice is heard regretting its disuse and arguing for its revival.

Before offering a few suggestions on homiletic preaching, I will invite a glance at the different forms which the homily assumes.

The first of these is to subject the Gospel of the day to a clear division, choosing from it the main topics and treating them in regular order. This method does not differ very greatly from that of a set sermon on the Gospel, for the discourse ranges over a number of points chosen from the Gospel about which are grouped the lessons and applications to which the preacher wishes to draw attention. There is this distinction, however, that the homily deals not with single texts or propositions, but with the whole extract, which serves as a background, and provides the points for the discourse. A greater freedom is thus allowed in the homily, since there need not be that care for logical sequence and for the unity exacted by a set sermon. Examples of this form of homily would be the treatment of the parable of the Pharisee and the publican under two heads : (1) the pride of the Pharisee's prayer, and (2) the humility of the publican's ; or again, the parable of the Sower could provide the preacher with points on (1) the necessity of the Word of God and (2) the reasons why so little fruit comes from its preaching.

A second method is to explain in the first part of the sermon the whole of the Gospel of the day, and then to deduce from it its practical and moral consequences—this is the plan usually followed by St John Chrysostom.

The preacher may adopt a third way of treating the Gospel of the day by explaining the Gospel phrase by phrase, introducing as he goes along, in a familiar commentary, the teaching he desires to draw from each passage. There will be no attempt to give unity to the discourse ; the lessons suggested by each short passage need have no intrinsic relation to one another. This form is usually called the " lesser homily" to distinguish it from the others, which bear a greater likeness to the set discourse.

There is much to be said in favour of the homiletic form of preaching. In the first place it conforms to the command, " Preach the Gospel," and is more immediately attached to the text of the sacred Scriptures than any other kind of sermon. Besides this ; its freedom, its simplicity, renders it more readily adaptable to the spiritual needs of the ordinary folk who form, as a rule, the greater part of a congregation. It is easier to introduce homely but important practical topics into a homily than into a more elaborate kind of sermon ; and moreover, being of its nature less rigidly logical and less subject to literary standards, it makes but little demand on the sustained attention of the people. A distraction may spoil the whole of a set sermon for a listener ; but the wandering mind, when it returns to attend to a homily, can secure something for its profit. In its advantages—and in its disadvantages too—it may be compared to those short pithy paragraphs of news which a humane journalism provides for those whose endurance cannot sustain long and elaborate leading articles.

Looking at the matter from the preacher's side, the homily has the advantage of being more easily prepared than the subject-sermon, since its course is already marked out by the narrative of the Gospel ; the pegs, so to say, are already in place upon which the reflections can be hung. Fate often decrees that the hard-worked priest, whose duties are exacting and whose chances of study are rare, is obliged to preach twice or sometimes three times a Sunday. The homily is a safe refuge for him ; it is easy to compose, easy to remember, and therefore easy to deliver. Nevertheless, it may be well to point out a few of the snares into which the homilist may unwittingly fall ; for even the homily is not so easy to prepare as to render all labour superfluous.

The preacher of the homily has to steer his course wisely between over-ingenuity and platitude—these would seem to be the chief defects to be avoided in this kind of discourse.

K

By over-ingenuity I mean the use of far-fetched and out-of-the-way commentaries on the text of the Gospel. We find many of these in the works even of the greatest among the Fathers, which we may be sure would not be there if these authors had lived in our day. For good or for ill, we have in great measure lost interest in symbolism of the more recondite sort ; and though the spiritual meaning of Scripture still awakens curiosity, it is a much more restrained curiosity than that of the Alexandrians, or that of the Milanese in the days of St Ambrose. The plain blunt man of our day is not voracious for allegory or for subtlety; and the more obscure meanings of things have little power to hold his attention. If we strive for subtlety we run the risk of amusing when we do not bore our hearers.[1]

As for platitude, this is easily achieved if we regard the homily merely as a paraphrase of the text of Scripture instead of an explanation and a commentary. The purpose of the homily is not to inflate a passage but to elucidate it by added material, drawn from the contemplation of its inner sense, or from explanations got from other sources which throw its meaning and implications into relief. Inflation does not add much light to the text ; it may even render a plain passage obscure, as it does in these instances which I extract from a book entitled, *Familiar Explanations of the Gospels*. The passage, " But I tell you the truth, it is expedient for you that I go," is paraphrased, " The thought of my quitting you seems to cause you much uneasiness, but it is inconsistent with reason to indulge any disquietude on this account, for I tell you with truth that it is entirely for your advantage that I withdraw myself from you." Again : " Prepare ye the way of the Lord " is rendered thus : " Remove every impediment that may be likely to obstruct His passage." " Now there was much

[1] For instance, one preacher explained the mystical sense of the parable of the Samaritan in great detail. Before he finished he had compared the Pope to the innkeeper. Another was much exercised why St Peter used the word " tabernacle " instead of some simple word, as " tent " or " house." The explanation he accepted at last was that " St Peter, being an uneducated man, would never have used a short word if he had happened to think of a long one."

grass in the place " was considered too simple and mono-syllabic. It became, therefore, " It happened fortunately that on the spot where the crowd was collected there was a sufficiency of herbage."

Excessive subtilty and commonplace paraphrase are both avoided if the preacher will take pains to meditate upon the Gospel, and consult a good commentary from which to select the considerations which strike him as apposite. Of these the best for his purpose are the scholarly works which have outlived many generations and contributed to the knowledge of each of them. Some, even of the best of them, may be picked up at a very low price from dealers in second-hand books.[1]

Besides a Commentary, it is good to have a Handbook or a Dictionary of the Bible for occasional consultation when questions of Biblical archæology, topography and history present themselves.[2] Lives of Christ like that of Fouard,

---

[1] The chief of these are :

(1) *Cajetan* (Tommaso de Vio Gætani, O.P.) wrote original and (it was then thought) startling Commentaries on many books of the Old and New Testament. He commented the Gospels. *In Evangelia Matthæi, Marci, Lucæ, Joannis* (pub. Venice, 1530); *In Sti Pauli Epistolas* (pub. Paris, 1532).

(2) *Maldonatus* (Juan Maldonado, S.J.), *Commentaria in quatuor Evangelia*, written about 1580. Eng. Trans., Davie. Cornely held this to have been the best Commentary on the Gospels ever written.

(3) *Cornelius a Lapide* (Cornelis van den Steen, S.J.), 1567-1637, wrote Commentaries on all the books of the Canon (with the exception of Job and Psalms). His Commentary on the Epistles and Gospels is of great value. Eng. Trans., Mossman.

(4) *Aug. Calmet, O.S.B., Commentaire littéral sur tous les livres de l'Ancien et du Nouveau Testament* (1707-1716). For a criticism of his work, see "Cath. Encyclopædia," *s.v. Calmet* : Eng. Trans., Oxford, 1726.

(5) *Piconio* (Henri Bernadine de Picquigny, O.S.F.C.), *Triplex Expositio in Sacrosancta Evangelia*, 1726. Also a triple exposition of St Paul's Epistles : Eng. Trans., Pritchard.

For a complete list of Commentaries, see "Cath. Encycl." (*s.v. Commentaries*). It may seem strange to quote these older works instead of the more recent, but modern authors are mainly concerned with matters of Biblical criticism, which are of great interest to Scripturists, but not to the ordinary laymen for whom sermons are composed.

[2] *Hastings* has edited a smaller edition of his well-known *Dictionary of the Bible*, taking as its basis the Index of the larger work in five volumes (T. & T. Clark, Edinburgh). A practical Catholic hand-

and books of Palestinian travel can help the preacher to construct a " composition of place " and render his presentation of the Gospel more concrete and actual.[1]

Perhaps this enumeration seems to open out too long a perspective of New Testament study. If this is so, I may mention one work of wisdom and scholarship planned for the very purpose of helping priests in the preparation of their Sunday Homily: *The Gospels for Sundays and Festivals*, by the Rev. Cornelius Ryan (2 vols., Dublin). There is first an Introduction descriptive of the scene of the Gospel History, which may be referred to when it is needed. For each of the Sunday Gospels the Greek and the Vulgate text are set in parallel columns. Then follows the English translation with parallel passages from the other Gospels. After this there is a combined narrative—the story is told again, with the parallel passages inserted in their place. Then verse by verse the Gospel of the day is set forth and minutely explained by illuminating scriptural, patristic and theological citations, all of them well chosen and definite. A fourth section follows which is entitled " Moral Reflections," sufficiently developed to supply points for two or even three instructions. The work is really an epitomized " Homilist's Library." Every Gospel is made clear in its local and literary setting and in its direct bearings upon the spiritual life. Half an hour's intelligent study will yield abundance of

book to the whole Bible is that of *Seisenberger* (Eng. Trans. from 6th German edition by A. M. Buchanan): its usefulness is increased by bibliographical references to special works.

Fr. Hugh Pope, O.P., has recently completed his *Aids to the Bible* by publishing the second volume (on the New Testament). The publisher is Washbourne, London.

[1] The two chief Catholic lives of Our Lord are those of *Fouard* and *Didon*—the latter is more oratorical but less informing than the former. *Edersheim, Life and Times of Jesus the Messiah*, is useful but naturally calls occasionally for some doctrinal modification.

Books of travel are abundant. The following are of service :—*The Holy Land*, W. H. Dixon, 2 vols. (Chapman & Hall, 1865) ; *The Holy Land*, J. Kelman, 1 vol. (A. & C. Black, 1902) ; *The Holy Land and the Bible*, Dr Cunningham Geikie, 2 vols. (Cassel, 1887); *The Land and the Book*, Dr W. M. Thomson, 3 vols. (Nelson, 1881). The illustrations in *J. J. Tissot's Life of Our Lord Jesus Christ* may help preachers in their descriptions of scenes from the Gospels.

material out of which a preacher may frame a thoroughly instructive and devout homily.

I have remarked that the Gospel and not the Epistle is usually chosen by the homilist. The reason for this is, perhaps, that the Epistles are as a rule more difficult matter for the commentator than the Gospels ; and hence preachers more often prefer to confine themselves to a single text rather than to venture upon a homily. Yet some of the Sunday Epistles lend themselves readily to treatment, especially if the preacher seeks assistance from a good commentary. This labour will be rewarded by the special interest that he will arouse in his people ; for many laymen who have heard an Epistle read year after year have never had it explained to them, while they have heard the Gospel explained many times.[1] This circumstance is worth considering when we are inclined to complain that the Sunday Scripture has been so often expounded that there is nothing fresh to be said upon it.

[1] For this reason a number of priests drew up a set of sermon plans (mostly homiletical) on the Sunday Epistles. They are published by the Kingcone Press, London : *Sermon Plans on the Sunday Epistles*, by the Rev. E. Carroll, edited by the Rev. W. M. Cunningham.

CHAPTER IX

DOGMATIC AND MORAL SERMONS

THE Gospel, as it was preached by Our Lord, was popular—that is, it was adapted to the intelligence of the fishermen and peasants who listened to it. The wisdom Our Lord brought from Heaven, which prophets and kings had desired in vain to hear, came to the world at last in the form of stories and parables, and of simple but earnest exhortations, accessible to the intelligence of the "little ones" who thronged the streets and journeyed out into the desert to hear this Word of Life. The Kingdom of God was preached to them in stories of sowing and reaping, of nets cast into the sea, of children playing in the market-place, of the disgraced agent and the penitent scapegrace, of the unjust judge, and the housewife seeking a lost coin.

Thus the Word was preached to the crowds of Galilee. Yet when the Pharisee Nicodemus desired to probe it more deeply, Our Lord set it before him in another guise, and planted in his soul the seeds of the mysterious doctrine of regeneration. It is of the essence of preaching, as of the Gospel, to be plastic, to be adaptable to every degree of intelligence ; it has milk for babes and meat for the strong. What is essential is that preaching shall instruct and edify, and incline men's hearts to the truth, in the measure that they can be brought to understand it. Neither the feeble nor the wise of the flock are to be forgotten —the preacher must become all things to all, that he may save all.

This practical consideration decides for the priest the measure of theological learning to put in his sermons. There seems to be something too formal and artificial in the distinction sometimes sharply drawn between catechetical and theological preaching. There is theology in all preaching worthy of the name; for what is a catechism but an elementary compendium of theology? A country priest who instructs a rustic congregation thoroughly, must preach theologically; and his sermons will be neither less intelligible nor less interesting if he can turn to account the fund of doctrine he has gathered from his professional studies.

I

When the Fathers of Trent recalled pastors to their duty of plainly instructing their people in the rudiments of Faith and Morals, they inaugurated a reformation for their own age; and at the same time laid the foundations of a solid and permanent policy. Their reform attempted to combat a kind of preaching that discourses about religion without teaching religion. People may assemble in church and listen to devout commonplaces or impassioned exhortations, without any consistent explanation of doctrine being set before them. It is not far-fetched or fantastic to imagine parishioners, even in our own day, listening to two sermons every Sunday without learning their religion; and hearing regularly something about doctrine and morality and spirituality without gaining accurate or profitable notions of any of them. "I have often remarked," wrote Fénelon in his *Dialogues on Eloquence*, "that there is no art or science in the world which its professors do not teach in a correct manner, by principles and with method. It is only religion which is not taught in that way to the faithful. There is given to them in childhood a little dry catechism, which they learn by heart without understanding the sense of it, and afterwards they have no more instruction than vague and detached sermons. I wish that Christians might be taught the first elements of religion, and thus be led in order to the greater mysteries." Here is a distinction. There are two planes of religious teaching, two orders, two methods—the one regards the elements, the other the profounder developments of sacred doctrine. Of these the first is the more important, because it is the basis, the groundwork of religious teaching; it supports, and is presupposed by the other. We cannot, to be just, speak of the primary instruction that children nowadays receive as a "little dry catechism." Without being by any means perfect, the teaching given to children in our schools is usually satisfactory. Still, we are wrong if we imagine that the child who satisfies his religious tests at school is thereby fitted with sufficient instruction to last him a lifetime. In very many instances what he learns does not bite very deeply into his thoughts or affections; as is evident from the ascertained fact that it may be, and sometimes is, so soon and so completely forgotten. An army chaplain wrote recently of his experiences among soldiers : " Hardly two people will agree as to the exact source of the leakage amongst Catholics, but no one can deny that intense ignorance is at least a proximate cause of the trouble. It is only a small consolation to know that non-Catholic ministers agree in saying that our own men are splendidly instructed compared to theirs : the fact that ignorance does exist amongst numbers of our people ought to be faced, and every effort ought to be made to apply an efficient remedy. Whether the evil be due to parental neglect, an inadequate method of teaching catechism, or sheer irreligiousness is a question I leave for others to discuss, but it is one that calls for attention." [1]

The men of whom this military chaplain speaks had probably lost their way to church some years before he made their acquaintance ; but his observation, which will be endorsed by any urban priest, is worth attention ; because it helps to dissipate any illusion as to the sufficiency or the effectual permanence of the religious instruction given to children. There is one obvious remedy; it is that suggested by the deliberations of the Council of Trent and the apostolic efforts made since then to promote the systematic instruction, not of children only, but of adults. The document of Pius X., *Acerbo Nimis,* which will be found in an Appendix, states the case clearly and fully. [2]

[1] *Irish Ecclesiastical Record,* Nov. 1916: "Pastoral Work in War Time," by "Ignotus."

[2] How the provisions are to be carried out among us is not so clear, as English-speaking countries are in a somewhat exceptional position,

Reading its provisions in their broad purport, the *Acerbo Nimis* insists that, for the regular and orderly teaching of adults a programme or scheme is absolutely necessary ; for instruction cannot have the abiding value of education, so long as it is given haphazard. Christian doctrine must be systematized and treated with order and method, failing this, it cannot but be incompletely presented ; some points will get too full and others too cursory a treatment ; important matters will be glossed over or omitted, while others of less moment are emphasized ; there will inevitably be useless repetitions, disorder, and general incoherence.

From the preacher's point of view, a settled programme is a boon. To say nothing of the relief its use gives to one's conscience, the use of a scheme saves a great amount of time. Many a priest spends more time in fixing on a subject than in preparing a sermon about it when he has found it. He takes up first one subject and then another, composes half a sermon, and then resolves to begin a fresh one ; sometimes, even, he finishes a sermon and then casts it aside as useless. All this irresolution and fickleness is swept out of the way where a priest has his subject fixed for him already ; he is brought up alongside a definite task, and has to make the best of it. As for the people, they will get the benefit of a complete and orderly view of their religion, and they will be spared that harping upon a few themes which is one of the banes of unsystematized preaching.

A genuine success in these instructions is not scored without the expenditure of labour. In preaching familiar and rather elementary doctrine the temptation is to treat it in the barest and dreariest way. This of course bores everybody who is thoroughly acquainted with the matter already ; nor does it greatly help even those who are ignorant of it, though it is for the benefit of these that it is chiefly intended. The priest who wishes to impart elementary instruction effectively must seek that art to which allusion is made by St Gregory in words which we often repeat in the Office :

owing to our denominational school system. In some dioceses the regular and systematic instruction of adults is secured by episcopal regulations, and a detailed scheme is drawn up to which priests are required to conform.

the art of " so expounding that the matter may be learnt by those who do not yet know it, without being burdensome to those who know it already." To follow this excellent hint a preacher must bring freshness and novelty into his treatment. People will soon get tired of these long courses of instruction if they discover that they are merely being taken through their catechism again.[1] But if the old subjects are handled newly, illustrated vividly, investigated more deeply, reinforced by uncommon scriptural references, there will be enough novelty to make the topics appear fresh.

II

Seminarists are often exhorted by their professors to get themselves ready to " popularize theology," but unfortunately they are not so often told how this is to be done. As we have already said, a priest " popularizes " theology when he brings his study to bear upon simple points of doctrine ; now, let us give attention to another matter, that of rendering more subtle points of doctrine intelligible, and even fascinating, to lay people. To clear the ground, I may say that there are portions of theology that cannot be popularized in preaching, except by a man with a consummate gift of exposition ; further than this, there are some parts of it that no mortal preacher can render intelligible to a mind untrained in the methods of the schools.

The theology of textbooks, to be made accessible, must be made less subtle ; no metaphysical treatise in divinity can be cut up into sermons and preached as it stands. A good example of the simplification of theology, the metamorphosis of a treatise into a sermon, has been pointed out by a modern

---

[1] Some priests use the Catechism as a basis of their course of instruction. This is not a bad plan, if they avoid the appearance of "re-catechising" the people. But it is surely better to take some account of the seasons of the Church's year, which can scarcely be done if the order of the Catechism is followed strictly. I heard of a priest who took the life of Our Lord as the framework of his instructions ; and fitted into it all that his people needed. It would be a useful work for anyone to undertake, to draw out and publish a well-thought-out plan of subjects and references, chosen in accordance with this excellent idea of connecting doctrinal and moral teaching with the Person of Our Lord.

writer in a work on St Augustine.[1] In his book on the Trinity, the saint has a long explanation of the analogy existing between the distinction of Persons in the Blessed Trinity and the distinctions of the faculties in the soul. In the treatise he draws it out thus : " Whoever is able to understand what is meant by a ' word ' not only before it is uttered in sound, but also before the images connected with it are considered in thought—for there is the word that belongs to no tongue, to wit, of those which are called the tongues of the nations, of which our Latin tongue is one— whoever, I say, is able to understand this is able now to see, through this glass and in this enigma, some likeness of that Word of whom it was said, ' In the beginning was the Word, and the Word was with God and the Word was God.' For of necessity when we speak what is true—that is, speak what we know—there is born from the knowledge itself, which the memory retains, a word which is altogether of the same kind with that knowledge from which it is born. For the thought when it is formed by the thing which we know is the word which we speak in our heart ; which word is neither Greek nor Latin nor of any other tongue."

The treatise *De Trinitate*, from which this passage is taken, was of course intended for theological readers who were assumed to possess enough subtlety of mind to unravel its meaning. Now the saint had occasion to speak of the same analogy popularly in a sermon (Sermon 52). Let us note the difference. First he warns his hearers that his illustration is but an analogy. "No one is to say, ' See what he is comparing to God ! ' I told you before and I tell you again, I warned you, and I warned you carefully. The things are widely distant, as low things from the highest, as mutable from immutable, as created from Creator, as human from Divine. . . ." He goes on : " So now I ask you, my friend, have you a memory ? If you have not, how can you remember what I have said ? But perhaps you have forgotten what I said a moment ago ? Well, then, this very word that I am now saying ' *dixi* '—you could not retain

[1] Montgomery, *St Augustine : Aspects of his Life and Thought*, chap. vii.

its two syllables unless you had a memory. For how would you know that there *were* two syllables unless you remembered the first while the second was being said. That need not delay us longer. It is clear that you have a memory.

"So I ask you a second question, Have you an intelligence? 'I have,' you say. If you had no memory, you would not remember what I had said; if you had not an intelligence, you would not recognize that you remembered it. So you have this too. . . . I ask you a third question. Do you *wish* to remember and understand? 'Certainly, I do,' you say. You have then also a *will*.

"These are the three things which I promised to tell you of. In you there are all these three things which you can count, but you cannot separate," and so on.

We must not leave this instructive example without noticing what has happened to the passage in the treatise on its becoming a part of a sermon. The idea of the analogy has been retained in substance, but the difficult points have been suppressed—they would have been too hard to follow. The style, too, has become personal and vivid. Starting from this one typical instance we may generalize to a method. Omission of abstruse matter, simplification of language, and the brightening of the manner of presentation—these are what is chiefly wanted, if one desires to transfer theology from the textbook to the pulpit.

There is another thing to be done also, not so much by way of change as by way of addition. Scholastic theology is usually unemotional; it reduces religion, as far as it is capable of being thus transposed, to terms of abstract thought. Now, religion as it is in a man, religion as we wish to preach it, is not shut up in intellectual categories; it seeks contact with all human faculties. Scholastic theologians constantly warn their readers of the danger of the imagination getting into the way of the intelligence and upsetting the speculative judgment. This is very well for theologians, but it is not so well for ordinary people, in whom the imagination and the feelings hold a dominant place.

Theology, then, as used in preaching, must be directed towards devotion; it should seize the affections as well as give understanding to the intelligence. Let me illustrate this. Thousands of sermons on the Sacred Heart have proceeded on this plan : the Heart of Christ is a part of the Sacred Humanity. Now as the Sacred Humanity is united hypostatically with the second Person of the Blessed Trinity, it is adorable ; and since the whole is adorable, so too are all the constituent parts. Therefore the Heart of Christ is adorable. As theology, this is, if not very profound, at least correct, but if a whole sermon is all taken up with it (as it has often been, in my experience) what spiritual benefit can the people possibly get from it ? They do not require the truth of the adorableness of the Sacred Heart to be proved to them by this theological algebra. What they do want is the same truth commended to them in terms of the imagination and the affections. We have only to open our Breviary to find this ready to our hand.

> Amor coegit Te tuus
> Mortale Corpus sumere,
> Ut novus Adam redderes
> Quod vetus ille abstulerat.
> Non Corde discedat tuo
> Vis illa Amoris inclyti :
> Hoc fonte gentes hauriant
> Remissionis gratiam.

Passing now to a final point : a young priest may sometimes wonder where he can best find theological stiffening for his sermons on dogma. He wants them to be substantial, to have a good basis of thought in them. He will seldom be disappointed if he takes up the index of the *Summa Theologica* and looks up the point he purposes to explain. He may not find exactly what he is looking for in the first or the second reference, but he is almost sure to light upon it before he has come to the end of them. Some think that the Summa is a very stiff book of theology, but taken on the whole it is not so ; it is certainly much easier and infinitely more interesting than most modern commentaries upon it. It is not all-sufficient, for when it has been consulted one has usually nothing more than a very solid framework. Still, after all, the framework is the main thing. To fill in the outline is not hard, when the outline is definite. Expansion of the central thoughts supplied by the Summa is obtained by developing the ideas and illustrations in the passage of the Summa itself, or by seeking it from sacred Scripture or other devotional sources. The superstition that the Summa is too subtle and abstract to be of much use for parochial preaching has perhaps frightened off many priests from having recourse to it ; as a fact, if they had gone to it they might have preached better sermons with much less trouble. Moreover, their sermons would have introduced their people to subjects in which they delight, and of which they seldom hear a word—such as the human operations of the soul of Christ, His prayer, His priesthood. The sermons of the priest who knows how to use his Summa and his Bible will not move in a narrow, cramped circle, nor stagnate into conventional commonplaces ; they will be rich in thoughts upon the abiding verities, and open up for his people generous fountains of living water.[1]

III

Thanks to the definite doctrinal and moral tradition living and acting in the Church, the work of a Catholic moralist— and the priest with the care of souls is the moralist of his parish—is much more easy than it could possibly be if this general agreement were absent, or if each priest had to count upon his sheer personal influence to establish his claims as the guide of his people. As it is, the priest knows that his people are at one with him in all essential beliefs, and that they admit his authority to expound the Christian law, to teach and to rebuke, as the representative of the Church and of God.

Individuals there may be among them ready to criticize and find fault, but the strictures of these do not, except in very rare instances, even touch upon essential matters.

[1] This division has been devoted to Dogmatic preaching. It is well to mention, at least in a note, that the *Prima Secundæ* and the *Secunda Secundæ partis* are excellent sources for Moral Sermons also. The teaching on the Virtues and Vices is wonderfully suggestive and shrewd.

A layman may recognize that his pastor is not exempt from limitations arising from want of knowledge, experience or tact, he may criticize, sourly or good-humouredly, a preacher's manner, temperament and so on, but such trifles are but superficial, and do not affect the well-recognized relation of teacher and taught subsisting between them. So true is this, that the faithful account it a somewhat feeble eccentricity in a priest if he harps upon his right to teach and their obligation to take his words seriously. Authoritative airs and graces, contentiously worded proclamations of the priestly dignity inherent in his person, would be received in a mood of bewilderment or amusement, should a preacher think fit to fall back upon such means of enhancing the influence of his teaching. This radical sympathy between priest and people, which we are inclined almost to ignore because it is so normal, is really of incalculable use to us, and it has often attracted the wistful attention and envy of others not so fortunately placed. How would a barrister not welcome a jury, or a political candidate a meeting of his constituents, so open to persuasion as is a Catholic congregation listening to its parish priest !

In this division of the chapter we are concerned with the priest in his character of moralist. The guidance of souls in the confessional is often spoken of as the " Art of all Arts," and the description is almost equally fitting to the office of publicly directing the collective conscience of a people from the pulpit. The difference between these functions lies mainly in this, that while the confessor directs individual souls, the preacher guides them assembled together. This difference renders the task of the preacher of moral sermons somewhat more complex than that of the direction of individual consciences, for the preacher, though he addresses a group, must manage to reach the conscience living in separate persons. He has to bring himself into contact not only with general but with particular needs. Hence, obviously, his teaching must be definite. General exhortations and general denunciations are of little avail ; it is not the universal and the vague, but the particular and the concrete that tells.

The field of moral teaching is wide, but it has to be viewed
by the people piece by piece, as well as under its general
aspects, and neither principles nor details must be neglected.
At the source, Christian morality is intimately connected
with Christian dogma.   In the issue, morality is dogma in
action.   There is no absolute division between dogma and
morality ; without dogmatic truth as its support moral
science is little more than a catalogue of ethical sayings ;
just as dogma, viewed apart from conduct, is a collection
of speculative propositions. Faith and life, truth and
right action, knowledge and morality, have in the Christian idea a mutual interdependence.   Further, not only
has Christian morality this indissoluble connection with
revealed truth, it keeps a fast hold also on natural
ethics.   How close this connection is can be judged
by the circumstance that the moral teaching of St
Thomas Aquinas embodies a not inconsiderable part of
Aristotle's ethical doctrine.   The task of the moralist,
then, is to educate his people in Christianity as a practical
scheme of life, based upon definite beliefs, the implications
of which embrace the whole range of human motives and
conduct.

Moral instruction, then, presents an extensive programme.   It is much more than the enumeration of
virtues and vices or even scraps of advice regarding
morality ; it is the education of the Christian in the
form of life of which the example and the teacher is Christ
Himself.   All that goes to make the doctrine of devout
living understood in its trials, its temporal and eternal
rewards, its daily sacrifices and duties, all that shows
what are the conditions of its growth, and the reasons
of its failures, is matter for moral teaching.   To render
the Christian ideal authoritative, and at the same time
attractive, to reinforce it by natural and supernatural
reflections, is the essence of moral instruction and
exhortation.

If this branch of our duty is left undone, where is there
hope for the preservation of an energetic religious life in our
Catholic people ?   The conscience is a God-given faculty,

but is not, for all that, perfect in its judgments or free from obscurities. What inner light it has flickers and fails unless it is well tended. Public opinion contributes its current notions on morality, its proverbs and tags exhorting to natural honesty and virtue, but little else besides. Then, too, there is the constant pressure of the lower appetites within, always tending to obscure even the natural judgments of conscience. In this struggle for moral existence and well-being, a definite and well-ordered education of the conscience is no luxury but an indispensable necessity. There is, moreover, little to reassure us in the signs that usher in the future ; on the other hand, unless we close our ears to warnings from many quarters, and our eyes to the facts of experience, the opposition between the standards of the world and those of the Church shows less chance than ever of a reconciliation. It is mainly upon clear, forcible, enlightened exposition of Christian morality that groups of Catholics —who form in some places a very small fraction of the population—will have to depend. If it is denied them, many will inevitably be swept away by the storm.

Let us turn now to our equipment.

Moral Theology holds, together with Dogmatic Theology, the chief place among the subjects taught in seminaries. It is, as every one knows, primarily directed to the preparation of a priest for his duties in the confessional ; but, secondarily, it is of the highest utility to him in his preaching. Not only has he been guided to survey in detail the laws of Christian conduct, but in that process he has, if he has fully profited by his course, gained an insight into the principles of moral action. The very number of the cases of conscience he has studied, and the solutions he has heard delivered, have the effect of gradually forming in him an instinct or a faculty expert in judging the moral aspects of human conduct. Casuistry is for many an ill-sounding word, but the casuistic habit is, if rightly employed, an indispensable instrument for moral teaching. Preaching that breaks loose from the principles of moral theology is certain to be unsatisfactory, because it will be obscure, meagre and indefinite. The background of moral preaching is then provided by the discipline gained in the study of moral theology.

Moral theology, however, is not the sole source of moral preaching. The view of life imposed by the study of it is too scientific and artificial to be in all senses satisfactory and complete. It neither represents the completeness of the Christian law nor the full range of possibilities in Christian conduct. It has the defects of its qualities ; being constructed for the confessional, it bears some analogy to a penal code, and in much the same way as the criminal enactments of a country give but a partial account of the standards of its citizenship, so moral theology falls short of supplying a full scheme of the duties and obligations arising from the perfect law of charity that is the code of God's Kingdom upon earth. It does not even profess to expound " the whole Counsel of God." As our preaching of Dogma is not restricted to matters strictly defined, so moral instruction goes beyond the *minima* of obligation with which casuistry chiefly deals. Moreover, because moral theology has the particular " case " and the individual man in view, there are parts of it which are un- suitable for public instruction. To take instances. It would be unwise to parade the opinion that wife-beating in moderation is sometimes excusable, or that " occult com- pensation " is allowable under certain conditions, or to enter into details of theological opinion on the question of " mental reservation." These are matters of casuistry to be taken into account in issuing a verdict when one is dealing with a special case of conscience, but inexpedient as matter for general moral instruction.

Especially is caution and delicacy needed when sins against the sixth commandment are in question. If prudence is exacted of confessors, even in instances where penitents are neither ignorant nor innocent, it must be still more rigorously practised where young and old, guiltless and guilty are present. It is better here to err on the side of reticence than to be carried away by undiscriminating zeal. In- struction on these matters should be given guardedly and seldom. Teaching which bears only indirectly upon this sub ject will usually suffice—such, for instance, as that conveyed by the preaching of mortification, self-restraint, avoidance of evil company. These can be so treated as to serve for warning where it is needed, without awakening curiosity or causing disedification where it is superfluous. To sum up in a word, Moral Theology is an instrument of moral teaching to be used only when it serves a good turn.

A complement, and in a manner a corrective, to what is provided by Moral Theology is the science of the spiritual life with its divisions into Ascetical and Mystical Theology. With this we group what may be called the Art of the spiritual life expressed with copious variety in the lives of the saints. It cannot be held that this is not the kind of teaching suitable to ordinary lay folk, for, as a matter of fact, it is this which is most needed. Every Christian requires counsel on prayer and distractions in prayer, on the meaning of suffering and trials, on despondency, on fervour and tepidity, on the difference between temptation and consent to evil thoughts. A little light thrown on such points even by a truism has often lifted a weight lying upon a conscience for years. Preachers sometimes imagine that plain explanation of simple matters such as these is not called for; they think everybody understands them already. Experience fully proves that exact knowledge on these points is not by any means universal, and one can well understand the trouble caused to devout people when it is wanting. I am not here advising preachers to expound to their parishioners the spiritual teaching of St John of the Cross, but I think they might do worse than give a few instructions every year on the principles met with in books like *The Spiritual Combat* or *The Devout Life*.

IV

The effectiveness of moral sermons is in a great measure dependent upon the preacher's power of observation and his knowledge of the human heart. Book-learning cannot give us either the one or the other, but books can help us to cultivate and increase our power of profiting by experience.

Besides the remote preparation afforded by his general education, a young priest needs special help to teach him how to apply experience to the improvement of his preaching. He is gaining and storing up knowledge of the world by his contact with his parishioners and others, by his pastoral visits, by his instruction of converts, by his duties in the confessional ; but this is not of itself always sufficient to render his preaching practical. He probably feels that it would help him greatly to find a good model of effective moral preaching. If he has the good fortune to be living with other priests capable of serving as such a model, he can learn a great deal from listening to them ; but this good luck does not fall to all young priests. Sometimes they have no opportunity of hearing sermons from others, sometimes the sermons they actually hear give them little help.

The resource left to him is to read sermons—not ordinary ones but exceptionally able ones ; to fix upon some preacher who is above all a practical moralist, and read enough of his work to acquire some tincture of his skill. A priest who is looking about for help of this kind must of course take care whom he selects as his example ; for if he makes the wrong choice, his preaching will rather suffer than benefit by his industry. One hardly knows which would be worse—to try to find one's way to passable preaching unassisted, or to study laboriously a model not worth imitating.

There is difference of opinion, of course, as to the merits of well-known preachers, past or present, but I think that most of those who have read his sermons will agree that Bourdaloue is one of the greatest Catholic moralists of all time.[1] Some critics place him on the same level with St John Chrysostom, others rank him even higher. Let critics decide such matters. From the Catholic Encyclopædia one learns that Bourdaloue is not much read nowadays, and if this is so, it is regrettable. Possibly some priests are kept away from his sermons because they have heard of him as a

---

[1] Louis Bourdaloue, born at Bourges, 1632, entered the Society of Jesus at the age of fifteen. Made his vows in 1666, and afterwards preached at Rouen, Orleans and elsewhere. Called to Paris, 1669, where he preached in the churches and before the court of Louis XIV. Died 1704.

court preacher, and judge from this that he would be of little use to them. The truth is, that though he preached often before the court, he was above everything a popular preacher. At Rouen " artisans left their workshops and merchants their country houses and doctors their patients " to listen to his sermons. " The whole town was turned upside down," writes a preacher who followed him next Lent ; " as for me," he adds, " when I preached the following year I restored everything to order. No one left his business."

It is not hard for a reader of his sermons to discover the reason of his hold upon the people. He possessed in an eminent degree the qualities that make a moralist. He was clear in his doctrine and plain in his language, and his sermons are invariably constructed on a transparently logical plan. But chiefly, the source of his power was the extraordinary talent he received from nature, and perfected with infinite industry, of reading the hearts of men. Consciences lay open before him ; he read them through and through, and what he saw there he was able to show to others. " Attend, I will make you see," is a phrase constantly recurring in his sermons ; and he does make us see. Of emotion or pathos he has very little—he relied entirely upon the depth of his penetration, the exactness of his portraiture and the inflexible logic of his deductions. Reading him, one cannot but be reminded of a physician who diagnoses his patient's malady with marvellous accuracy, understands completely the course the disease will take if unchecked, yet never admits it to be incurable. The remedy is at hand, and if the patient will rouse himself and take it, he will infallibly recover. Every type of moral sickness appears in his amazing sermons—greed, impurity, self-deception, ambition. He depicts their victims with pitiless truth, adding line to line, until the portrait stands out complete. Yet he is no satirist ; he does not mock, nor exhibit airs of superiority or aloofness. Over against these cruelly true descriptions you are shown the austere majesty of the Divine Law. Nor is he a rhetorician, ranting and denouncing. To Bourdaloue we may go for an education in the method of making moral sermons live.

Does this mean that preachers should become, in Boileau's phrase, "the apes of Bourdaloue"? Not at all. His sermons are three times too long for a modern audience, and he has, moreover, a failing I have already hinted at— he appeals scarcely at all to the affective emotions. An anonymous Jansenist, who heard Bourdaloue preach a Lenten course in 1679, criticized him in an open letter.[1] He represented to the preacher that the sermons would be all the more effective if they were shortened to one division only, instead of running into two or three, and if an appeal to the emotions were added, with a suggestion of appropriate resolutions, after the manner of St Francis of Sales. Though Bourdaloue himself did not take the hint, it may be found useful to priests who have the wisdom to seek assistance from him in their preparation of moral sermons.

[1] Quoted in Griselle, *Bourdaloue, Histoire critique de sa prédication*, T. i. p. 468.

CHAPTER X

THEOLOGY and the faith which it enshrines rest upon a substructure of historical truth. Their province is revelation, the unmerited communication of God to man ; hence, the fact of revelation being rejected, Christian beliefs and the theological system which binds them organically together collapse for want of foundations.

There exist schools of thought outside the Church intent upon preserving Christian ideals while refusing credence to the historical basis upon which tradition has consistently held them to be reared ; but the view of such schools is utterly alien from Catholic theology and sentiment. A Catholic regards it as certain that the facts upon which his religion is based really occurred, and, moreover, that these facts transcend the natural order. So far as this principle is concerned, there is no distinction between the faith of the learned and that of the unlearned : the scholar may be in a position to give a reasoned and scientific account of the relations between supernatural doctrine and its rational and historical basis, while the unlettered man can not ; still, the belief even of the unlearned leans upon a conviction that God powerfully and graciously interfered with the course of history to reveal His will more plainly than He has done in the processes of nature or in the interior dictates of the human conscience. This will sound very truistic to every priest, since the method of our theological education presupposes the principle, and during our studies it is re-affirmed at every step ; I mention it here only to introduce what appears to be a matter calling for very earnest thought.

The countries in which we live are no longer saturated with Protestant dogmatism. The number of people interested in the theory of Justification by faith alone and the other beliefs dear to primitive Protestants is very small ; relatively small also is that school of Anglicanism which has adopted many opinions almost identical with the traditional faith of Catholics. The centres of interest for the populations of these countries are no longer what are called denominational controversies ; the place of these is usurped by more radical questions, such as those of the existence of a future life, the validity of any claim to authority in religion, the Divinity of Christ. Hence the need for the preaching of Christian apologetics. Priests must look to the underpinning as well as to the embellishment of the edifice of faith.

Years ago Mgr. Dupanloup, alive to the religious situation in France, held that in every large town there should be a pulpit devoted especially to apologetic preaching, and this not only for the enlightenment of men alienated from the Church, but for the instruction of Catholics in the groundwork of belief. It may be objected that the situation of France is very different from that obtaining in England. This may be so, yet, I think, it is not so different as is sometimes imagined. One notices the quickened vigilance of progressive Catholic Societies in England, such, for instance, as the Catholic Truth Society, for the provision of apologetic literature : one hears read at Catholic conferences, papers by men of practical experience proclaiming the necessity of "fortifying the layman " in the intellectual reasons underlying his faith. The opinion is gaining ground that teachers in our primary and secondary schools should go through a course of apologetic instruction as a necessary part of their training. Unless all this is the startled cry of alarmists, plainly something needs to be done, not only by the press and by pamphlets, but by the pulpit.

Conservative priests will say perhaps that the Catholic laymen whom they know are in no need of "fortification " ; that there is danger to be apprehended in broaching questions which may raise doubts or uneasiness in the minds of the simple and devout ; that their experience has not shown them any sign of trouble from this quarter ; that pontifical pronouncements in recent years have insisted on simple instruction rather than on courses of apologetic. Conservatism is usually plausible; yet if one listens to less optimistic witnesses, our people are not passing through the fire without some singeing. Some years ago Father Martindale, proofs in hand, showed that the danger to souls was greater in some places at least than many of us imagined, and urged immediate action for meeting it. "Clearly," he wrote, "in view of an attack, especially in so well-organized a one as this, no one can be content to sit, like Vergil's shepherd, with folded hands, singing hymns. But worse than all inactivity (because their conscience pricks the inactive) is the resolution which expresses itself in the phrase that "something must be done," as if it were a case of drains and the proper person was waiting outside with all his tools, and just had to be sent for. If we think that the remedy exists, is to be easily obtained, is recognized as desirable, we assume easily that some one is sure to seek it, and meanwhile no one does anything and we all catch typhoid." [1]

Even the most conservative among us will admit that, dangerous influences being of the strength they are, there may be some reason for fear at no very distant future. They cannot reasonably object to what our French neighbours call "the vaccination of souls," preventive measures in view of the possible attacks of disease. That I may not be accused of merely contenting myself with the narcotic formula "that we must be up and doing," I purpose to trace in this chapter what would seem to be the lines along which this prophylactic plan may proceed with a fair chance of success.

I

At the outset it must be clear that formal apologetic should not come to be regarded in the light of a substitute for dogmatic and moral instruction. There is implicit apologetic in every good sermon, whatever its subject may be, and in some localities normal preaching supplies all the defence of the faith that is needed. Apologetic sermons

[1] *The Month*, Oct. and Nov. 1910, p. 471.

are to be looked upon as exceptional efforts to counteract or to ward off certain dangers, if they are either present or reasonably to be expected. If the reader will turn to the Appendix and read the Letter on Sacred Preaching issued at the command of Pope Leo XIII., he can easily assign the place of the apologetic conference in our homiletic scheme. There he will see that the intention of the Pope was to restrict their use and to prevent them from occupying too prominent a position in preaching. Their purpose is to defend the outworks of Christian doctrine ; that aim being achieved, there still remains in its entirety the pastoral duty of explaining the truths of religion and morality. Condensed to the utmost brevity, the Pope's views were these : (1) Conferences (as distinct from dogmatic and moral sermons) are occasionally necessary ; (2) they demand a more than ordinary measure of knowledge and study in the preacher ; (3) they should be popular, and suited to the special audience before which they are delivered ; (4) they should not turn on abstract and abstruse topics nor take on a pompous and high-flown style ; (5) they should be so composed as to avoid the danger of distressing the more simple folk who listen to them. These being the general canons and cautions for this kind of preaching, let us pass to their application.

The kind of apologetical discourse I have in my mind as suitable to our time is not directly controversial ; the sermons are best thrown into the form of positive exposition. Whatever refutation of anti-Christian opinion they contain is implicit ; they shun the atmosphere of wrangling and disputation, and aim at constructiveness, being in this respect more closely analogous to dogmatic than to polemical sermons. Demonstration, not denunciation, is their keynote. As to their content, what is chiefly required in them is solidity of information. Old arguments, old views of history or science or philosophy are to be maintained in them only on the condition that they are still respected by the well-informed.

The preacher is not required to give to his exposition all the rigidity of scientific handling, but in the preparation of his material he needs to be alive to the demands of sound modern criticism. The subjects he chooses should not be antiquated or academic, but closely adapted to his own place and time ; he is not concerned with the past except inasmuch as it has its place in the heritage of the present ; for since no arguments he uses can possibly reach dead unbelievers, there is nothing to be gained by disinterring and flagellating the corpses of heresiarchs and doubters long since dead and forgotten. Similarly, as there are adversaries whose opinions are as dead as themselves, so also some of the weapons formerly employed against them have become useless or rusty. Many of them, let us hasten to say, are rusty rather than useless. Even modern fashions of defence which at first sight seem new can be dimly traced far back into the past.

And now let us take stock of the equipment we have brought to this task from college. We came from the seminary with a considerable yet undoubtedly incomplete knowledge of Apologetics. Some of our fund came to us from the professor of Dogmatic Theology, and some of it from the professor of Apologetics. The latter introduced us to one good manual at least, which is now in our bookshelves. Let us take it down. It is in Latin, it is scientifically arranged, it is, after the fashion of textbooks, complete. It is severe in style and in arrangement, there is little light and shade in it, and no emotion, unless that quality may appear in an occasional citation from some actual orthodox or unbelieving champion. We read through the table of contents and then the people think of whom we are to instruct. How much we find in our manual unsuitable to most of these men and women whom we are to address !

Here are metaphysical chapters on the possibility of revelation, and of miracles ; and long proofs, establishing the dates of the four Gospels. How few among our people would be capable of following these close demonstrations with attention, not to speak of interest. These chapters might be of use if we were preparing a lecture for an audience familiar with the problems already, but the audience with which we have to deal is not to be of that kind, but merely the congregation assembling Sunday by Sunday, at evening services, with the addition, it may be, of a few people attracted by their curiosity or their interest in these special subjects. These abstruse portions of our textbook, then, we had better leave alone.

Let us now turn back to the portions of the manual which do seem susceptible of popular treatment. The body of apologetic doctrine as set forth in the book is divided up into theses, and scholia, and corollaries, and objections followed by their solutions. Obviously this is not the method " understanded of the people." Still, we feel that it contains information and argument likely to be of use. When we have mastered all that the manual contains on the point we intend to treat, we are in possession of a nucleus of fact and demonstration ready to grow into an organically connected train of ideas. Have we now sufficient material for an apologetic conference ? The answer is Yes or No, according to the circumstances. If we light up this textbook information with a little originality and imagination we undoubtedly have sufficient material out of which to make a useful and sound sermon. Yet no one would hold that preparation of this kind, gathered from a few pages in a manual, can do more than supply us with a passable sermon. If the occasion calls for something better than the ordinary, a discourse on a special occasion, for instance, or an adver-tised course of sermons, we shall set about preparing for it in a different way—a way that I will describe in the next section.

II

There is an incomparably better and sounder way of preaching apologetics than the one just indicated, and one most needed in our day, when thoughtful Catholics of every class are becoming acquainted by reading and conversation with the conclusions of historical and philosophical science. To be of real help to them, and to keep their knowledge of the foundations of the faith at the same level as their general culture, a penetrating apologetic must be at hand to explain or supplement what they read in neutral or biased authors. It may be said that keenly intelligent Catholics are not dependent upon sermons, they can have recourse to Catholic books. This is so, but it must not be forgotten that Catholic books are not always accessible, and that at present the production of apologetic literature of this standing is slow.[1] We have been late in beginning, and have much leeway to make up. Catholic apologetic literature needs to be supported, and, where it has not been able to keep pace with the demand, to be supplemented, by the spoken word.

It may be objected, again, that this more learned kind of apologetic calls for the expert rather than the average man. I answer, by a distinction ; for original research, Yes ; for popularizing work, No. It calls for study, and even special study, but not for that grinding concentration that makes the specialist. The popularizer has the shoulder of the expert to stand upon.

Again the conservative interposes, " Apologetic sermons of this kind are useful only in large towns, in centres where there is intense curiosity among large groups of reading men, but the clergy in large towns are just those who have little time to give to study." Is this true ? I can only answer for my own experience, but it happens that the most intellectually active priests I have known were in town parishes. But, granting the objection to the full, it ought to be possible for some less occupied priests to devote themselves to a matter of this kind. The country clergy of studious tastes might give their activities a practical and unselfish turn by issuing forth occasionally from their rural paradises and placing the benefit of their studies at the disposal of their brethren

---

[1] At present we depend mainly upon works written on the Continent. The C.T.S. has done good work in late years to supply the need of a native Apologetic by publishing such books as the series on the History of Religions : Sir Bertram Windle's *Church and Science*, the cheap edition of Devas's *The Key of the World's Progress*, etc. *The Westminster Lectures* (or at least the less technical of them) set a good standard for apologetic preaching. Then Mr E. I. Watkin's *Thoughts on Apologetics* (published by The Catholic Library) is a book full of hints upon certain new lines of thought along which Apologetic can be profitably developed. Father Walshe's latest addition to the Westminster series, *The Principles of Christian Apologetics*, will be found very useful.

in towns. We have already specialism in preaching—retreat-giving and conducting missions, for instance ; what is there to forbid a similar specialized assistance in the preaching of popular apologetics ?

Whatever system is decided upon, it is to be hoped that the " vaccinators of souls " will begin in real earnest before the hospitals are seen to be manifestly overcrowded.

It is time now to say something more definite about this deeper Apologetic. Its special character and its special usefulness is in this : that it carefully and thoroughly investigates the stock apologetic proofs of religion, polishes the arguments, and states them with exactness and precision, even modifying them where necessary, in order to bring them into line with the actual positions of contemporary knowledge and ways of thinking.

The old rational proofs of religion are not superannuated, but they need retouching and rejuvenating. By the old proofs I mean those contained in the older manuals, and copied with slight modifications into the newer ones, *e.g.* the arguments from miracles, from prophecy, from the rapid diffusion of Christianity, from the constancy of the martyrs, from the social and moral benefits proceeding from the Catholic Church. All these, and others like them, are susceptible of profound treatment, and have more significance than a superficial examination of them reveals. They lead to problems which can only be solved by some study and some subtilty. We will experiment upon one of them as a specimen.

The Vatican Council cites as an argument in favour of Christianity " its marvellous diffusion throughout the world." The Church has progressed and conquered a whole civilization in spite of every kind of obstacle set in its way—the reluctance of man to submit his intelligence to authority, and his passions to rule, the persecutions of open force and the betrayals of domestic enemies, the poverty of the means available for its astounding enterprises. Have we not here a sign of the supernatural assistance of God and the divinity of the Christian religion ? No : say the naturalistic historians. Christianity prospered—they allege—from causes incidental to the historical conditions under which it made its appeal, and its victory was brought about by the natural processes of history. The fifteenth chapter of Gibbon's *Decline and Fall of the Roman Empire* pleads this view, and assigns five causes, all of them natural, for the early expansion of Christianity in the Græco-Roman world. Now these five causes are not wholly the false dream of a bitter controversialist such as Gibbon was. They did actually operate, and it is for the apologist to show that their working does not exclude the special and providential action of God. To get to the bottom of the matter, and to define our position exactly, requires some study of psychology, history, and philosophy. The situation has to be reconsidered in a concrete setting, it becomes a definite problem for the philosophy of history. Newman has so treated it, and in masterly fashion, in the *Grammar of Assent*. I am not dealing with apologetics as such, but with popular methods of apologetic, so I must not go out of my province into the details of the argument. But I will cite Newman's introduction as a specimen of an apologist's way of getting to the heart of the subject instead of wrangling over it or escaping from it through some trapdoor of rhetoric.

"As is well known, various writers have attempted to assign human causes in explanation of the phenomenon : Gibbon has especially mentioned five, viz., the zeal of Christians inherited from the Jews, their doctrine of a future state, their claim to miraculous power, their virtues and their ecclesiastical organization. Let us briefly consider them.

"He thinks these five causes, when combined, will fairly account for the event ; but he has no thought of accounting for their combination. If they are ever so available for his purpose, still that availableness arises out of their coincidence, and out of what does that coincidence arise ? Until this is explained, nothing is explained, and the question had better have been left alone. These presumed causes are quite distinct from each other, and, I say, the wonder is, what made them come together ? How came a multitude of Gentiles to be influenced with Jewish zeal ? How came zealots to submit to a strict ecclesiastical régime ? What connection has a secular régime with the immortality of the soul ? Why should immortality, a philosophical doctrine, lead to belief in miracles, which is a superstition of the vulgar ? What tendency had miracles and magic to make men austerely virtuous ? Lastly, what power was there in a code of virtue, as calm as that of Antoninus, to generate a zeal as fierce as that of Maccabæus ? Wonderful events before now have apparently been nothing but coincidence, certainly ; but they do not become less wonderful by cataloguing their constituent causes, unless we also show how these causes came to be constituent." [1]

This subject of the Expansion of Christianity has in more recent times been taken up by Harnack, and our apologist, in fitting himself for his discourse, would read as a preliminary task Harnack's work, *The Mission and Expansion of Christianity in the First Three Centuries*.[2] He would also study the work of the Abbé J. Rivière, who goes over the same ground and rectifies some of the German professor's statements and conclusions.[3] It must be obvious that a man who had studied the point thus, would be in a position to treat the question with greater actuality and thoroughness than one who had been content with the meagre information supplied by a manual, nor would his discourse be less comprehensible to ordinary people by reason of the deeper insight he had gained.

III

The central demonstration of traditional apologetic is that which establishes the divinity of the Christian religion by proving the divinity of its Author. The evidence of Divinity, radiating from the human history of Christ, supports both the confidence of simple faith and the intellectualism of ordered theology ; and the principal aim of apologetic is to render this evidence intelligible and convincing, especially

[1] *Grammar of Assent*, pp. 457 and 458.
[2] Eng. Trans. by Moffat (London and New York, 1908).
[3] *The Expansion of Christianity*, Eng. Trans. (Herder, 1915).

to those who, whether deliberately or in their own despite, are driven by doubt or urged by curiosity to examine the foundations upon which individual or collective faith is raised. Reasons do not directly produce faith, but they remove obstacles from its path ; they confirm and embolden the assent to supernatural truth. It is no matter either for blame or for surprise that believers should manifest interest in Christian evidences. We have elsewhere noted that the Gospel was ushered into the world in company with an apologetic, and as the Gospel is embodied in a Person, that apologetic has always moved round the question of His Divinity. But the changes of time bring about changes of outlook, and according to this law Christian evidences will naturally accommodate themselves to altered modes of thought. New arguments will be searched for to meet new questionings, and old ones will be adapted to fresh fashions of approaching problems which are at once old and new. Here I am not dealing with the science of apologetics, but with its art and practice. The special point I wish to make now regards the most effective way of presenting a portion of apologetic demonstration to non-theological minds. How is it best accomplished, this task of presenting the traditional proofs of Our Lord's Divinity to lay audiences, in a way that avoids arid and unintelligible and complicated discussion on the one side and a meagre and diluted treatment of the question on the other ? I can do no more here than outline what appears to be a feasible scheme, and if the following pages appear to err by excessive condensation, a consultation of the sources and passages given in the notes will considerably fill up the outline and clothe the bare skeleton of the text with flesh. My purpose is to indicate a line of treatment, not the points of a sermon or even of a course of sermons.

One observes that the ordinary method of setting forth the arguments for Our Lord's Divinity is to gather together passages from the Gospels, in which Our Lord claims to be divine, and then to show how He made good His claim by prophecy and miracle. This is on the whole a good, and probably the best plan, but it is susceptible of modifications which cannot but add to its definiteness and therefore its effectiveness. To mention at present only one point, in which improvement can obviously be made, a distinction is not always drawn between the evidence of the Synoptic Gospels and that of St John. Seeing the difference there is between the outlook and method of these two classes of sources, the testimony ought not to be confounded, as though they were on the same plane.

What, first of all, is to be the point of departure? Some would make a beginning with the Mosaic revelation and the authority of the Old Testament. Now this appears to approach the subject from too long a range. Others set out from a demonstration of the authority of the New Testament. That is open to the objection that it introduces questions of date and authorship and similar critical matters not very interesting to lay people. The habit of beginning at this point probably survives from the time when the ideas of Strauss and others of that school held the field, and when it was consequently thought necessary to establish the Gospels as sources of contemporary witness to the events they related. Nowadays the positions of criticism are changed, and we may assume, even with the assent of most liberal critics, that the Gospels in their substance were written at a date quite close to that of the history they recount. As to inspiration, that scarcely enters into the question. For our purpose it is sufficient to accept the documents we employ as invested with the authority of contemporary evidence and not as being, besides, divinely inspired.

There remains, then, as a point of departure, the historical surroundings and the Palestinian atmosphere in which the life of Our Lord was lived. The primitive setting of the Gospel was that of Palestinian Judaism, and the manner in which Our Lord's claim was stated was accommodated to the outlook of the men in whose hearing He spoke. For this the Synoptic Gospels are the main sources. It is true that before the New Testament was completed the Gospel had been poured into another mould, yet it is useful to commence with the primitive stage first, and then proceed to treat the later period represented in the later New Testament literature.

The primitive phase of the Gospel is seen to be saturated

with Messianism.[1]   Religion, literature and politics were deeply impressed with national expectations and chimeras. This ancient hope of Israel permeates the Synoptic Gospels. The recent loss of political independence intensified the desires, bequeathed by the prophets and fantastically embellished by apocalyptic visionaries, of a great national King and Prophet who should bring peace and, happiness to God's people and set up the eternal rule of property and justice.[2] The preaching of St John the Baptist announced the imminence of the Messianic appearance and reign.   Our Lord was the Messias promised, and He must break the news to people whose ideas of what He was to be were confused and unspiritual.   His claims, then, must be set forth cautiously and discreetly, and under such modes as to forestall and exclude untrue and misleading interpretations.   His hearers must be so educated as to accept their Messias as a spiritual Lord and teacher, and a Kingdom that is not of this world. Not until late in His ministry did He accept the title.[3]   But from the beginning He suggested His Messiahship in a veiled and implicit fashion.   He compared His vocation and works to those which the prophets had attributed to the Messias.[4] His purpose was slowly to unseal the eyes of those about Him to His dignity and spiritual function.   After His reading in the synagogue of Nazareth of a Messianic passage of Isaias, the evangelist relates that "the eyes of all the synagogue were fixed upon Him," and in the same chapter His claims are seen to rouse indignation in some and wonder in all.[5]

The title under which He was known was obscurely Messianic: "The son of Man." [6] On an occasion which forms a turning-point in the history of His self-manifestation He accepts from St Peter another and more dignified title, that of "The Christ the Son of the Living God," as a

---

[1] See, for example, Matt. xii. 23, xvii. 10 ; Luke ii. 38, iii. 15. See also Acts iii. 18, v. 42, viii. 37, ix. 22, xvii. 3, xviii. 5.

[2] See Hastings, *Dictionary of the Bible*: "Messiah"; and Tixeront, *History of Dogma*, chap. i., para. 2.

[3] On two occasions : Matt. xvi. 16, 17, and Mark xiv. 61, 62.

[4] *E.g.* Matt. xi. 3-5; Luke vii. 19-23.   *Cf.* Isa. xxxv. 5, 6.

[5] Luke iv. 16-42.

[6] Found over seventy times in the Synoptics.   *Cf.* Daniel vii. 13, 14.

testimony coming not from " flesh and blood," but from an inspiration of the Father.[1]

The claims He makes in other passages throw a vivid light upon the way in which these titles were understood by Himself. He was Master of the Sabbath, greater than Jonas, wiser than Solomon, higher in authority than the Baptist or Elias or Jeremias.[2] He exacted a complete surrender of his disciples' will to Himself as well as to the Father.[3] He would be with His disciples to the end whenever two or three should meet in His name, and to the end also His doctrine would stand firm.[4] Finally He was the Judge, before whom the good and the evil must render an account of their works [5] after heaven and earth had passed away. Read in this light, the Synoptic Gospels reveal a gradually worked out scheme of education the purpose of which was to stimulate curiosity and allow the traits of the Messianic character to be divined by His apostles and disciples.

The fourth Gospel is at once a work of history and theology, in which the human career of Our Lord and the meditation of the beloved apostle unite and mutually compenetrate. From early times the difference between its outlook and that of the Synoptists was noted. " John," wrote Clement of Alexandria, " the last of all, seeing that the bodily facts had been reported by the other evangelists, at the instance of other disciples and by the inspiration of the Spirit composed the Spiritual Gospel." [6] St John completes the Memoirs of the synoptic writers by viewing the facts and sayings of Christ with the eye of a divine.[7] Hence the discourses of Our Lord have to be understood as being grouped and synthesized according to the Apostle's didactic purpose. The intrinsic relations between Christ and the Father are emphasized and

---

[1] Matt. xvi. 16 and collateral texts. For a discussion of this title see Lepin, *Jésus Messie et Fils de Dieu*, pp. 145 and foll. (1st edition) ; also a very pertinent treatment of the text in Batiffol [E. T.], *Primitive Catholicism*, Excursus A.

[2] Matt. xii. 8 ; xiii. 16-17 ; xvi. 13-17.

[3] Matt. xi. 25-30 ; xix. 29 ; xxiii. 9-11.   [5] Matt. vii. 21-23 ; xxv. 31-46.

[4] Matt. xix. 28 ; xxiv. 35.

[6] Euseb., *H. E.*, vi. 14, 7.

[7] See Barry, *The Tradition of Scripture*, pp. 169, 170, 264, 265.

brought into relief. He works with the Father.[1] He raises men from death as does the Father.[2] To know Him is to know the Father.[3] He knows the secrets of the Father, and even as a Shepherd He knows His flock.[4]

He pre-existed with the Father before He took up His human existence. His office of manifesting the Godhead is described at length to His disciples, when His last hour is approaching, in a discourse which abridges the testimony He renders to His claims (St John, chapters xiii.-xvii.). These chapters form a comment on the whole purpose of the Gospel as set forth in its prologue ; and that purpose was to declare the Word made Flesh.

Such are the principal teachings of Our Lord on His own Person and authority. Miracles and prophecy are the proofs, and they are so closely integrated with the very organism of the Gospel that their violent amputation would bring it to its death.

In popular apologetic it is not required to enter upon highly metaphysical discussions on miracles, for the plain man's philosophy is not of the kind which disallows God to work freely in His own universe, nor is he so foolish as to deny miracles and then to rhapsodize about the symbolic significance of supernatural events which never happened. I may dispense myself from enumerating and classifying the miracles of Our Lord, for that is done in every manual. It is a good thing for apologists to give detailed treatment to the great miracle of the Resurrection, with the view of showing the place it held in the primitive preaching of the Gospel from the beginning.[5] Especially, also, is it useful to show how the apostles insist on the fact of the Resurrection not only as a conclusion of Apologetic, but as a premise for further spiritual teaching.[6]

Our Lord prophesied future events—His rejection, sufferings, death and resurrection.[7] He foresaw the harvest of

---

[1] John v. 17.   [2] John v. 21.
[3] John viii. 12-19.   [4] John x. 14, 15.
[5] See, *e.g.*, Acts i. 22, iv. 33, xvii. 18.
[6] St Peter i. 3, iii. 21 ; Acts ii. 33, iv. 10-12, v. 31 ; 1 Cor. xv. 12 and foll. ; Romans viii. 11 ; 2 Cor. v. 1-5, etc.
[7] Mark viii. 31-34, ix. 11, 30, x. 32-34, xii. 1-12, etc.

souls to be reaped in future ages by the Church in Gentile
fields.[1] His words prepared the apostles for the trials He
saw in store for them on their mission.[2] It would not seem
advisable in such apologetic conferences as I have been
sketching to enter upon the thorny problems of the eschato-
logical prophecies, where even practised Scripturists are
puzzled by the complexity of the questions which they
involve. If the circumstances should demand this treatment,
an apologist may turn for guidance to the article, " Jesus
Christ," contributed by Fr. de Grandmaison to the French
Dictionnaire d'Apologétique. The whole article will be found
of immense use as a source of excellent ideas for the
apologetic presentment of Christian evidences. It is
thoroughly modern and at the same time in the best sense
traditional, and is not likely to be surpassed or superseded
for many years to come.

IV

In a Constitution of the Vatican Council (*De Fide catholica,
cap. III.*), we read :' 'To the Catholic Church alone belong
those signs, so numerous and so marvellous, which have been
designed by God to manifest the credibility of the Christian
Faith. More than this, if one considers its wonderful expansion, its eminent holiness, and its inexhaustible fecundity
in benefits of every kind, the Church itself, in its unity
embracing all ages and places, in its unchanging stability, is
a great and perpetual motive of credibility, and a victorious
witness to its divine mission. It follows that the Church,
like a standard lifted up in the midst of nations, calls to its
breast those who do not yet believe, and renders its own
children still more confident that the faith they profess
rests upon an assured foundation."

Here is a summary of many themes, deserving of development at the hands of Catholic apologists. These questions
have filled volumes of apologetic, and one of the needs of our
time is to bring into the open the demonstrations hidden

---

[1] Matt. viii. 10-12, xiii. 31-33, 38, xxi. 43 ; John iv. 20-24.
[2] Matt. x. 16-18, xxiv. 9.

in learned volumes of scholarship, and to pass them on in popular guise to our own people and to others. They are frequently treated in sermons, but, it must be confessed, rather rhetorically than with precision. Has not the time come when those of our number who have a bent for historical study might with advantage apply themselves seriously to these important and attractive questions? It is not in my province to do more than suggest methods of handling the various matters treated in preaching, and in this instance I must be content to refer priests to a book with which many will be already familiar, the author of which seems to have happily hit upon the right way of treating the proofs referred to in the Constitution just cited. The book I mean is the *Key of the World's Progress*, by C. S. Devas. Vividly written, cautious, erudite, candid, it is worthy to become a sort of guide and model for the popular apologist. Perhaps its balanced moderation may try the patience of those whose taste is for wide and vague generalities and who attribute much virtue to sonorous phrases, but it will prove a sure help to all who are alive to the need of getting beneath the surface of these problems. However aptly these subjects seem to lend themselves to rhetoric, they belong to the province and claim the exactitude of historical treatment. But we know that history, even ecclesiastical history, is a picture in which light and shadow are set over against each other. It is as childish to shut one's eyes to the light because there is shadow, as it is to deny the shadows because there is so much light. There would be far less talk among our adversaries of our " pretensions " if we developed with care and exactness the witness of history to the supreme part the Church has played in embodying in its visible, tangible reality truths and principles which must have faded and perished unless they had been absorbed into a living society.

Besides this historical method of apologetic, there is another, proceeding from psychological data, and drawing its arguments from the attentive study of our human faculties, needs and instincts. Its principles, and its exact place in the scheme of Catholic apologetic, would carry me into longer explanations than would be desirable. I must be content to leave it with a bare mention, and the general observation that it can be made to serve, even in popular apologetics, as an auxiliary to the more objective method to which this chapter has been confined.[1]

[1] See in the Catholic Encyclopedia the last part of the article *Immanence* and the attached bibliography.

CHAPTER XI

SOME OTHER TYPES OF SERMON

A YOUNG priest may find himself at a loss, when a sermon is required from him of a different type from the customary forms. This chapter, with its rather miscellaneous contents, is written for his guidance, and contains hints upon preaching sermons of a type different from the ordinary. A section is devoted to each of the following : (1) Five-minute sermons at Low Mass ; (2) Controversial sermons ; (3) Panegyrics of the Saints ; (4) Funeral sermons ; (5) Charity sermons ; (6) Sermons for Children.

The same general rules and cautions apply to the preparation of these as of others ; but as there is something special about them, I have indicated what logicians call the " difference " which distinguishes them from other types and demands some corresponding modification in their structure or treatment.

Five-Minute Sermons

A large number of Catholics, attending Mass regularly every Sunday, go from the beginning of the year to the end without hearing a single sermon. The Epistle and Gospel are read at Low Masses, preceded usually by a lengthy list of announcements, but not one word of personal instruction is added by the priest. In many places there is good reason for this, for the congregations attending the early masses usually contain a fair proportion of busy people, who can afford to give but a very small portion of their Sunday morning to public worship. These come, sometimes at no small sacrifice of their convenience, to the Low Mass. Servants, housewives, invalids, have each different but quite adequate reasons for choosing the shorter services. There are others

185

who come from less satisfactory motives—the people who do not like singing, or sermons, or long ceremonies. It was a good thought to introduce for the benefit of Low Mass congregations the custom of preaching very short sermons of five or six minutes in length. The first to put the idea into practice was Father Algernon Brown, an English convert who had joined the Paulist congregation in America, and who inaugurated the custom about forty years ago in the Paulist Church in New York. Other parishes followed the example, and the practice is now fairly common.

The restriction of time, which is an essential feature in these discourses, entails a special type of composition. There is no time for an elaborate introduction ; the preacher must plunge into the heart of his subject without delaying over preliminary explanations, or leading up to his points. Economy of words and condensation of thought must be his aim throughout; there is no room for elaborate developments or long drawn-out illustrations. Above all, the point to be treated should be very definitely conceived, and the strictest unity should exist in the scheme of the discourse. That perfection which makes small objects, such as miniatures and gems so precious, comes to them from the special delicacy of artistic detail : and so it is with the short sermon. It is almost sure to fail unless it is well thought out beforehand ; and a preacher who believes that because the time assigned to him is short, he can trust himself to chance inspirations, will in all probability produce nothing better than a confused medley of detached sentences, thrown to the congregation at a chance and without effect.

Sensible people do not expect from a five-minutes exposition what they look for in more ample and leisurely efforts ; they well know that the subject must be circumscribed to accord with the time permitted for its treatment. What such reasonable folk expect, we ought to manage to provide. If we choose a wide subject the sermon will resemble a table of contents or a jerky *précis* of a longer discourse. The tendency must be rigorously suppressed " to delight in the spacious liberty of generalities as in a champaign region and not in the enclosures of particularity." One single

principle treated without haste but with a fitting thoroughness, one text commented upon in such a way as to bring
out its meaning plainly, one religious practice explained,
will take up the allotted time. The little sermon must
be definite without being bare, concise without being
cramped, and it must make swiftly and unerringly towards
its mark.

These discourses are much to the taste of the people, and,
if conscientiously prepared, strike deeper and more surely
than any other kind. The substance of the sermon need
give but little trouble to the preacher. A point taken from
a longer discourse will provide all its material. Nevertheless,
there must be nothing fragmentary, nothing which might
give the impression that the sermon is a mere scrap. The
pattern on its fabric must be complete, otherwise it will
appear to be made of mere shreds and clippings from some
larger piece.

These suggestions apply equally to other forms of the
short sermon—the " few words " introductory to ceremonies
such as blessings, processions, and so on, the sermonettes
customary at May Devotions and other services of that kind.
There should be nothing random, nothing straggling about
them, each should be an orderly, well-constructed sermon,
with a beginning, middle and end.

Controversy

During the Advent of 1835 and the Lent of the following
year, Dr Wiseman drew large congregations to the Sardinian
Chapel and the Church at Moorfields to listen to his discourses
upon the points of dogma and practice in which Catholics
and Protestants disagree. The experiments were remarkably
successful, and worked a great change in English estimates
of Catholicism. The preacher, in a letter written to a friend
in December of 1835, optimistically related his own impressions. " I have two lectures every week. The effect
has been a thousand times beyond my expectations. The
chapel is crowded to suffocation, every seat is occupied half
an hour before the Compline, and if it were three times as

large, it would be full. I have never preached less than an hour and a half, generally an hour and three quarters, yet no one has found it long, nor has attention once flagged. Last week I treated of Church Authority, and this of the Real Presence ; next week the Supremacy and Indulgences, etc. The common people say they can follow every word, and that ' I make them quite sensible ' ; the priests come in shoals, and they and all the congregation tell me that the whole system and the form of treatment throughout is quite new to them all. Indeed they wish that I should stay till Lent and give a fuller course, but this is out of the question. Nay, *entre nous*—for I write to you as a friend—they say I ought not to go back at all. But I am thus *vainly* full with you, because it will convince you of what I have often said, that the method I have followed in school was as applicable to a congregation if simplified and reduced to a popular form, and in this I always thought that I could succeed. Every one agrees that a most successful experiment has been made and that proof has been given of the interest which may be thrown round the Catholic doctrines by a little exertion." [1]

The novelty of which this letter speaks was the lecturer's departure from the style of controversy to which they had been accustomed, and of which we have a classical specimen in Milner's *End of Religious Controversy*. Wiseman's method was to approach men of unsympathetic and sometimes contemptuous minds by the gate which gave the readiest access. Instead of imposing the claims of the Church as an obligatory teaching which they were bound to accept, or of directly attacking the views to which they were attached, he strove to convince them that the doctrines of the Church were very different from what their prejudice imagined them to be ; and that deep in their own minds and hearts there were principles and affinities cognate to, and in fact logically leading towards, Catholicism. He told them, for instance, that they already received the religion they professed from authority, and not, as they themselves imagined, from the

[1] Ward, *The Life and Times of Cardinal Wiseman*, vol. i. pp. 233, 234.

dictates of their own private judgment ; from this he went on to justify the Church's claims to their attention as responding in the most perfect degree to aspirations in them, of which they were but vaguely conscious.

This way of approaching disputed questions is familiar to us now, but it was a novelty then, and less than a quarter of a century before Wiseman's experiment Bishop Milner had strongly condemned the well-known London preacher, Dr James Archer, on the ground that " he soothed rather than roused the apprehensions of his non-Catholic hearers " by his disdain of controversy.[1]

It seems certain that Dr Wiseman's method is the one most suitable to our day, as it was to his own. One is often told that the world is tired of controversy, and the saying is true, if by controversy is meant a direct attack upon the religious convictions of others. Controversy is, after all, strategic and opportunist, and it is obviously poor strategy to direct an attack upon positions most strongly fortified and most obstinately defended. Wiseman's tactics, here and in his more important controversies of a later period, were designed to allay the irritation set up by direct polemic ; and to win his adversary rather than to confound him. It was a change of plan, not of substance. The content of his controversy is not unlike that of the older school, but he presented it more agreeably.

His success was due to the fact that his method was true to psychology. All of us love our own opinion, and resent direct attacks upon our convictions. The heretic is no exception ; not because he is a heretic but simply because, being human, his instinct is to set himself stiffly against a violent assault upon his beliefs, even if they should be founded on nothing more solid than prejudice. He does not like being written down an ass. Wiseman in his letter mentions that his policy is that of the theological schools, which we know—if we know anything— is that of distinguishing frequently and denying seldom, according to the cautious principle of St Thomas that error

[1] See Gillow, *Biographical Dictionary of English Catholics*, s.v. Archer.

lives only because it is mixed with some truth.[1] In the truth common to the Church and the sects is the starting-point of discussion, for all rational disputation must proceed from some agreement.

To pass now from the manner to the substance of controversy. The arguments to be sought for and developed clearly are such as have the best chance of being seized by the audience. It may be that the controversialist will have to sacrifice what he considers his best reasons. He should be prepared to do so, if they are above the reach of his hearers or too complicated to be treated adequately. But, even if those he retains are to his mind not the best that can be adduced, they must at all costs be valid. Sham reasons and fallacious logic are no auxiliaries to truth, and an argument faulty at its roots is worse than none. There are some reasons, St Thomas has ironically remarked, so feeble that they appear to give probability to the opposite side. In controversy the statement of the objection and its refutation ought to be straightforward and unsophistical. It was a common saying of a good lawyer that there is no first-class advocacy without a good measure of frankness, and this is as true in the pulpit as in the law courts.

The form in which the proofs are displayed must receive good attention. St Francis of Sales, the most apostolic and successful of disputants, advises preachers to give their reasoning *le lustre de la spéciosité*—a graceful dress and appearance. Clear synthetic arrangement aids the intelligence, and vivacity of manner and diction keeps interest from flagging—a matter of much moment where the drift of an argument is lost altogether unless all its stages are closely followed.

Finally, the more courteous we are towards opponents the better effect our words will produce. " Insulting and injurious epithets," writes Suarez, " ought to be avoided as evil in themselves and unfitting in a Christian man engaged in a serious affair. And, besides, they may prevent any

---

[1] Sicut illud in quo est falsitas vel malitia est aliquod ens sed non est ens completum, ita etiam illud quod est malum vel falsum est aliquod bonum vel verum incompletum. In Sent. xix. 5, 1.

fruit coming from the discussion." [1] It might seem unnecessary to mention this; but I recently saw it stated in a Catholic newspaper that the question of controversial courtesy is unimportant, since disputants must expect to receive hard knocks and be ready to give back what they get. Even if this were true in newspaper controversy, it would be false in that of the pulpit. Newspaper correspondents sometimes allow themselves to treat their opponents as ignorant little boys, or, following the older fashion, as unpardonable scoundrels and shufflers. But the utterances made in a church should not be lacking in the restraint due to the sacred place; and moreover, the spoken word, if it is unguardedly violent, wounds more deeply than the written word. Granted, it is difficult to keep due measure when our contest is with an awkward or disingenuous adversary. In these circumstances, trying as they are, it is better to bring the discussion as quickly as may be into a calm and impersonal region, and to pass from the adversary to his reasoning. The priest whose words are most sure to carry conviction, or at least to disarm prejudice, is he who shows no signs of a mania for disputation, but who is ready, at the call of duty, to come forward as a defender of the faith, without forgetting the reverence due to the sacred place in which he stands. Some of our people who dearly love a fight may feel disappointed at the rather unexciting performance, but the wiser ones will be gratified to find vigour of thought and cogency of reasoning allied to a perfect regard for the peaceable courtesies of civilized life.

Panegyrics in Honour of the Saints

The first stage in the preparation of the panegyric of a saint is a study of the facts of his life, for what distinguishes this class of discourse from others is the predominance of the historical element. A sermon cannot rightly be said to centre round a saint unless it goes to his life for its inspiration. A devout anecdote or two, a general but impersonal eulogy of sanctity, a number of reflections which have no very obvious connection with one saint more than another do not

[1] Suarez, *De Fide*, xx.

give enough of the biographical turn to a sermon, the essence and interest of which ought to lie in the description of a human being. There can be no history without a good framework of facts. It is advisable, then, to begin by reading the best biography of the saint that we can lay our hands on ; a work of the first order does not take longer to read than a second-rate one, and the impression it leaves is more distinct. I may say that by the *best* biography I do not necessarily mean the most devotional one, or the one with most frequent apostrophes and notes of exclamation ; but rather the most exact and the most graphic. It would be away from my subject to wander into the question as to what qualities in religious biography are best suited to our time; it would be superfluous also, for the matter was threshed out well some decades ago, on the appearance of the Oratorian Lives of the saints.[1]

Two points, however, may be touched upon. The first regards the prominence given to the miraculous and extraordinary incidents recounted in the lives of saints. We are agreed that God is able to set, and often has set the seal of miracle upon the life and work of those who have given themselves to Him, withholding nothing for themselves. This truth, isolated from all controlling criticism, has determined the fashion in which many saints' lives have been written. Miracles seem to some hagiographers as natural to saints as strange coincidences are to ordinary people. In our time and country it is better to be cautious, and to require some proof of the marvels of which biographers are often too prodigal. We may be sure that a saint's life, viewed correctly, will be edifying. Moreover, as the career of a saint is set forth as a model of the practicability of the Gospel, it will lose nothing, but will rather gain, if it is presented in its most imitable light. This is not to be understood as a warning to gloss over the supernatural ; but rather as a counsel to exercise a " sanctified common sense " in determining the proportion of marvellous and natural incidents in hagiography.

[1] See Ward, *The Sequel to Catholic Emancipation*, ii. pp. 244 and foll., and the references provided there.

The other point turns upon the mention or the omission of faults that may be discerned in the saints. To emphasize them regardless of proportion would be irreverent and disedifying; it would be intolerable in speaking even of commonplace people, living or dead. Yet no scandal can be given to sensible Christians when they hear that the saints, like themselves, were subject to the trials, and even the frailties, inseparable from the discipline of their earthly pilgrimage. What lessons of encouragement would have been lost had the Evangelists, out of fear of giving disedification, suppressed the lapses of St Peter or the doubts of St Thomas![1]

The life having yielded material, it remains to shape it into a discourse. Obviously, our sermon must not resemble an arid index, it must be a portrait; and as a painter cannot show both the smile and the frown of his sitter in one picture, we must pass over many possible aspects and

---

[1] Tillemont treats this matter very judiciously: "Comme cet ouvrage est destiné à rechercher la verité de l'histoire, on sera obligé d'y remarquer quelquefois des fautes dans les plus grands Saints. C'est une nécessité dont on eût voulu pouvoir être dispensé : mais si on ne peut pas cacher ce qui paroît dans les monumens publics, au moins on tâchera d'en parler avec le plus de modestie qu'il se pourra, et avec le respect que l'on doit à ceux qui seront un jour nos juges ; en prenant pour modèle la manière si sage dont S. Augustin parle de l'erreur de S. Cyprien sur le batême. Après tout, il faut que les fautes mêmes des Saints nous puissent être utiles, puisque Dieu qui dispose tout pour l'avantage de ses élus, a permis qu'elles arrivassent, et qu'elles vinssent jusques à nous. Elles nous peuvent en effet servir à ne nous pas décourager dans nos foiblesses, à ne pas trouver étrange que les plus gens de bien ayent aussi quelques défauts, à ne pas mépriser le bien que Dieu a mis en eux, à cause des restes de l'infirmité humaine qu'il n'a pas encore guéris. S'il ne paroissoit aucune foiblesse dans les saints, on pourroit croire qu'ils étoient d'une nature différente de la nôtre. Mais en voyant qu'ils étoient foibles comme nous, nous avons lieu d'espérer de la grace toute-puissante de Jésus-Christ, que nos foiblesses ne nous empêcheront pas de participer à la force qu'ils en ont receuë pour devenir Saints. Enfin on voit dans les bonnes actions des Saints ce que nous avons receu par le sang et par la mort de nôtre Sauveur ; et on voit dans leurs défauts combien nous sommes éloignez de la perfection qu'il nous donnera quand nous lui serons unis dans le ciel ; comme on voit dans les méchans dont on est souvent obligé de parler, ce que nous serions sans la grace" (*Mémoires pour servir à l'Histoire Ecclésiastique des six premiers siècles*, T. i., *Avertissement*).

N

choose the one under which we intend to represent our hero. Usually this is not difficult ; for the dominating purpose of a saint's life is often some simply-grasped principle revealing itself constantly, insistently throughout his career. In St Francis of Sales it is a zealous mildness, in St Francis of Assisi a devotion to evangelical simplicity, in St Francis Xavier a consuming zeal for the conversion of infidels, in St Francis Borgia contempt for worldly honour. If, as happens in some saints, the dominant motive is more complex, some little skill is needed to give unity to the discourse ; still, with the history of the saint before us, there ought to be no great difficulty even there. Each preacher will naturally arrange his facts and lessons according to his own conceptions ; and it would be senseless of me to dogmatize as to the most suitable way of doing this, when there are so many ways equally suitable. Instead, I will add a few warnings which have been suggested by sermons I have heard or read.

1. Be cautious of superlatives. It is profitless to set about proving that your saint was absolutely the greatest among Confessors or Bishops or Martyrs.

2. Avoid profuse moralising. Recount the actions of the saint in such a way that they yield their own lesson.

3. Do not analyse the saint into a bundle of abstract virtues and preach a complete little sermon on each one of them.

4. Keep before you the human facets of the saintly career. A description of the appearance of the saint, or of his circle, or (especially if he had a large influence on public affairs) a neat historical background, help to make your picture life-like. For this reason note in any biography you may read, any personal touches of description, for sometimes they tell more about a saint than pages of incident. For example, how much we seem to know of St Bede from the letter of his disciple Cuthbert, relating his death. His whole life and spirit seem to be abridged for us in those few pages.

5. As language should attempt to rise to the level of its subject, a graphic and eloquent style is fitting to a public tribute to this triumph of Christ in the persons of His saints.

Funeral Sermons

There are many resemblances between a Funeral Discourse and the Panegyric of a saint. Each is a solemn tribute rendered to the virtues of the dead; each relies for its effect upon the personal element prominent in the discourse; elevation of style and language is demanded in each. But there are manifest differences. The saint in the glory of heaven is the object of religious devotion, the Christian over whom a funeral discourse is pronounced is assumed to be undergoing the discipline of penal purification. The saint is commended as an intercessor; the soul appearing before the judgment seat of Christ is in need of earthly intercession. In the funeral sermon, moreover, thought is taken for the relatives and friends afflicted by the sorrow of loss and separation. The spirit of a Christian farewell to the dead is expressed by St Paul, " Now we would not have you ignorant, brethren, touching them that sleep, that you grieve not, even as the rest who have no hope. For as we believe that Jesus died and rose again, God will likewise bring with Jesus those who have fallen asleep through Him." [1]

The discourse is a plea for prayers, and a solace to the sorrows of the survivors, who need to be consoled in their loss by the promises held out by Christian hope. As for its spirit, we shall naturally go to the funeral liturgy—in which the sermon is a sort of interpolation—as a reliable guide. All recognize that the Requiem and the Funeral Service of the Church is a masterpiece of devotion and of spiritual tact, so there will be nothing of bad taste in a funeral sermon so long as a preacher keeps close to the spirit of the liturgy. [2] The chief difficulty in this form of sermon arises from the circumstance that the preacher is expected to offer something in the way of personal appreciation; and it is for this reason that a friend of the dead man is chosen to deliver

[1] 1 Thess. iv. 13, 14.
[2] The *spirit* of the liturgy is a guide; but the doctrine of a sermon may of course go beyond the doctrine expressed in the funeral service. The liturgy is a prayer for salvation, and purgatory is not explicitly mentioned in the Mass for the Dead or the Funeral Service.

it. His estimate of the dead person is not expected to exhibit punctilious and well-weighed calculation such as that required of a reviewer or a biographer; it is rather the interpretation of a life as seen through the eyes of a friend. There is no extravagance in generous eulogy, nor does a preacher offend when he emphasizes those good qualities on which his admiration and affection have dwelt during the days of their intimate converse. The only praise to be deprecated is that which is insincere and unreal. It may be that both the preacher and his hearers are aware of blemishes which marred the perfection of the one who has passed away; but Christian charity demands, and common humanity endorses, a generous appreciation of virtues which may have co-existed side by side with blemishes and shortcomings. Hardness and coldness, then, must be avoided equally with the extravagance and insincerity of flattery. No mechanical rule is discoverable for guiding a discourse between these two extremes; nothing avails but an instinctive sense of proportion and sobriety of judgment.

One other point may be usefully mentioned. The congregation at a funeral is usually of an exceptional kind, the proportion of non-Catholics being notably larger than at other times. Respect for the dead brings to our churches many who are not often seen there; they come to testify their friendship for the dead man and their sympathy towards his relatives. Among them are those who have been associated with him in social and civic life—his professional acquaintances, for example, or colleagues in commercial or municipal enterprises. It is sometimes remarked that, probably out of deference to the presence of such people, the preacher dwells rather lengthily on the character and doings of the dead man in their civic and worldly aspect. There is at times something of snobbishness—or, if that word is too uncomplimentary, something of secularity—in the preacher's appreciations; and the spirit of Samuel Smiles dominates the discourse rather than the spirit of the Catholic liturgy. Trivial successes and titles (sometimes incredibly unimportant) are made much of, and catalogues of achievements and dignities are rehearsed. There may be some among the audience to whom such lists are interesting, but most men must think them as inappropriate as an untimely parody. Would not even those who judge titles and honours at too high a rate be equally impressed—to say the least—if reflections of the preacher were more definitely spiritual? In the ordinary course of their lives they may have lamentably few opportunities of being brought face to face with serious views on life and death, and is it not something worse than time wasted to confirm in them unspiritual ways of thinking, by magnifying achievements to which their worldliness is prone to attach an excessive value?

Charity Sermons

Preaching the Gospel and talking about money are two uses of the faculty of speech that are not easily united with propriety.[1] Disinterestedness is one of the signs of the genuine apostolic spirit—the shepherd has it, the hireling has it not. Still, money has to be spoken of sometimes: the most apostolic man has to pay his bills when they become due, churches and schools have to be built and kept in repair, heavy burdens of debt have very often to be lifted from parishes—not infrequently by rectors who have had nothing to do with contracting them. Talking about money is fatally easy to some men, and a " business " sermon needs scarcely any preparation. But when begging and dunning take a disproportionate place in pastoral addresses, the efficacy of preaching is diminished and nullified.

This is a delicate subject even to mention, for the clergy as a whole is acknowledged to be generous and self-sacrificing. Still, it would be foolish to deny that some priests disedify their people by the energy and determination which they devote to their financial problems. A passage in Archbishop Ullathorne's *Ecclesiastical Discourses* sums up the case: " The good shepherd spending his life for his flock, the flock from duty, gratitude and devotion supporting the life that is expended for them, presents one of the most beautiful combinations in the whole divine structure of the Church.

[1] Under this heading I include all sermons dealing with money matters.

Each party has a work and a sacrifice for the other, and
whatever is cherished by sacrifices is dear to them who make
the sacrifice.   In these obligations of mutual service, Our
Lord proves the bonds of higher confidence and closer love.
But for this whole reason there can be nothing more injurious
to the filial devotion of the people towards their spiritual
father, than for him to be constantly reproving them and
driving at them, in ways that reveal a hankering after their
money.   It makes the Church and the priesthood odious
in their eyes.   It displays an utter want of spirit, sense and
spiritual tact.   Such a one will ask me—Then how am I
to live ?   What am I to do ?   Our Lord will tell you, ' Give
and it shall be given to you.'   If you are really generous
to your people's spiritual wants they will be generous to your
temporal wants.   Wise, prudent and laborious priests will
all tell you this.   It works as Our Lord intended it should
work, with the regularity of a law of nature, that if the
pastor gives himself heart and soul to the spiritual interests
of his people, without distinction of person or class, they
will never see him want.   Nay, if he sets himself to provide
needful charities, his resources will grow in proportion.   But
if his people see him more zealous for money than for souls,
they will close their hearts to his most passionate pleadings." [1]

I may here remind a young priest that his wisest course
is to speak as little about money from the pulpit as possible.
Being an assistant priest, he has no financial responsibility,
and words which would be, I will not say welcomed, but
tolerated, from an older man, would be bitterly resented
coming from him.   He need not delude himself, moreover,
that the scoldings which older priests sometimes allow to
themselves as a precious perquisite are greatly enjoyed by
the parishioners.   The people endure them, first with repugnance and afterwards with indifference or amusement.
Excited language often repeated begins to sound histrionic,
and as a performance the dunning is accounted either as dull
or as diverting—never as pathetic or tragic.   The people
compare their persistent pastor with other priests of their
acquaintance who manage to create the spirit of generosity

[1] Ullathorne, *Ecclesiastical Discourses*, xi.

in their parish without noise and without loss of dignity. How do these other priests achieve this ? Chiefly, it would seem, by educating their people to an intelligent and devout appreciation of almsgiving as a spiritual work. A charity sermon is really effective in proportion as it keeps well in sight the Christian view of temporal goods and their use. Every good charity-sermon one hears or reads has the Gospel for its basis, and is in a true sense theological. Read, for example, St Cyprian's pastoral instruction on almsgiving, and you will see how he lifts the subject into the region of supernatural charity. While he pleads for generous giving he is exhorting to virtue, and his thoughts keep returning to great spiritual truths—the beneficence of God in creation and redemption, Christ's promises to the merciful, the vanity of hoarded riches, the presence of Christ in the persons of the poor.

Almsgiving is with him " excellent and divine," " the saving work, the great solace of believers, the defence of hope, the guardian of faith, the remedy for sin," " God's true and greatest gift, necessary for the weak, glorious for the strong, giving spiritual grace, earning Christ as a judge, making God Himself a debtor." In reading through that ancient charity-sermon one is conscious that our modern scolding is, compared with its manly vigour, " as water unto wine " ; and yet it is nothing more than a commentary upon the words of Holy Scripture, and no Christian who heard it could criticize its spirit without laying irreverent hands upon the teaching of the Faith.

Sermons to Children

The scope of this book does not embrace the ministry of catechizing children. This has its own laws, and a special volume would be required to treat it adequately. Here, then, I confine myself to a few brief suggestions on preaching to children. No one can doubt that the art of instructing children well, is an extraordinary gift, and many a man would find it much easier to address a congregation of Doctors of Divinity than a church full of children. Nearly always, the lapse of years separates a grown-up man from his childhood so completely that he cannot re-create the world of thoughts in which he lived in that bygone time. Yet, to speak to children with effect he must enter their universe and speak their language. Even goodwill and sympathy are not always able to build a bridge over the gulf, though these qualities are the foundation of the gift whenever it is possessed. The ugly word *polypsychism* has been invented to describe the genius of entering into the conceptions of minds differently constituted from our own, and one of its rarest degrees is the power that older people sometimes have for understanding and thus influencing the inner life of children.

Gerson is a case in point. Theologian, reformer and mystic though he was, his interest in children was insatiable. " It is by the children that the reform of the Church must be begun," was one of his axioms ; and his devout reflections on the words of the Gospel," Suffer little children to come unto me," reveal a side of his character unsuspected by many who know him only by the part he played in the embroiled ecclesiastical politics of his age. They are a rebuke to those of us who think little of the importance of our pastoral duties towards children. " O good Jesus," he writes in his treatise *De parvulis ad Christum trahendis,* " who will be ashamed after Thee to be lowly towards little ones ? Who, puffed up by his greatness or his knowledge, will despise their ignorance and weakness, when Thou who art God blessed for ever, Thou in whom are hidden the treasures of wisdom and knowledge, dost meekly lower Thy blessed arms to the pure embraces of little ones."

In English-speaking countries we have given less attention to this occupation of our ministry than we might have done, had the duty of instructing children fallen completely upon us. Catechism is in the hands of others, of religious and lay teachers, and work on our part may seem almost superfluous. Yet it is not really so, as experience is constantly showing. Zealous priests often remark that nowadays children learn more of their religion than formerly, yet, in spite of this, they are not more religious. The reason of this is not simple, for there are many causes contributory to the lamentable effect.   Home ties count for less nowadays than they did formerly, and there are many temptations in the way of children that arise from a laxity altogether of our own time.   Here we are not concerned with the investigation of these evils, but with the best method of applying what remedy is possible.   Besides a general oversight of the catechizing, we have opportunities for instructing children from the pulpit.   How shall we best use these ?   Some seem to answer the question in practice by increasing the dose of catechism.   Others act on the view that something other than catechizing is wanted, and in this they seem to be taking the more reasonable course.   When the religious teaching in a school is in good hands (as it usually is), the children know their religion very satisfactorily. Considering, however, the conditions under which school instruction is imparted, it is not unnatural that children are unable to grasp the difference that there is between the purpose of religious and of secular instruction.   But when they are instructed in church they are fully in a religious atmosphere, they are in the building in which they confess and pray and hear Mass.   Is it not wise, then, for a priest to occupy himself with giving in church a thoroughly devout and practical direction to the knowledge they have received in the shape of information at school ?

The first thing to be done is to take the measure of their capacity and discover the way to their hearts and minds. As in dealing with adults, so with children, nothing can be done unless they are interested in the subject.   The preacher must provoke their curiosity, so that they listen to him not from duty, but because they are eager to hear him.   They have their ways of speech and thought, and he must make himself familiar with them.   I say ways of *thought* with a reason, for it is not enough that a preacher uses only such words as are contained in a child's vocabulary ; he has further to bear in mind how they do their thinking. Their power of reasoning is small ; general and abstract ideas, so common in even the ordinary thinking of adults, have no grip upon a child's mind, which moves naturally though confusedly in the tangible and concrete.   The

imagination of most children is strong, and hence truths
are best presented to them under the envelope of images—
comparisons chosen from the familiar things of daily life,
plain examples and stories.

Children are less able to endure monotony than adults,
so a preacher must vary, not his ideas and illustrations only,
but his tone, his rate of utterance, and his attitude. Above
all, unsuitable length must be shunned ; if it is not, nothing
that is said at the beginning will be remembered at the end.

Sermons should be arranged to lead directly to action—
at a tender age the *act* of piety should be more immediately
sought than any full understanding of the principles that
underlie it. These will grow upon the child as acts often
repeated turn into habits and as continued instruction
gradually unfolds a more reasoned appreciation of the
practices of religion. In a word, religious *practice* is the
result to be directly aimed at in sermons to children. The
theoretical knowledge of the Faith, given in the Catechism,
is thus immediately reinforced, when the child learns from
one whom he looks upon as his religious guide the manner
in which conduct is built up on the truths of faith. To
square practice with belief is the lifelong occupation of
every Christian ; and this is best begun as soon as the intelligence is opened to religious impressions. A priest,
therefore, will have accomplished a great deal if he has
thoroughly convinced the children in his parish that religion
is not only something that has to be learnt, but something
that must be used.

APPENDIX I

*Letter on Sacred Preaching issued at the command of Pope Leo XIII.
by the Congregation of Bishops and Regulars, addressed to
the Bishops of Italy and to the Superiors of Religious Orders
and Congregations.*

HIS HOLINESS POPE LEO XIII., who has so much at heart the
apostolic ministry of preaching, so necessary, especially in these
days, for the right guidance of Christian people, has learnt with
much pain that grave abuses have for some time crept into the
fashion of preaching the Divine Word, so that modern preaching
has become either contemptible or barren and unprofitable.
Following in the footsteps of his predecessors, he commanded
this Congregation of Bishops and Regulars to address themselves
to the Ordinaries of Italy and to the Superiors of Religious
Orders and Congregations, so as to stimulate their zeal and
watchfulness, in order that they may, to the best of their power,
remedy these abuses and destroy them altogether. In obedience
to the commands of the Holy Father, this Sacred Congregation
sets before the eyes of the Right Reverend Bishops and Heads
of Religious Orders and pious congregations the following rules,
and bids them to strive zealously and perseveringly to observe
them :—

1. In the first place, let them beware of entrusting so sacred
a duty to anyone who is not endowed with true Christian
devotion and love of Our Lord and Saviour Jesus Christ, for
without this he can do nothing better than " sounding brass
and a tinkling cymbal," [1] and can have none of that true zeal
for God's glory and the salvation of souls which ought to be
the sole aim and motive of the preaching of the Gospel. This
piety, so necessary to Christian teachers, ought to shine forth in
their outward conduct, which should never be in opposition
to their teaching, nor suggest in any way the spirit of the world.
It should be that which is becoming in members of Christ and
dispensers of the mysteries of God [2] ; if it is not so, the saying
of the Angelic Doctor is realized, " If the teaching is good and
the teacher is bad, occasion is given for blasphemy against
God." [3] Knowledge, too, should be combined with devotion
and virtue, since it is manifest and proved by constant experience

---

[1] I Cor. xiii. I.   [2] I Cor. iv. I.   [3] *Comment. on Matt. v.*

that wholesome, orderly, and efficacious preaching is looked for in vain from men who, untinctured by solid theological and other study, and relying on their glibness of speech, rashly enter the pulpit with little or no preparation. Men of this kind are merely beating the air; unconsciously they bring the Divine Word into contempt and derision; it is clearly to such that the words were addressed, " *Because thou hast rejected knowledge, I will repel thee, that thou perform not the office of the priesthood before me.*" [1]

2. Not before, but after the priest has become qualified in these ways may the Ordinaries and Superiors of Religious Orders entrust to him the great ministry of the Divine Word, seeing to it, at the same time, that he confines himself to matters proper for sacred preaching. The Divine Master Himself indicates these matters when He says, " *Preach the Gospel.*[2] . . . *Teaching them to observe whatsoever I have commanded you.*" [3] Conformably to this the Angelic Doctor wrote, " Preachers should illuminate faith, direct right action, show what is to be avoided, and appeal to men, both by threats and by exhortations." [4] The Holy Council of Trent thus speaks, " Announcing to them what sins are to be shunned and what virtues are to be practised that they may escape eternal pain and attain to the blessedness of heaven." [5] Still more fully is this explained by the Supreme Pontiff Pius IX. of blessed memory as follows, " Preaching not themselves but Christ crucified, let them announce the sacred truths and commandments of our holy religion according to the doctrine of the Catholic Church and the Fathers, clearly and plainly in grave and eloquent fashion of speech. Let them deter all from vice, and inflame all to devotion, so that the faithful, nourished by wholesome teaching, may depart from all evil, and follow the way of holiness, thus escaping eternal penalties and reaching the glory of heaven." [6] Hence it clearly appears that the Creed and the Commandments, the precepts of the Church and the Sacraments, virtues and vices, the duties of particular states of life, the Day of Judgment, and such eternal truths, should form the standard material of sacred oratory.

3. Many preachers of our time unworthily neglect these serious themes, " *seeking what is their own and not what is Jesus Christ's,*" [7] for they know that these are not themes which will bring them the reputations they ambition; therefore they leave them alone, especially in Lent and on other solemn occasions; and changing the name as well as the thing described by it, substitute for the old-fashioned sermons a strange kind

---

[1] Osee iv. 6. [2] Mark xvi. 15. [3] Matt. xxviii. 20.
[4] *Comment. on Matt.* v. [5] Session v., c. 2 *de Ref.*
[6] *Encyc. of Pius IX.*, Nov. 1846. [7] 1 Cor. xiii. 5.

of *conference*, adapted rather to attract the mind and fancy than to move the will and reform the heart. They do not reflect that while moral sermons were suitable to all, these are adapted only to a few; and that even these few, if they were better instructed in the way of virtue, and helped to become more pure, humble, obedient to the Church, would have their minds purged of many prejudices against the Faith, and better disposed to receive the light of truth. For errors in religion, especially among Catholics, usually have their root in the passions of the heart rather than in the vagaries of the mind; according to the Scripture, " *From the heart proceed evil thoughts, blasphemies,*" etc. Hence St Augustine wisely comments the words, " *The fool hath said in his heart there is no God,*" [1] by the wise reflection, " in his *heart*, not in his mind."

4. It is not intended, however, to absolutely condemn the use of these conferences, which may sometimes, when properly conducted, be most useful in rebutting the many objections raised against the truths of religion. But it is desired to banish utterly from the pulpit pompous discourses, treating of speculative rather than practical arguments, discourses more secular than religious, more showy than fruitful, such as are perhaps not out of place in journalism or debating clubs, but are out of place in a sacred edifice. With regard, then, to conferences that aim at the defence of religion from hostile attacks, these are occasionally necessary; but this kind of discussion is a weight not suited to all shoulders, but only to the more robust. Even the most skilful orators must practise it with discretion; for such defences should be made only in such localities and in such churches, and to such audiences as need them, and where real benefit may reasonably be looked for from them. It is evident that the Ordinaries are the best judges as to these conditions. The demonstrations employed should have deep foundations in sacred doctrine, rather than in human and natural reasonings; they should be composed with such solidity and clearness as to avoid the danger of imprinting error more deeply than truth, since with some minds objections are prone to carry more weight than their refutation. Above all, the danger must be avoided of allowing an excessive vogue of conferences to bring moral sermons into disesteem and disuse; as if they were subordinate matters, of less importance than controversy and fit only for common preachers and their audiences. The truth is that it is moral preaching which is more necessary to the faithful at large, and no less sublime; hence the ablest and most distinguished orators should sometimes at least treat it with a living zeal, however distinguished and numerous their auditory may be.

5. Not only are there notable abuses in the choice of subject,

[1] Psalm xiii. 1.

but others no less deplorable, in the form of treatment. In reference to this St Thomas Aquinas teaches truly that, if the preacher is really to be the light of the world, "he must have three qualities—the first, stability to keep him from erring from the truth; the second, clearness that he may not be obscure in his teaching; the third, utility by which he seeks God's glory and not his own." [1] Unfortunately the form of modern sermons is not only far removed from that clearness and evangelical simplicity which ought to distinguish them, but it is implicated in cloudy circumlocutions and abstruse topics quite above the understanding of the generality of people, so that the pitiful complaint suggests itself to the mind, "*The little ones asked for bread, and there was no one to break it for them.*" [2] But the worst defect is the frequent absence of that sacred impress, that air of Christian piety, that unction of the Holy Spirit in virtue of which the Messenger of the Gospel ought always to be able to claim, "*My speech and my preaching is not in the persuasive words of human wisdom, but in the showing of the spirit of power.*" [3] These preachers, on the contrary, relying on the persuasive words of human wisdom, care little or nothing for the divine word of sacred Scripture which should be the well-spring of their eloquence. "This peculiar and special virtue of the Scriptures, proceeding from the inspiration of the Holy Ghost, adds authority to the sacred orator, confers on him an apostolic freedom of speech, and grants him a nervous and persuasive eloquence. Whoever brings to his preaching that spirit and strength of the Divine Word, speaks not "*in word only, but in power and the Holy Ghost and much fulness.*" [4] Hence those who hold conferences on religion and proclaim the divine counsel may be held to behave unreasonably and imprudently, if they lean rather upon their own than upon divine reasoning, bringing to their task nothing or next to nothing except the words of human knowledge and human prudence. Their speech, however luminous it may be, must languish and freeze if it lacks the fire of the Divine Word, and if it is unlike that which relies on the divine strength of God's Word, for "*The Word of God is living and efficacious, and sharper than a two-edged sword, penetrating even to the division of soul and spirit.*" [5] It is perceived even by the learned of this world that there exists in the sacred writings a marvellously varied eloquence worthy of the subjects of which it treats. This St Augustine saw and eloquently noted, and his view is confirmed by the best among sacred preachers, who have confessed that "they owed their success, under God, to a constant and devout study and meditation of the Holy Scriptures." [6]

[1] *Comm. in Mattheum.*   [2] Lam. iv. 4.   [3] 1 Cor. ii. 4.
[4] 1 Thess. i. 5.   [5] Heb. iv. 12.
[6] From the *Encyc. on Sacred Scripture*, Nov. 1893.

6. Here, then, is the chief source of sacred eloquence, the Bible. But these preachers of novelties, instead of drawing their eloquence from the fountain of living water, turn, by an intolerable abuse, to the parched cisterns of human wisdom ; instead of using the divinely inspired texts, or those of the Fathers and the Councils, they quote in abundance, secular writers, modern, sometimes even living authors who—themselves and their works—are very frequently open to equivocal and dangerous interpretations.

It is a great abuse, also, to treat religious subjects exclusively from the standpoint of this present life, passing over in silence the life to come ; to enumerate the advantages conferred upon society by the Christian religion, yet saying nothing about the obligations enjoined by it ; to depict the Divine Redeemer as all charity, without even a mention of His justice.

Preaching such as this has but little point ; the man of the world comes away persuaded that, provided he can say, " I believe in Jesus Christ," he is a good Christian even though he makes no attempt to change his life for the better.

But what do such preachers as these care about fruits ? They seek other things ; chiefly, they wish to attract auditors " of itching ears," [1] and if the churches are full, they care little that souls are empty. They never speak of sin or of the Day of Account, or of other grave truths which might awaken a saving contrition ; they speak " pleasing words," [2] and this with eloquence more suitable to the demagogue than the apostle, more profane than sacred, which earns for them hand-clapping and applause long ago condemned by St Jerome when he wrote : " When you speak in the church let groans and not applause be aroused ; let the tears of your hearers be your praise." [3] Hence it is that all their preaching seems to be enveloped, whether in the church or elsewhere, in the atmosphere of the theatre, which robs it of its sacredness and of all superhuman efficacy. Hence again, in the people, and indeed to some degree in the clergy, the decline of taste for the Divine Word, the scandal of the devout, the slight profit to sinners and unbelievers, who, even though they sometimes throng to listen to such " pleasing words " (particularly if attracted by high-sounding language about progress, patriotism, and modern science) leave the church as they entered it after applauding the orator " who knows how to preach " ; " they are amazed but not converted." [4]

7. Desirous, then, in conformity with the esteemed command of His Holiness, of remedying such hateful abuses, this Sacred Congregation addresses itself to all the Most Reverend Bishops and Superiors General of Religious Orders and pious Ecclesiastical

[1] 2 Tim. i. 3.
[2] Is. xxx. 10.
[3] *Letter to Nepotian*.
[4] Aug. *In Matt*. xix. 25.

Institutes, that they may, with apostolic severity, oppose these customs and strive to extirpate them. Mindful of the prescriptions of the Council of Trent " only to choose fitting men for the sacred office of preaching," [1] let them apply themselves to this matter diligently and prudently.

As to priests in their dioceses, let them be firm in not entrusting to them so grave a ministry, without having first tested them, either by examination or in some other suitable way, " unless they are approved in their life, knowledge and conduct." [2] If it is a question of priests from other dioceses, let them accept no priests to preach, especially on solemn occasions, unless they present letters vouching for their good conduct and fitness from their Ordinaries or Superiors. No Superior of Religious, of whatever Order, Society or Congregation, should permit any subject of his to preach, still less give him commendatory letters to any Bishop, without having first satisfied himself both of his moral conduct and of his correctness in handling the Divine Message.

If Ordinaries, after having accepted some preacher on the strength of recommendations presented by him, should see him deviate from the rules and admonitions contained in this letter, they should recall him to his duty by an opportune remonstrance ; if this does not suffice, they should at once remove him ; even adding, if the case requires it, canonical penalties.

In conclusion, since the Sacred Congregation knows that it can count on the zeal of the Right Reverend Ordinaries and Superiors of Religious Orders, it is confident that, chiefly through their co-operation, this novel fashion of announcing or rather of adulterating the Divine Word will be speedily reformed ; and that sacred preaching, stripped of this mundane ornament, will regain its native and venerable majesty and its superhuman power, for God's glory, the salvation of souls, and the universal advantage of the Church and of the world.

Rome, from the Secretariate of the Sacred Congregation of Bishops and Regulars, July 31st, 1894.

ISIDORE CARDINAL VERGA (*Prefect*).
LUIGI TROMBETTA (*pro-Secretary*).

---

[1] Session v. c. 2 *de Ref.*   [2] Council of Trent, *ibid.*

APPENDIX II

Encyclical of Pope Pius X. on the Teaching of Christian Doctrine.

IN this time of bitter stress and difficulty the secret counsel of God has raised us to the Office of Chief Pastor, and laid upon us the charge of ruling the whole flock of Christ. Long has the enemy been prowling round the sheep-fold and lying in wait with cunning astuteness, so that now specially, that has come to pass which the Apostle foretold to the elders of the Church of Ephesus, " *I know that ravening wolves shall enter in among you, not sparing the flock.*" [1] Whoever still has zeal for the glory of God is searching for the causes and reasons of the present decadence of religion. Opinions are divided, and many ways suggest themselves of securing and restoring the Kingdom of God upon earth. We agree with those who believe that, though other causes are at work, the main reason of the indifference and torpor of this age, with its many attendant evils, is to be found in the prevalent ignorance of religious truth. This fully bears out what God Himself spoke by the prophet Osee. "*And there is no knowledge of God in the land. Cursing and lying and killing and theft and adultery have overflowed, and blood hath touched blood. Therefore shall the earth mourn, and every one that dwelleth in it shall languish.*" [2]

Frequent, and, alas ! too well founded complaints are uttered that there are many Christian people in our day who live in complete ignorance of matters necessary for salvation. And when we speak of Christian people, we mean not only the masses and those of humble station who are excused somewhat from blame, because they are so much in the power of hard task-masters that they have little time left to think of themselves and their concerns ; not only these, but more especially others of some learning and culture, and endowed with abundant knowledge of profane matters, live altogether without concern and without care for religion. It would be difficult to convey a true description of the thick darkness surrounding them, and their case is all the more pitiable, because they feel their misfortune so lightly. They are heedless of God, the Creator and Ruler, and of the wise teachings of Christian faith. They know nothing of the Incarnation of the Word of God, nor of the restoration of human kind which was His work ; nothing of Grace which is the chief means of gaining eternal gifts, nothing of the august Sacrifice or of the Sacraments through which

[1] Acts xx. 29. [2] Osee iv. 1.

O

grace itself is acquired and preserved. Of the wickedness and foulness of vice they make no account; hence there is no anxiety of avoiding it or of casting it away, and so their last day comes upon them, and the priest, anxious for their salvation, has to occupy these last moments which should rightly have been devoted to stimulating the love of God, in giving summary instruction upon the rudimentary articles of faith. Often it happens even, that the dying man has become so involved in his culpable ignorance that he deems it superfluous to summon the priest, and thus, without seeking reconciliation with God, he sets out calmly on that terrible journey to eternity. Our predecessor Benedict XIV. had good reason when he wrote: "This we affirm, that the greater number of those who lose their souls, fall under this eternal condemnation through ignorance of the mysteries of faith which must be known and believed by all who are to be counted among the elect." [1]

Under these circumstances, Venerable Brethren, what is there to cause surprise when we find corruption of morals and degeneracy of life, not only among uncivilized peoples, but even in the very midst of Christian populations? Paul the Apostle, writing to the Ephesians, uttered this warning: "*Fornication and all uncleanness or covetousness, let it not be so much as named among you, as becometh saints, nor obscenity nor foolish talking.*" [2] He bases this holiness and this modesty, which restrains the passions, upon a foundation of supernatural wisdom. "*See therefore, brethren, how you walk circumspectly, not as unwise but as wise. Therefore become not unwise: but understanding what is the will of God.*" [3] And for this he had good reason, for the will of man preserves some vestiges only of that love of rectitude and goodness with which it was endowed by its Creator, and which dragged it (so to speak) not towards the apparent, but towards the real good. Depraved by the corruption of Original Sin, and almost forgetful of God, its Maker, its affections are turned to the love of vanity and the search after deceit. A guide is needed to point out the way to the will, which is wandering blindly among its perverse passions; a guide that will prevail upon it to seek the path of justice from which it has so wickedly strayed. That guide, not presenting itself at random, but provided by nature, is the intelligence. But if that too be lost in the darkness, being lacking in the knowledge of supernatural truths, then the blind will lead the blind and both will fall into the ditch. "*The light of thy countenance is signed upon us,*" cried holy David, thanking God for God's revelation of His truth; then in gratitude for its effects he adds, "*Thou hast given gladness to my heart,*" the gladness that fills the heart and sets men running in the way of the Divine Commandments.

[1] *Instit.*, xxvi. 18.   [2] Eph. v. 3, 4.   [3] Eph. v. 15, 16.

The truth of all this is evident on a little reflection. Christian revelation brings us much farther than human wisdom can do, towards a thorough knowledge of God and the Divine perfections. What is the result ? The same doctrine commands us to honour God by faith—the homage of the mind ; by hope—the homage of the will ; by charity—the homage of the heart ; and thus brings the whole nature of man to the service of God, its Author and Ruler. In like manner the doctrine of Jesus Christ, and that alone, reveals the true and sublime dignity of man ; since it shows man that he is the son of a heavenly Father, Whose likeness he bears, and with Whom he will live in happiness for ever. Moreover, from this dignity and from man's recognition of it, Christ proves the duty of all men to love one another as brothers, of living as becomes the sons of light in this world ; " *not in rioting and drunkenness, not in chambering and impurities, not in contention and envy.*" [1]

Likewise, Christ commands us to cast all our anxieties upon God, for He has care of us ; to prefer everlasting advantages, to the passing pleasures of time. Not to enter too much into detail, is it not the doctrine of Jesus Christ that inspires the proud man with a love of humility, thus showing him his true glory ? " *Whoever shall humble himself . . . this one is greater in the kingdom of heaven.*" [2] By the same doctrine we are taught spiritual Prudence, by which we are delivered from the prudence of the flesh ; Justice, by which we give to each his due ; Fortitude, that we may be ready to suffer without fainting for God and for everlasting happiness ; and finally, Temperance, which makes it possible to love even poverty for the sake of the Kingdom of God, and actually to glory in the Cross, without heeding its shame. The wisdom of the Christian faith is equal to lending light to the mind in its search after truth, and warmth to the will whereby we follow after God by uniting ourselves with Him by the practice of virtue.

Far be it from us to assert that moral goodness is inevitably connected with religious knowledge. Would that there were not so many facts in open contradiction with such a notion. What we do contend is that, while the mind is enveloped in crass ignorance, there can be no rectitude of the will nor purity of morals. A man may miss his path, even walking with his eyes open ; but if blind, he is sure to lose his way. Besides, there is always some hope of moral reformation, so long as the light of faith is not altogether extinguished ; whereas, if want of faith is added to corruption as a result of ignorance, the damage is almost irreparable, and the path to everlasting ruin lies wide open.

Such are the evil effects—many and grave—proceeding from ignorance of the principles of religion ; such is the necessity and utility of religious instruction ! It is vain to expect a

[1] Rom. xiii. 13.   [2] Matt. xviii. 4.

Christian man to fulfil his duty as long as he is unaware of it;
let us ask now, whose is the duty to save minds from such
damaging ignorance and to equip them with the necessary
knowledge. Venerable Brethren, there cannot be the least
doubt that this office falls to those, whoever they may be, who
exercise the care of souls. Christ's command to them is that
they shall know their sheep and pasture them; but pasturing
means, in the first place, teaching, for the shepherds promised
by God through the prophet Jeremias were teachers, " *I will
give you pastors according to my own heart, and they will feed
you with knowledge and doctrine.*" [1] Hence, too, Paul the
Apostle said: " *Christ sent me not to baptize but to preach the
Gospel,*" [2] thus intimating that the first duty laid upon those
who are entrusted with the government of the Church is that
of giving instruction to the faithful.

It would be superfluous to speak here of the sublimity of this
duty and of its merit in the sight of God. Who would deny that
the zeal and labour spent upon the instruction of souls, for their
eternal welfare, is more meritorious than that devoted to the
passing interests of the body; though indeed charity to the poor,
and help rendered to relieve their distress, is of great value before
God? What could be nearer and dearer to the heart of Jesus
Christ our Saviour, who spoke of Himself by Isaias the prophet,
" *To preach the Gospel to the poor hath He sent me?* " [3]

For our present purpose it will be sufficient to maintain with
urgency that no obligation is so strict nor so appropriate to the
priestly state. Is it not a truth beyond question that a priest
ought to combine piety with sound knowledge? " *The lips
of the priest shall keep wisdom.*" [4] Most certainly the Church
requires this in candidates for the priesthood, for it is from priests
that the Christian people look for the knowledge of the divine
law, and it is to this work that God has called them. " *And
they shall seek the law from his mouth; for he is the messenger
of the Lord of Hosts.*" [5] Hence the Bishop addresses those who
present themselves for ordination: " Let your teaching be the
spiritual medicine to the people of God, let them be prudent
fellow-workers with us in our sacred order, so that, meditating
day and night on his law they shall believe what they read,
and shall teach what they believe." [6]

Now if what we have just said is applicable to all priests, how
much more closely are they bound who possess the name and
exercise the function of parish priests; and thus by virtue of
their rank, and by a sort of contract take upon themselves the
care of souls. These, in a certain degree, may be regarded as
the teachers and doctors, designated by Christ in order that

[1] Jer. iii. 15.
[2] 1 Cor. i. 17.
[3] Luke iv. 18.
[4] Malach ii. 7.
[5] Malach, *ibid.*
[6] *Roman Pontifical.*

the faithful may be no longer as children tossed to and fro and carried about by every wind of doctrine by the wickedness of men, but rather " *working truth in charity, they may in all things grow up in Him who is the Head, even Christ.*" [1] Wherefore the Sacred Synod of Trent, treating of the pastoral office, lays down its first and chief duty to be the instruction of the faithful. It ordains that priests must speak to the people on the truths of religion on Sundays and the more solemn festivals, and do so daily, or at least three times a week, during the holy seasons of Advent and Lent. Not content with this, it adds that parish priests are bound, either themselves or through others, to instruct the young, at least on Sundays and Festivals, in the principles of faith and their duty of obedience to God and to their parents. [2]

It enjoins upon them also to explain in the vulgar tongue the efficacy of the sacraments for the reception of which the children are being prepared.

These prescriptions of the Council of Trent have been epitomized and still more plainly stated by our predecessor, Benedict XIV., in his Constitution, *Etsi minime*, in the following words : " Two chief obligations have been imposed by the Council of Trent on those who have care of souls : the first being that they should speak on divine things to the people on feast days ; and the second, that they instruct the young and the ignorant in the rudiments of the law of God and of the Faith."

Rightly, then, does that wise Pontiff make a distinction between the sermon—commonly known as the explanation of the Gospel—and the Catechism. Perhaps there are some who are desirous of saving themselves trouble, by counting the explanation of the Gospel as if it serves also for the catechetical instruction. This view is untenable, as a little consideration will show. The sermon on the Gospel is addressed to those who may be presumed to know already the rudiments of faith— one might call it the bread that is broken to feed the grown-up. Catechetical instruction, on the other hand, is that milk which the Apostle Peter desired to be sought for without guile by the faithful as new-born babes.

The task of the catechist is to take one or other of the truths of faith or Christian precept and to explain it fully and in detail. Since reformation of life is the aim of this kind of instruction, he ought to show the difference that there is between what God requires men to do and what they actually do. Then he should, by the aid of examples drawn from sacred Scripture, or from the history of the Church or from the lives of saints, show his hearers how they should set about the reformation of their conduct : then he should make an ending by urging all present

[1] Eph. iv. 14, 15.
[2] Session v., c. 2 *de Ref.* : Session xxiv., c. 4, 7 *de Ref.*

to shun vice and pursue virtue. We are aware that the office of catechizing is little sought after, for it is not commonly held in high repute, nor does it gain any great measure of applause. In our opinion those who undervalue it thus do so out of light-mindedness and not because their judgment is sound. We ungrudgingly admit the merit of those pulpit orators who, out of zeal for God's glory, devote themselves either to the vindication of Catholic truth, or to the exaltation of the saints. But for their labour to be fruitful, the Catechist must already have done his work, and if he has not, there is no foundation to be built upon, and the builders' work is vain. It happens too frequently that highly ornate sermons which win the applause of crowds fail to touch the heart; they merely tickle the ears.

On the other hand, however lowly and simple catechetical instruction may be, it is the word of which God Himself speaks in Isaias : " *And as the rain and the snow come down from heaven and return no more thither, but soak the earth and water it, and make it to spring and give seed to the sower, and bread to the eater ; so shall my word be which shall go forth from my mouth : it shall not return to me void but shall do whatever I please, and shall prosper in the things for which I sent it.*" [1]

We have the same opinion of those who write books requiring much time and labour to illustrate the dogmas of faith ; we think their activity is worthy of great praise. But how many readers are there who derive sufficient profit from such volumes as would correspond to the labour required to produce them ? But the teaching of the Catechism, if rightly performed, never fails to be useful to those who listen to it. But (let us repeat it once more, for the sake of inflaming the zeal of ministers of the Sanctuary), there are multitudes nowadays, and their number is always increasing, who are either utterly ignorant of Christian truth, or know so little of it that they lead the life of pagans.

How many these are, not children merely, but adults, yes, and even old men, who know nothing of the principal mysteries of faith, and who, on hearing the name of Christ, can only ask, " *Who is He, that I may believe in Him.*" [2]

Ignorant as they are, they think it no crime to excite and cherish hatred against their neighbour, to become parties to unjust bargains, to engage in dishonest speculations, to rob others by usurious practices, and to commit other horrible crimes of the same kind. Further, they are unaware that the law of Christ forbids not only immoral deeds, but condemns deliberately indulged immoral thoughts and desires ; even when restrained by some motive from sensual actions, they feed on evil thoughts without scruple, multiplying iniquity beyond number of the hairs of the head. Again we must repeat that such persons are found, not only among peasants and the poorer classes, but

[1] Is. lv. 10, 11.　　　　　　　　[2] John ix. 36.

among persons of high social position, and even among those who, puffed up with knowledge and relying upon a vain learning, allow themselves to make a jest of religion and *" blaspheme what they know not."* [1]

It is vain to expect a harvest where no seed has been sown; how, then, can we hope the coming generations to be more moral, unless they are early instructed in the faith? If faith is languid in our day, if it has almost disappeared in multitudes of men, the reason is that catechetical teaching is either superficially performed or else neglected altogether.

It is no excuse to say that faith is a free gift bestowed upon each one at baptism. All baptized in Christ have, it is true, the infused habit of faith; but this supernatural germ left to itself, and, so to speak, cut off from aid from without, *" does not grow or put forth great branches."* [2] Man has within him at birth the faculty of intelligence, but he has need of the mother's word to awaken it, as it were, and to bring it into play. So, too, the Christian, born again of water and the Holy Ghost, has faith within him, but he requires the word of the Church for its nourishment, development and fruitfulness. Hence the Apostle wrote, *" Faith comes by hearing, and hearing by the word of God,"* and, to show the necessity of teaching, he adds, *" How shall they hear without a preacher?"* [3]

If what we have written sufficiently proves the supreme importance of instruction, it follows that we ought to do all that is possible to maintain and revive, wherever it has fallen into disuse, the custom of catechetical teaching which Benedict XIV. has described as the most effective means of promoting the glory of God and securing the salvation of souls. [4] Desirous, Venerable Brethren, as we are of fulfilling this most important duty of the supreme apostolate, and to introduce uniformity in this matter of such moment, we command with authority that the following precepts shall be observed in every diocese:

1. On all Sundays and Festivals throughout the year, without exception, parish priests, and all who have care of souls, shall, with the text of the Catechism, instruct for the space of a full hour the young of both sexes in what they must believe and do to be saved.

2. They shall, at stated times during the year, prepare boys and girls, by continued instruction lasting over several days, to receive the Sacraments of Penance and Confirmation.

3. Every day in Lent, and, if necessary, on other days after the Festival of Easter, they shall, by suitable instructions and exhortations, carefully prepare boys and girls to receive devoutly their first Communion.

4. In each parish the Confraternity of Christian Doctrine

[1] Ep. of St Jude ii. 10.   [2] Mark iv. 32.
[3] Rom. x. 17.   [4] Bened. xiv. Const. *Etsi minime.*

is to be canonically instituted. By its means parish priests—
especially where clergy are scarce—will secure valuable assistance
from devout lay people who will give their time to this good
work, for the glory of God, and to the end of gaining the many
indulgences which the Roman Pontiffs have attached to its
performance.

5. In large towns, especially in those which contain uni-
versities, colleges and grammar schools, religious classes should
be arranged at which instruction is given in the truths of faith
and the practice of Christian virtues, for the benefit of the young
people attending public schools from which religious instruction
is excluded.

6. Since in these days, not only the young, but adults also,
stand in need of religious instruction, all parish priests and
others having care of souls shall, in addition to the usual homily
on the Gospel delivered at the parochial Mass on all Festivals
of obligation, explain the Catechism for the faithful, in a simple
fashion, suited to the understanding of their hearers, at an
hour convenient for their people, but not at the same time as
that arranged for the instruction of the children. They shall
make use of the Catechism of the Council of Trent, dividing
the matter in such a way as to allow them to treat, within
four or five years, of the Apostles' Creed, the Sacraments,
the Decalogue, the Lord's Prayer, and the Commandments of
the Church.

We hereby prescribe and commend this, Venerable Brethren,
by virtue of our apostolic authority.

It is for you to promptly put it into execution in your dioceses,
and to provide that these prescriptions of ours are not neglected
or—what is the same thing—are carelessly and irregularly
obeyed. To avoid this, you must not cease to recommend and
to require that your parish priests do this duty thoroughly
and prepare themselves for it diligently ; let them not speak
words of human wisdom, but " *with simplicity of heart and in
the sincerity of God,*" [1] imitating the example of Jesus Christ,
who, through the revealed mysteries hidden from the beginning
of the world, yet spoke " *always to the multitudes in parables,
and without parables did not speak to them.*" [2] The same was
done by the Apostles taught by Our Lord, of whom Pope Gregory
the Great said, " They took the greatest care to preach to the
ignorant, not sublime and difficult matters, but those that are
easy and intelligible." [3] Nowadays in matters of religion the
majority of men must be considered as ignorant.

We do not wish it to be supposed that this studied simplicity
of preaching exempts anyone from the duty of labour and
meditation ; on the contrary, more than any other kind, it requires

[1] 2 Cor. i. 12.   [2] Matt. xiii. 34, 35.
[3] St Greg., *Moral* 2, xviii. 25.

both. It is much easier to find a preacher capable of delivering a long and eloquent discourse than a catechist altogether successful in his method of imparting instruction. It must be carefully borne in mind, therefore, that whatever facility of ideas and language a man may have inherited from nature, he cannot dispense himself from preparing himself thoughtfully when he undertakes to catechize either the young or those of more mature age, and it is a mistake to suppose that because the common people are not highly cultivated there is no reason for taking pains. On the contrary, the more uncultured the hearers, the more diligent the teacher ought to be ; for he has to bring home to their minds sublime truths which are far above the native capacity of the multitude, and which must yet be known by all, lettered and unlettered, in order that they may attain eternal salvation.

Lastly, Venerable Brethren, permit me to address to you the words of Moses, " *If any man be on the Lord's side, let him join with me.*" [1] We pray and entreat you to reflect on the ruin of souls which is wrought solely by ignorance of supernatural truth. Doubtless you have done much that is useful and praiseworthy in your respective dioceses, in the interests of your flock, but before all else, and with all possible zeal, diligence and perseverance, provide that the knowledge of Christian doctrine penetrates and pervades the minds of all. " *Let everyone,*" as St Peter says, " *as he has received grace, minister the same, one to another, as good stewards of the manifold grace of God.*" [2]

Through the intercession of the Most Blessed and Immaculate Virgin may your care and diligence be made fruitful by the Apostolic blessing, which, in token of our affection and as an earnest of heavenly favours, we impart to you, to your clergy, and to the people entrusted to the care of each one of you.

Given at Rome, at St Peter's, on the 15th day of April 1905, in the second year of our Pontificate.

PIUS X., POPE.

APPENDIX III

Encyclical Letter of Pope Benedict XV. on the Pres...
of the Word of God.

WHEN Jesus Christ by His death o...
the Redemption of the human ra...
obeying His precepts to becom...

[1] Exodus xxxii. 26.

other means than the voice of His preachers, commanding them to declare to mankind what they must believe and do to be saved. " *It pleased God by the foolishness of our preaching to save such as believe.*" [1] Therefore He chose the Apostles, and when He had infused in them by the Holy Spirit the gifts proportionate to so great an office, " *Go,*" He said, " *and preach the Gospel to the whole world.*" [2] This was the preaching which renewed the face of the earth. For if the Christian faith has converted the minds of men from error to truth, and their souls from the filth of their vices to the perfection of every virtue, certainly it was through the medium of this preaching. " *Faith, then, comes by hearing, and hearing by the word of Christ.*" [3]

Thus, since by the purpose of God things are preserved by the same causes which furnished them with being, it is evident that the preaching of Christian Wisdom must be applied to continue the work of Eternal Salvation; and therefore must be counted among the most important and serious of duties. Hence it must be the chief subject of Our cares and thoughts, especially on those points where it appears to have deviated from its original design, not without loss to its fruitfulness.

This, then, Venerable Brethren, is added to the other misfortunes of these times, about which We before all others are solicitous. Looking round we find that the number of preachers is probably greater than it ever was before. When We inquire into the State of public and private manners and customs, there is to be observed among the common people a daily increasing contempt and forgetfulness of the supernatural; the standard of Christian Virtue is lowered, and life is gradually sinking to pagan levels. The causes of these evils are many and various, yet no one would deny the lamentable fact that the ministers of the Word do too little to remedy the disease. Has the Word of God ceased to be what the Apostle said it was, living and efficacious and more piercing than a two-edged sword? Has daily use dulled the edge of this weapon? If in many places this is so, is it not the fault of the ministers who do not wield it rightly? It cannot be alleged in excuse that the Apostle lived in better times than ours; when men were more willing to listen to the Gospel, or less rebellious against the law of God.

As the duty of Our Apostolic office warns us and the example of Our two immediate predecessors urges Us, We feel that We ⸺ earnestly, as befits so grave a matter, bring back the ⸺ the Divine Word to the standard set by Our Divine ⸺ ⸺crees of the Church.

⸺⸺le Brethren, it behoves us to seek the ⸺⸺ the right path. These can be ⸺⸺ing is undertaken by unfitting ⸺⸺h due care, or the necessary

[3] Rom. x. 17.

method is not observed. This office of preaching is by the Council of Trent "the chief one of Bishops."[1] The Apostles likewise, whose successors the Bishops are, considered this a most especial part of their duty. Thus spoke St Paul, " *For Christ sent me not to baptize but to preach the Gospel.*"[2] This was also the opinion of the other Apostles. " *It is not reason that we should leave the word of God and serve tables.*"[3]

This duty by right devolves upon the Bishops alone; nevertheless because they are so variously occupied with the many departments of church Government and hindered from discharging their obligation in its fulness, they must needs satisfy it through the instrumentality of others. Hence those who are not Bishops are, when they are preaching, performing the episcopal duty.

Let this first be understood that on one shall undertake the office of preaching on his own responsibility and without that lawful authority only to be given by a Bishop. " *How shall they preach unless they be sent.*"[4] For the Apostles were sent, yes, sent by Him who is the *Shepherd and Bishop of our souls*[5]; the seventy-two disciples were likewise sent, and St Paul himself, although constituted by Christ a vessel of election who might carry His name before the Gentiles and Kings, only then assumed the apostolate, when the elders obeying the command of the Holy Spirit, " *Separate me Paul for the work* "[6] of the Gospel, having imposed hands upon him, sent him forth; and this was ever the custom in the Early Church. For all those who were raised to holy orders, as Origen, and others who were afterwards elevated to the episcopate, such as Cyril of Jerusalem, John Chrysostom, Augustine, and other ancient doctors of the Church, were each granted the power to preach by his own particular bishop. Now, Venerable Brethren, another custom seems to have come into use. Among sacred orators there are not a few against whom you could aptly apply what the Lord spoke by Jeremias, " *I did not send prophets, yet they ran.*"[7] For nowadays whoever is lead from personal taste or any other such reason has easy access to the pulpit, and finds an opportunity of exercising himself there as if he were an actor in a public spectacle. Therefore, Venerable Brethren, it is your duty to see that such an evil custom is removed from our midst; and since you must render account to God and the Church, of the pasture provided for your flock, it is only just that you should allow no one against your command to enter into the fold and feed the flock of Christ at his own choice. No one in your diocese should be allowed to preach unless called and approved by you.

---

[1] Session 24 *de Ref*. c. 4.
[3] Acts vi. 2.
[5] Ph. x. 25.   [6] Acts xiii. 2.
[2] 1 Cor. i. 17.
[4] Rom. x. 15.
[7] Jerem. xxii. 21.

To those, then, whom you commission to this work you must pay the greatest attention. Regarding this matter it is decreed by the Council of Trent that the Bishops are permitted to choose only the suitable, that is, those who can fruitfully fulfil the office of preaching. " *Fruitfully* " is the word used, and note it, for it sets the standard in this matter—it does not say eloquently, nor with the applause of hearers, but with fruit to souls, for this is the end to which all teaching is directed. If you wish Us to define more closely who are really to be considered " suitable," we may say that they are those in whom you find signs of a divine vocation. The same condition is demanded of a fitting and worthy preacher, as that requisite for a candidate to the priesthood. " *Neither doth any man take the honour to himself, but he that is called by God.*" [1] This calling is easily discerned—Christ our Lord and Master, when He was about to ascend into heaven, did not order His Apostles to set out at once and preach, but said, " *Stay you in the City until you be endued by the power from on high.*" [2] The sign that any one is divinely called to this duty is the virtue from on high with which he is endued. Its nature can be judged, Venerable Brethren, from what we know happened to the Apostles as soon as this power had descended upon them. Leaving on one side the miraculous gift added to them, the descent of the Holy Spirit changed their ignorance and weakness into learning and perfection. There is no reason why a priest endowed with a fitting degree of knowledge should not be commanded by a Bishop to preach, provided (lest God be tempted) that he has the necessary natural qualities. Such is the wish of the Council of Trent, when it decrees that a Bishop shall allow only those to preach who are approved in morals and doctrine. The Bishop should discover by close observation the capacities both as regards learning and conduct of those whom he proposes to send as preachers. A bishop who is remiss and negligent on this point, is guilty of grave fault, and on his head rests the blame for the errors of the unlearned preacher and the bad example of the unworthy one. To render your duty the easier, Venerable Brethren, faculties for preaching shall henceforth be subjected to this twofold test, as is done already in the instance of those who are appointed as confessors, and whoever is found wanting in either respect should be refused an office, for which he is considered unworthy. Your dignity and the well-being of Holy Church demand this. Since preachers are your substitutes, they, if any one, should appear as the salt and the light of the world.

After these considerations it may seem superfluous to go further and explain what should be the end and fashion of preaching. If the rule which we have quoted as to the choice of sacred orators is put in force, what doubt can there be that

[1] Heb. v. 4.   [2] Luke xxiv. 49.

men thus chosen will set before themselves the true aims and ideals in preaching. However, it may be an advantage to illustrate further these two points, by showing how preachers sometimes fall short of the true standard.

The test that a preacher can use in judging his manner of preaching is this—Can he say what St Paul said, " *For Christ we are ambassadors.*" [1] If they are ambassadors of Christ they should wish, in discharging their office, to do what Christ Himself wished in bestowing it on them, nay, more, what He set Himself to do when He lived upon earth. For the Apostles and the preachers after the Apostles were sent to no different purpose than that of Christ. " *As the Father sent me I also send you.*" [2] Why Christ came down from heaven we know, for He told us openly. " *For this I came into the world, that I should give testimony of the truth,*" [3] and again, " *I came that they might have life.*" [4]

Two things, therefore, must be done by preachers. They must spread abroad the light of the truth delivered by God, and they must awaken and foster supernatural life in their hearers ; in a word, they must promote God's glory by seeking the salvation of souls. "For as no one can rightly be called a healer unless he heals, or a teacher unless he teaches some art, so every preacher is unworthy of the name who does not strive to bring men to the fuller knowledge of God and to their eternal salvation. A pompous declaimer he may be called, but he is no true preacher of the Gospel. Would that there were no such declaimers ! Yet there are such, and what are their motives ? With some, the empty wish for reputation. They care little for sense and much for sounds. Feeble-minded people make much of them, but they save no souls. They will not speak of plain and homely things, for fear they should be suspected of knowing nothing besides. Their pride forbids them to feed the little ones with milk." (*Abbot Gilbert, Serm.* 27, *On the Canticle.*) And though Jesus Christ, led by the lowliness of His audience, showed that He was the expected Messiah, " For the poor have the Gospel preached to them." [5] What efforts do not these men make to have glory reflected on their sermons by the celebrated cities or the churches of the first rank in which they preach ! And although God's revelation contains truths which are terrible to the weakness of our human nature, and which for that reason attract no crowds ; these they cautiously avoid, and instead, deal with matters that have nothing sacred about them except the place in which they are delivered. Often in the very middle of a discourse on the eternal truths they lapse into politics, especially if anything of that kind makes an intense appeal

[1] 2 Cor. v. 20. [2] John xx. 21. [3] John xviii. 37.
[4] John x. 10. [5] Matt. xi. 5.

to the audience. Their one object would seem to be to please their hearers and satisfy the bent of those denounced by St Paul as having " itching ears." [1] Hence those gestures, not calm and grave, but such as actors and platform-speakers use; hence that exaggerated softening of the voice, those tragic tones, that language smacking of the daily paper, that gush of opinions borrowed not from the Scriptures or the Fathers, but from the writings of infidels and non-Catholics, and finally that volubility astounding the ear and exciting the wonder of the audience. And yet the sermon is profitless, and the faithful are sent empty away. How astoundingly self-deceived these wretched preachers are ! They woo the applause of the ignorant with laborious irreverence—let them have it ! Yet is it worth their while ? For men of judgment will despise them, and worse than that, they must face a strict and terrible account at the hands of Christ. The search of praise is not the only way in which men wander from the right form and method. There are other objects even less honourable which they pursue ; for not a few forget the saying of St Gregory, " A priest should not preach to eat, but he should rather eat, that he may preach." (*On* 1 *Kings, Bk.* 3).

These, disdaining other work which would give them an honourable livelihood turn themselves to preaching, not as a sacred ministry, but as a means of making money. Their anxiety has nothing to do with the good of souls, but rather with the payment which comes from their preaching. Nothing but harm and scandal can follow from such practices ; it must be your especial care, Venerable Brethren, to remove without delay from office anyone whom you find abusing this ministry for the sake of glory or gain. For anyone who does not hesitate to disgrace such a sacred function is not above suspicion of stooping still lower and disgracing himself first of all, and then, further, the sacred office which he unworthily performs.

The same severity should be exercised towards those who preach unfittingly, because they have neglected the discipline necessary to prepare them for their office. What these are, can be learnt from his example whom the Church calls the " preacher of truth," Paul the Apostle. Would that by God's mercy we had many more preachers like him !

What we first learn from him is this, how well prepared and fitted the preacher should be. We do not speak here of his doctrinal studies which he had pursued under his master Gamaliel. The knowledge which he acquired by revelation thrust into the shade and almost overwhelmed that which he had acquired by his own industry, though even this latter was profitable to him, as we see from his Epistles.

Yet knowledge, as we have said, is necessary to the preacher,

[1] 2 Tim. iv. 3.

scarcely keep the root of faith, their intelligence is darkened because their souls have been corrupted.

Finally St Paul preached, not to please men but Christ. *"If I yet pleased men I should not be the servant of Christ."* [1] He sought nothing but the glory of Christ, because his soul was burning with the love of Christ. O would that all who labour in the ministry of the Word would truly love Jesus Christ, then they might say with St Paul, *"And on account of Him (Jesus Christ) I have suffered the loss of all things,"* [2] and *" For me to live is Christ."* [3] Only those who burn with love can kindle fire in others. Thus St Bernard admonishes the preacher, " If you are wise you will show yourself to be a reservoir and not a water-pipe " (On the Canticle), that is to say, be so full of your own message that it must needs overflow upon others. But the same Doctor adds, " To-day in the Church we have many water-pipes, but very few reservoirs (Sermon on the Canticle, xviii.).

Strive then, Venerable Brethren, with all your might that this may not come to pass again. For it is your duty to raise up many preachers after God's own heart to silence the unworthy, to choose, train, and direct the worthy. May the merciful and eternal Shepherd, Jesus Christ, look compassionately upon His flock, so that, by the intercession of the Holy Mother of the Incarnate Word, Queen of the Apostles, the apostolic spirit may be renewed among the clergy, and the number of those may be increased who strive *" to present themselves approved unto God, workmen that need not to be ashamed, rightly handling the word of truth."* [4]

We lovingly bestow the Apostolic Benediction upon you, your clergy and people, as a pledge of divine gifts, and in witness of our goodwill towards you.

Given at St Peter's, Rome, on this the fifteenth day of June, the Feast of the Sacred Heart of Jesus, in the year 1917, the third of our Pontificate.

BENEDICT XV., POPE.

APPENDIX IV

A COURSE OF SERMONS FOR THREE YEARS

The following plan suggests subjects for a three years' course of instruction in Christian doctrine. The references are made to the following works only :—

    I. The Holy Scriptures.
    II. The *Summa Theologica* of St Thomas Aquinas.
    III. *The Catechism of the Council of Trent.*
    IV. *The Catholic Encyclopædia.*

---

[1] Gal. i. 10.   [2] Philipp. iii. 8.   [3] *Ibid.*, i. 21.   [4] 2 Tim. ii. 15.

P

V. *Letters on Christian Doctrine*, by Fr. Zulueta, S.J.
VI. *The Christ, the Son of God* (2 vols.) and *St Peter*, by the
Abbé Fouard.
VII. Works by Cardinal Newman: *Sermons on Various
Occasions; Discourses to Mixed Congregations; Anglican
Difficulties*, vol. ii. ; *Parochial and Plain Sermons.*
(Those Parochial and Plain Sermons only are referred
to which occur in the Selection adapted to the Seasons
of the Ecclesiastical Year.)
VIII. Works by Bishop Hedley: *Our Divine Saviour; The
Christian Inheritance ; The Light of Life ; A Bishop
and his Flock ; A Retreat; The Holy Eucharist.*
IX. Leo XIII. Collection : *The Pope and the People.*
X. Hurter : *Sanctorum Patrum Opuscula Selecta.*

FIRST YEAR.

ADVENT. Revelation.

1st Sunday. God's Existence. Hedley: *The Christian Inheritance* ; The Science of God.
2nd Sunday. Mysteries. Hedley: *The Christian Inheritance*,
" Mysteries." Newman: *Parochial and Plain Sermons*;
" The Mysteriousness of our Present Being."
3rd Sunday. Divine Providence. *Cath. Encycl.*: Providence
(Divine).
4th Sunday. The Word of God. Psalm cxviii. ; Hebrews, chap. i.

CHRISTMAS TO LENT. The Incarnation and the Blessed Virgin.

1st Sunday. The Fitness of the Incarnation. *Summa*, iii.
q. i. art. 1 and 2.
2nd Sunday. Original Justice and Original Sin. Romans v.
8-21. *Summa*, i. q. xciii. art. 1 ; q. xcv. art. 1 ; ia, iiæ, q.
lxxxi. art. 1.
3rd Sunday. The Immaculate Conception. *Cath. Encycl.*:
Immaculate Conception.
4th Sunday. The Divine Maternity. II. *Orationes Procli, En-
comium Cyrilli in Dei Genetricem* (Hurter, *Opuscula* xii.).
Newman: *Sermons to Mixed Congregations*, " Glories of
Mary " (2).
5th Sunday. Devotion to Our Lady. S. Bernardi *Sermo de
Aquæductu* (Hurter, *Opuscula* xii.). Hedley: *The Light of
Life*, " Ark of the Covenant"; *The Christian Inheritance*,
" The Virgin Mother."
6th Sunday. The Word made Flesh. Hedley: *Our Divine
Saviour*, " The Word made Flesh."
7th Sunday. The Sacred Humanity. Philippians ii. 5-10 ;
Hebrews v. 1-10. *Cath. Encycl.*: Jesus, section iv.

8th Sunday. The Hidden Life. Newman: *Sermons on Various Occasions*, "Omnipotence in Bonds." Hedley: *A Bishop and his Flock*, "The Holy Family."

LENT TO EASTER.   Redemption.

1st Sunday. The Value of the Precious Blood. Hedley: *Our Divine Saviour*, "The Redemption."

2nd Sunday. The Agony in the Garden. Newman: *Discourses to Mixed Congregations*, "The Mental Sufferings of Our Lord in His Passion." Fouard: *The Christ, the Son of God*, vol. ii. book vi. c. v.; book vii. c. i.

3rd Sunday. The Condemnation of Christ. Fouard: *The Christ, the Son of God*, vol. ii. bk. vii. c. iii., iv.

4th Sunday. The Way of the Cross. Fouard: *The Christ, the Son of God*, vol. ii. bk. vii. c. v.

5th Sunday. The Supreme Sacrifice. Fouard: *The Christ, the Son of God*, vol. ii. bk. vii. c. vi.

6th Sunday. The Death and Burial. Fouard: *The Christ, the Son of God*, vol. ii. bk. vii. c. vii.

EASTER TO PENTECOST.   Grace and the Theological Virtues.

1st Sunday. Divine Grace. Zulueta, vol. ii. Letter i.

2nd Sunday. Indwelling of the Holy Ghost. John iii. 5; Romans viii.; 1 Cor. iii. 16-17, vi. 19; 2 Cor. vi. 16; Eph. i. 13, 14; Gal. v. 22, 23.

3rd Sunday. Faith. Hedley: *The Light of Life*, "The Divine Gift of Faith"; *Our Divine Saviour*, "The New Testament Teaching as to what Faith is."

4th Sunday. Hope. Luke xii. 31, 32, xxi. 28; 1 Peter i. 3, iii. 15; Romans viii. 18-25; Titus iii. 7; *Summa*, ia, iiæ, q. xl. art. 1.

5th Sunday. Charity towards God. *Summa*, iia, 2æ, q. xxvi. art. 1, 2, 3.

6th Sunday. Charity towards our Neighbour. Hedley: *The Light of Life*, "Christian Charity."

PENTECOST TO ADVENT.   The Commandments.

1st Sunday. God the Lawgiver. Hedley: *A Bishop and his Flock*, "The Service of God."

2nd Sunday. The Christian Law. *Cath. Encycl.*: Morality.

3rd Sunday. Sin, Mortal and Venial. *Cath. Encycl.*: Sin. *Summa*, ia, 2æ, q. lxxi. art. 6; q. lxxii. art. 5.

4th Sunday. Occasions of Sin. *Cath. Encycl.*: Occasions of Sin.

5th Sunday. The First Commandment: (1) Adoration of the True God. Zulueta, vol. i. Letters ii. and vii.

P*

6th Sunday.   The First Commandment: (2) Heresy and Schism, Mark xvi. 15; 1 Tim. i. 19, 20; 2 Peter ii. 1-17. *Summa,* 2a, 2æ, q. xi. ; q. xxxix.

7th Sunday.   The First Commandment: (3) Communication with Heretics. *Cath. Encycl.*: Toleration.

8th Sunday.   The First Commandment: (4) Spiritism. *Cath. Encycl.*: Necromancy, Spiritism.

9th Sunday.   First Commandment: (5) Despair and Presumption.   Zulueta, vol. i. Letter vi.

10th Sunday.   The Second Commandment: God's Name holy. Zulueta, vol. i. Letter xiii.

11th Sunday.   The Third Commandment: (1) Observance of Sunday, Obligation of hearing Mass. *Cath. Encycl.*: Sunday. Zulueta, vol. i. Letter xvi.

12th Sunday.   The Third Commandment: (2) Observance of Sunday, Rest from Servile Work.   Zulueta, vol. i. Letter xvii.

13th Sunday.   The Fourth Commandment: (1) Duties of Parents, Education.   Zulueta, vol. i. Letter xviii.

14th Sunday.   The Fourth Commandment: (2) Duties of Children.   Zulueta, vol. i. Letter xix.

15th Sunday.   The Fourth Commandment: (3) Masters and Servants.   *The Pope and the People,* The Condition of the Working Classes.

16th Sunday.   The Fifth Commandment: (1) The Preservation of Human Life.   Zulueta, vol. i. Letter xxi.

17th Sunday.   The Fifth Commandment: (2) The Sin of Scandal. Zulueta, vol. i. Letter xxii.

18th Sunday.   The Fifth Commandment: (3) Intemperance. Hedley: *A Bishop and his Flock,* "Our Responsibility for Intemperance."

19th Sunday.   The Sixth and Ninth Commandments: (1) Purity. *Summa,* 2a, 2æ, q. cliii. art. 4, 5.   *Cath. Encycl.*: Chastity.

20th Sunday.   The Sixth and Ninth Commandments: (2) Safeguards of Purity.   Zulueta, vol. i. Letter xxiv.

21st Sunday.   Seventh and Tenth Commandments: (1) Dishonesty.   Zulueta, vol. i. Letter xxv.

22nd Sunday.   Seventh and Tenth Commandments: (2) Restitution.   *Summa,* 2a, 2æ, q. lxii. art. 2, 6, 8.   *Cath. Encycl.*: Restitution.

23rd Sunday.   Seventh and Tenth Commandments: (3) Avarice. Newman: *Parochial and Plain Sermons,* "The Danger of Riches."

24th Sunday.   The Eighth Commandment: (1) Our Neighbour's Good Name.   Zulueta, vol. i. Letters xxvi.-xxviii.

25th Sunday.   The Eighth Commandment: (2) Kind Words. Hedley: *A Bishop and his Flock,* "Kindness in Speech."

SECOND YEAR

ADVENT.   The Messias.

1st Sunday.   The Testimony of the Prophets.   *Cath. Encycl.*:
Messias.
2nd Sunday.   The Jewish World.   Fouard: *St Peter*, c. 1, 3.
3rd Sunday.   The Gentile World.   Fouard: *St Peter*, c. 15-17.
4th Sunday.   The Testimony of the Baptist.   Fouard: *The
Christ, the Son of God*, I., bk. ii. c. 2 and 4.

CHRISTMAS TO LENT.   The Teaching of Christ.

1st Sunday.   The Sermon on the Mount.   Fouard: *The Christ,
the Son of God*, vol. ii., bk. iv. c. 3.
2nd Sunday.   The Parables.   *Cath. Encycl.*: Parables.
3rd Sunday.   Christ and the Pharisees.   Matt. vi. 1, 2, 5, 16,
xxiii. (all); Mark vii. 1-23, xii. 28-34; Luke xiii. 10-16,
xviii. 9-14; John iii. 1-21.
4th Sunday.   Christian Perfection.   Faith: Mark iv. 35-40,
xi. 22-24; Luke xvii. 5, 6.   Simplicity: Matt. xviii. 1-5;
Mark x. 13-16.   Charity: Luke vi. 32-36, 41, 42, xiv.
12-14.   Unworldliness: Matt. vi. 19; Mark ix. 32-34;
Luke xii. 13-15.
5th Sunday.   His Teaching on Prayer.   (1) Example: Matt.
xiv. 19; Luke vi. 12, xxii. 43, xxiii. 34; John xi. 41.
(2) Precept: Luke xi. 1-13, xviii. 1-8.
6th Sunday.   His Authority.   Matt. vii. 21-27, xii. 38-42, xiii.
37-42, xix. 29, xxiv. 35, xxv. 31-41; Luke v. 20-24;
John v. 19-46.
7th Sunday.   His Declarations as to His own Person.   Matt. v.
17, x. 37-39; Mark i. 22; Luke iv. 16-21; John iv. 1-26,
vi. 51, viii. 12, xi. 25, xiv. 6.
8th Sunday.   Christ and Sinners.   Luke vii. 36-50, xiii. 6-9;
ibid., 23-30, xv. (all); John viii. 31-36.

LENT.   Prayer.

1st Sunday.   Necessity of Prayer.   *Catechism of Trent*, pt. iv.
c. 1, 2.
2nd Sunday.   How to Pray.   *Catechism of Trent*, pt. iv. c. 3.
3rd Sunday.   Objects of Prayer.   *Catechism of Trent*, pt. iv.
c. 4.
4th Sunday.   Public and Private Prayer.   Hedley: *A Retreat*,
xxi. and xxii.
5th Sunday.   The Our Father.   First part (Praise) *Catechism
of Trent*, pt. iv. c. 9-12.
6th Sunday.   The Our Father.   Second part (Petition) *Catechism of Trent*, pt. iv. c. 13-16.

EASTER TO PENTECOST. The Church.

1st Sunday. The Church in the New Testament. *Cath. Encycl.*: Church, sections 3, 4, 5, 6. Hedley: *The Christian Inheritance*, "The Religion of Jesus Christ."

2nd Sunday. Apostolicity. *Cath. Encycl.*: Apostolicity.

3rd Sunday. Catholicity. *Cath. Encycl.*: Catholic.

4th Sunday. Unity. *Cath. Encycl.*: Unity, Mark of the Church.

5th Sunday. Sanctity. *Cath. Encycl.*: Sanctity, Mark of the Church. Hedley: *A Bishop and his Flock*, "The Lives of the Saints."

6th Sunday. Authority. *Cath. Encycl.*: Infallibility, secs. i., ii., iii., a iv., v.

PENTECOST TO ADVENT. The Sacraments.

1st Sunday. The Sacraments and Sanctification. Hedley: *Our Divine Saviour*, "The Good Things of Christ."

2nd Sunday. Definition of a Sacrament. *Cath. Encycl.*: Sacraments, sec. ii.

3rd Sunday. Classification of the Sacraments. *Cath. Encycl.*: Sacraments, sec. iv. (3).

4th Sunday. The Minister and Subjects of the Sacraments. *Cath. Encycl.*: Sacraments, sections vi. and vii.

5th Sunday. Baptism. Institution and Necessity. Zulueta, vol. ii. Letter 3.

6th Sunday. Baptism. Administration. Zulueta, vol. ii. Letters iv.-vi.

7th Sunday. Confirmation. Zulueta, vol. ii. Letter vii.

8th Sunday. Penance. Institution. Zulueta, vol. ii. Letter xxv. Hedley: *A Bishop and his Flock*, "The Sacrament of Penance."

9th Sunday. Examination of Conscience. Zulueta, vol. i. Letter xxxiv.

10th Sunday. Contrition and Attrition. Zulueta, vol. ii. Letters xxix. and xxx.

11th Sunday. Confession. Doubts and Scruples. Zulueta, vol. ii. Letter xxxv.

12th Sunday. The Seal of Confession. Zulueta, vol. ii. Letter xxxviii.

13th Sunday. Indulgences. Zulueta, vol. ii. Letters xli., xlii.

14th Sunday. Holy Communion. Institution. Hedley: *The Holy Eucharist*, chaps. i., ii.

15th Sunday. Transubstantiation. Hedley: *The Holy Eucharist*, c. iii., iv.: *Our Divine Saviour*, "The Abiding Presence."

16th Sunday. Preparation for Communion. Zulueta, vol. ii. Letters xiii.-xv.

17th Sunday. Effects of Holy Communion. Hedley: *The Holy Eucharist*, chap. vii.; *The Light of Life*, "Divine Union."

18th Sunday. Frequent Communion. Hedley: *The Holy Eucharist*, chap. viii.

19th Sunday. The Mass. Sacrifice. Hedley: *The Holy Eucharist*, c. ix.

20th Sunday. Calvary and the Mass. *Cath. Encycl.*: Sacrifice, sec. iii. Hedley: *The Holy Eucharist*, chap. xii.

21st Sunday. Value of the Mass. Zulueta, vol. ii. Letter xxiii. Hedley: *Our Divine Saviour*, "The Harvest of the Holy Mass."

22nd Sunday. Extreme Unction. Zulueta, vol. iii. Letters i., ii.

23rd Sunday. Holy Order. Hedley: *A Bishop and his Flock*, "The Christian Priesthood"; *The Christian Inheritance*, "The Pastoral Office."

24th Sunday. Matrimony. *Cath. Encycl.*: Marriage, Sacrament of.

25th Sunday. Profanation of Matrimony. *Cath. Encycl.*: Divorce. *The Pope and the People*. Christian Marriage. Zulueta, vol. i. Appendix III.

THIRD YEAR

ADVENT. Creation.

1st Sunday. The Power of God. *Summa*, i. q. xxv. art. 3.

2nd Sunday. The Blessed Trinity. *Cath. Encycl.*: Trinity, secs. i., ii., iv.

3rd Sunday. The Creation of the World. Job xxxviii., 4, xxxix. 30; Isaias xl. 12, 21, 22; Ecclus. xxxix. 30-41; *Summa*, i. q. xlv. art. 1, 5, 6.

4th Sunday. The Creation of Man. Hedley: *A Retreat*, "God."

CHRISTMAS TO LENT. (1) The Pope. (2) The Laws of the Church.

1st Sunday. Primacy of the Roman See. *Cath. Encycl.*: Pope, sec. ii.

2nd Sunday. Institution of the Primacy. Fouard: *The Christ, the Son of God*, vol. ii., bk. ii. c. ii.

3rd Sunday. Infallibility. *Cath. Encycl.*: Infallibility, secs. i., iib, iv., v.

4th Sunday. The English Reformation. *Cath. Encycl.*: Reformation, secs. i., ii., iv.

5th Sunday. Reunion. *Cath. Encycl.*: Anglicanism; England (since Reformation); *The Pope and the People*; The Reunion of Christendom.

6th Sunday. Nature and Extent of Papal Authority. *The Pope and the People*; The Christian Constitution of States. Newman: Letter to the Duke of Norfolk, sections 2, 3, 4 (*The Difficulties of Anglicans*, vol. ii.).

7th Sunday.   The Laws of the Church.   Zulueta, vol. i. Letter xxix.

8th Sunday.   The Special Laws on Impediments to Matrimony. *Cath. Encycl.*: Impediments.   Zulueta, vol. i. Letter xxxiii.

LENT.   Devotions.   Hedley: *A Bishop and his Flock*, "The Spirit of the Gospel."

1st Sunday.   The Sacred Heart.   Hedley: *A Bishop and his Flock*, "The Sacred Heart."

2nd Sunday.   Benediction.   *Cath. Encycl.*: Benediction and Exposition.

3rd Sunday.   Sacramentals.   *Cath. Encycl.*: Sacramentals.

4th Sunday.   The Rosary.   *Cath. Encycl.*: Rosary.

5th Sunday.   Superstition.   Zulueta, vol. i. Letter ix.

6th Sunday.   Relics.   *Cath. Encycl.*: Relics.

EASTER TO PENTECOST.   Christian Holiness.

1st Sunday.   Devotion.   Hedley: *The Light of Life*, "The Sacrament of Piety."

2nd Sunday.   The Three Vows.   *Summa*, iia, iiæ, q. clxxxvi. art. 3, 4, 5.

3rd Sunday.   Heroic Sanctity.   *Cath. Encycl.*: Heroic Virtue. *Summa*, iia, iiæ, q. lxxxi. art. 8.

4th Sunday.   The Religious Life.   *Summa*, 2a, 2æ, q. clxxxvi. art. 1, 2, 6; *ibid.*, q. clxxxix.

5th Sunday.   Spiritual and Corporal Works of Mercy.   *Summa*, 2a, 2æ, q. xxxii. art. 1, 2, 3, 4.

6th Sunday.   Almsgiving.   Deut. xv. 4; Ps. xl. 1-4; Prov. xiv. 21, 31; Ecclus. xxix. 11-15; Matt. xxv. 41-46; Luke x. 30-37, xvi. 1-9; 1 Tim. vi. 17-19.

PENTECOST TO ADVENT.   The Trial and Destiny of Man.

1st Sunday.   The Meaning of our Life.   Newman: *Discourses to Mixed Congregations*, "God's Will the end of Life."

2nd Sunday.   Probation.   *Cath. Encycl.*: Man, section iii.

3rd Sunday.   The Use of Time.   Newman: *Parochial and Plain Sermons*, "The Lapse of Time."

4th Sunday.   Right Intention.   Hedley: *A Retreat*, "Our Life and its Surroundings."

5th Sunday.   Conscience.   Newman: Letter to the Duke of Norfolk, section 3 (*The Difficulties of Anglicans*, vol. ii.).

6th Sunday.   The Law of the Gospel.   *Summa*, iia, iiæ, q. cvi. art. 1, 2.

7th Sunday.   The Finality of the New Law, *Summa*, 1a, 2æ, q. cvi. art. 3, 4.

8th Sunday.   Natural and Supernatural Virtue.   *Cath. Encycl.*: Virtue.

9th Sunday. Merit. *Cath. Encycl.*: Merit.

10th Sunday. God's Justice and Mercy towards Men. Job xxxiv.; Jeremias iii. 1-25; Matt. vii. 21, xi. 25-27; Luke xviii. 14; John iii. 16; Rom ii. 1-11; Eph. i. 1-23; 1 John ii. 1-6, iv. 14-18.

11th Sunday. Purgatory. *Summa*, Appendix ad Supplementum, q. i. art. 1, 2.

12th Sunday. Mass for the Dead. Hedley : *The Holy Eucharist*, chap. xii. pp. 235-245.

13th Sunday. Prayers for the Dead. *Summa*, Supplementum, q. lxxi. art. 2, 4, 6.

15th Sunday. Hell. (1) General Doctrine. *Cath. Encycl.*: art. Hell.

16th Sunday. Hell. (2) The Pain of Loss. Matt. xxv. 41, 46; 2 Thess. i. 9; Apoc. xiv. 11, xix. 3, xx. 10; *Summa*, Supplementum, q. lxix. art. 3.

17th Sunday. Final Perseverance. *Cath. Encycl.*: Perseverance (Final).

18th Sunday. The Resurrection of the Just. *Summa*, Supplementum, qq. lxxxii.-lxxxv.

19th Sunday. The Beatific Vision. Hedley: *The Light of Life*, "Life Everlasting."

20th Sunday. The Differences of Glory. *Summa*, Supplementum, q. xciii.

21st Sunday. The Court of Heaven. Gen. xxi. 17; Tobias xii. 15; Matt. xviii. 10, xxii. 30; Apoc. vii. 11, 12, viii. 3-5. *Cath. Encycl.*: Angel.

22nd Sunday. The Reign of God and of Christ. (1) The Blessedness of God. *Summa*, i. q. xxvi. art. 1, 2, 3.

23rd Sunday. The Reign of God and of Christ. (2) The Victory of Christ. Philippians ii. 5-11; 1 Cor. xv.; Apoc. xix., xxi.; *Summa*, iii. q. lviii.

24th Sunday. Christ the Mediator. *Summa*, iii. q. xxvi. art. 1, 2.

25th Sunday. The Happiness of Heaven Eternal. Is. xxxv. 10, li. 3; Daniel vii. 14, 18, 27; Mark x. 21; Luke xii. 33; 2 Cor. v. 1; 1 John iii. 2; Apoc. xxii. 4.

BIBLIOGRAPHY

The following books are chosen from a great number bearing directly or indirectly on Preaching.

I. GENERAL

THE PRINCIPLES OF COMPOSITION AND RHETORIC

Aristotle, Rhetoric : Oxford Variorum Edition. [Eng. Trans. by Jebb, Cambridge University Press.]

Cicero, Oratorical Treatises : Ciceronis Rhetorica in the Bibliotheca Scriptorum Classicorum, Oxford. [Eng. Trans. by J. S. Watson in Bohn's Classical Library, 2 vols.]

Quintilian, Institutio Oratoria. Lipsiæ, 1854. [Eng. Trans. by J. S. Watson in Bohn's Classical Library, 2 vols.]

Whateley, The Elements of Rhetoric (Longmans).

Quiller-Couch, The Art of Writing (Cambridge University Press) ; The King's English (Clarendon Press).

Henderson and Freeman, Essay Writing (Bell & Sons).

Schleiniger, On Eloquence (Kegan Paul).

Fleming, The Art of Reading and Speaking (Arnold).

Greenough and Kettridge, Words and their Ways in English Speech (Macmillan).

II. SPECIAL

PREACHING

Newman, Lecture on University Preaching in " The Idea of a University " (Longmans).

Potter, Sacred Eloquence ; The Art of Extemporary Preaching ; The Pastor and his People. (The first two published by Simpkin & Marshall, the third by Duffy.)

St Augustine, De Doctrina Christiana and De Catechizandis Rudibus. Translated by Baker and Bickersteth (Mowbray).

Feeney, A Manual of Sacred Rhetoric (Herder).

Scheuch, O.S.B. The Priest in the Pulpit (Burns & Oates).

Boyd Carpenter (Anglican), Lectures on Preaching (Macmillan).

Ford (Anglican), The Art of Extempore Preaching (Elliot & Stock).

234

Audisio, Eloquenza Sacra (Stamperia Reale, Torino), 3 vols.
Hamon, Traité de la Prédication (Gabalda, Paris).
Monsabré, La Prédication (Lethielleux, Paris).
Mourret, L'Art de Prêcher (Bloud, Paris).
Bouchard, Formation de l'orateur sacré (Vitte, Paris).

There are chapters on preaching in most works of Pastoral Theology; for instance :

Manning, The Eternal Priesthood.
Oakeley, The Priest on the Mission.
St Charles Borromeo, Pastorum Instructiones.
Hogan, Clerical Studies.
Hedley, Lex Levitarum.
Stang, Pastoral Theology.
Bishop Ward, The Priestly Vocation.
Cardinal Gibbons, The Ambassador of Christ.

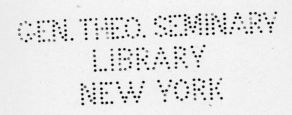
*Printed in Great Britain
by Turnbull & Spears, Edinburgh*

THE WESTMINSTER LIBRARY

A Series of Manuals for Catholic Priests and Students

Edited by the Right Rev. BERNARD WARD, Bishop of Brentwood,
and the Rev. HERBERT THURSTON, S.J.

Crown 8vo

THE PRINCIPLES OF CHRISTIAN APOLOGETICS. An Exposition of the Intellectual Basis of the Christian Religion. Specially written for Senior Students. By the Rev. T. J. WALSHE. 6s. net.

THE PRIESTLY VOCATION. A Series of Fourteen Conferences addressed to the Secular Clergy. By the Right Rev. BERNARD WARD, F.R.Hist.S., Bishop of Brentwood. 5s. net.

THE HOLY EUCHARIST. By the Right Rev. JOHN CUTHBERT HEDLEY, O.S.B., late Bishop of Newport. 4s. 6d. net.

THE MASS: a Study of the Roman Liturgy. By the Rev. ADRIAN FORTESCUE, D.D. 7s. 6d. net.

THE NEW PSALTER AND ITS USE. By the Very Rev. E. H. BURTON, D.D., Canon of Westminster Cathedral, and the Rev. EDWARD MYERS, M.A., President of St Edmund's College, Ware. 4s. 6d. net.

THE PRIEST'S STUDIES. By the Very Rev. THOMAS SCANNELL, D.D., late Canon of Southwark Cathedral. 4s. 6d. net.

THE TRADITION OF SCRIPTURE: its Origin, Authority, and Interpretation. By the Very Rev. WILLIAM BARRY, D.D., Canon of Birmingham. 4s. 6d. net.

NON-CATHOLIC DENOMINATIONS. By the Very Rev. Monsignor ROBERT HUGH BENSON. 4s. 6d. net.

THE EARLY CHURCH IN THE LIGHT OF THE MONUMENTS. A Study in Christian Archæology. By the Right Rev. Monsignor A. S. BARNES, M.A., Chamberlain of Honour to H.H. Pius X. With Illustrations. 6s. net.

THE PRIEST AND SOCIAL ACTION. By the Rev. CHARLES PLATER, S.J., M.A., Professor of Psychology at St Mary's Hall, Stonyhurst. With an Introduction by the Bishop of Northampton. 4s. 6d. net.

PREACHING. By the Rev. W. B. O'DOWD, of St Charles' House, Oxford.

LONGMANS, GREEN & CO.

39 PATERNOSTER ROW, LONDON, E.C.4